THREE
BILLION
NEW
CAPITALISTS

THREE BILLION NEW CAPITALISTS

The Great Shift of Wealth and Power to the East

CLYDE PRESTOWITZ

BASIC
BOOKS

A Member of the Perseus Books Group

New York

Copyright © 2005 by Clyde Prestowitz
Published by Basic Books,
A Member of the Perseus Books Group

Books published by Basic Books are available at special discounts for bulk purchases
in the United States by corporations, institutions, and other organizations. For more
information, please contact the Special Markets Department at the Perseus Books
Group, 11 Cambridge Center, Cambridge MA 02142, or call (617) 252-5298 or
(800) 255-1514, or e-mail special.markets@perseusbooks.com.

Design by Jane Raese
Text set in ITC Century Book

A CIP catalog record for this book is available from the Library of Congress.
ISBN 0-465-06281-4

05 06 07 / 10 9 8 7 6 5 4 3 2 1

For my grandchildren:

Kiele, Jay, Makaela, and Carolyn

We See Globalization as a "mega-trend" . . .
that will shape all other trends.
> —NATIONAL INTELLIGENCE COUNCIL'S
> PROJECT 2020

Intel will be okay no matter what. We can adjust.
But in addition to being Chairman of Intel,
I am also a grandfather, and I wonder what
my grandchildren are going to do.
> —CRAIG BARRETT, CHAIRMAN, INTEL

CONTENTS

> The United States is on the
> comfortable road to ruin.
>
> MARTIN WOLF

It is January 25, 2005, and as I sit down to write this prologue, I see today's *New York Times* on the table next to my computer with a headline saying:

DOLLAR'S STEEP SLIDE ADDING TO TENSIONS U.S. FACES ABROAD

Under the *Times* is yesterday's *Financial Times*. Its front page lead headline reads:

CENTRAL BANKS SHUN U.S. ASSETS

On page two of the *FT* is another headline:

DOLLAR AT THE MERCY OF SMALL GROUP OF CENTRAL BANKS

Under the *FT* is yesterday's *Wall Street Journal*. The lead headline on page A2 reads:

CHINA ON PATH TO OVERTAKE U.S. ECONOMY

At the bottom of the same page, another headline:

BIG SILICON VALLEY FIRMS THRIVE, BUT JOBS ARE FEW

Then, toward the bottom of the stack, today's *FT*:

STRATEGIC DIALOGUE POINTS TO THAW IN BEIJING–NEW DELHI RELATIONS

The text begins: "This is a quiet watershed in global diplomacy. If you look at the decades ahead and at the economic rise of China and India then this will be one of the world's most critical relationships."

Last but not least, the *Washington Post*, with another arresting headline on the front page of the business section:

LOCKHEED TEAM WINS REDESIGN OF MARINE ONE

Marine One is the presidential helicopter, and a Lockheed/European consortium has beaten Sikorsky's all American bid to build a new squadron of choppers for ferrying the President. The deal may be the first step toward renewal of the Pentagon's entire helicopter force. Although Lockheed is the American face on the deal, the key elements of the choppers will be largely designed and built by Italy's Augusta Westland. A key factor in this decision is that U.S. chopper technology seems to be lagging while the European Union's is surging in response to the same kinds of government subsidies that have helped make the Airbus the world leader in commercial jetliners.

I am struck by two things. First, all these headlines come from just two days' worth of big newspapers that are widely read in American policy and journalistic circles. Second, no one is talking about what these headlines mean. Each by itself suggests a significant trend with enormous potential consequences, but none of the papers editorializes on even one of those trends, let alone connects the dots. If you read the newspapers and watch the TV news and talk shows, you probably think that the most important events for the United States during the first weeks of 2005 were the elections in Iraq, the appointment of Condoleeza Rice as Secretary of State, and President Bush's inaugural address. But the real news is the serious flaw at the heart of the global economy, the uncertainty surrounding the dollar, the loss of U.S. financial sovereignty, the decline of U.S. technological leadership, and the rise of China, India, and the European Union. These developments add up to a shift of the global balance of influence away from the United States.

Granted, these subjects aren't visually dramatic and stirring like Iraq, Rice, and the inaugural, but they are more important, both strategically for the United States and the rest of the world and for you personally. As the headlines attest, important people in China, India, Japan, and Europe are getting worried and paying a lot of attention to these issues. So while your eyes may glaze over at mention of the *trade deficit* or *competitiveness*, you ought to be a bit alarmed that in the United States even the people whose job it is to pay attention—the policymakers, academic economists, media analysts, and bureaucrats charged with keeping America's economy running so that it will be morning in America for your children as it was for you—aren't.

It should concern you even more that while key American business leaders say they "want to be part of China's strategy" of economic development, America doesn't have a strategy. The economic views now dominant in the United States hold the very consideration of such a strategy to be contrary to America's interests. That American rates of saving are near zero and are accompanied by huge federal budget deficits is not a problem, goes the thinking, because both stimulate economic growth. That the deficits have to be financed by ever more borrowing from abroad, and that this strategy is mortgaging large U.S. assets to foreign lenders, it is argued, should be of no concern because the foreigners will always put their money here since America will always yield the best returns. And if tax holidays, bureaucratic pressure, and managed exchange rates are luring U.S. factories to foreign shores, not to worry. These are gifts to U.S. producers and consumers. Sure, some workers will lose their jobs, but that will only free them up to do more productive work somewhere else.

Or so it is argued. But the economic thinking that allows American leaders to take these positions and the worldview this thinking supports are badly out of touch with reality. Whether it recognizes the fact or not, the United States has a de facto economic strategy, and right now it is to send the country's most important industries overseas.

Consider 9/11. The terrorists who attacked the World Trade Center and the Pentagon left many clues about their intent, and suspicious developments were not lacking. The problem was a failure of imagination by the U.S. government and the public at many levels. No one connected the dots because no one was prepared to realize that new and powerful forces were coming into play. No one imagined that the United States could be vulnerable. No one could put their feet into the shoes of the Jihadists and think like them. Are America and the world in for another kind of 9/11 disaster—an economic one? Of course, it wouldn't kill people, not directly, but it would create great hardship around the world.

Let me tell you where I see the dots leading. We know the U.S. trade (current account) deficits—about $650 billion in 2004—are filling the coffers of the world's central banks with dollars, so many dollars, in fact, that several key central bankers are saying they have too many and that the United States may not be able, or may not intend, to make good on its international financial obligations. These bankers see that, even if the dollar devalues dramatically, America may no longer have the capacity to raise its exports sufficiently to balance the trade accounts. For the first time since the end of World War II there is a possible alternative to the dollar as the world's money, the euro. For the first time in memory, countries are reducing their dollar holdings. Russia is shifting its monetary reserves from 70 percent dollars and 30 percent euros to the reverse. The OPEC countries have reduced their dollar holdings from 67 percent of reserves to about 50 percent. Other big dollar holders, like Japan and China, are nervous.

The nightmare scenario—an economic 9/11—is a sudden, massive sell-off of dollars; a world financial panic whose trigger might be as minor, relatively speaking, as the assassination of a second-rate archduke in a third-rate European city. A collapse of the dollar and its consequent abandonment as the world's reserve currency would create a deep recession in the United States. Gas and fuel prices would soar, anything imported would suddenly become much more expensive, interest rates would jump, as would unemployment. The "stagflation" of the 1970s—slow growth and high unemployment combined with double-digit inflation and double-digit interest rates—would look like a walk in the park. And since the United States is at present the world's only major net importer, all of the exporters that depend on it for their economic stability would suffer severely as well. It's the thought of these consequences that makes the big dollar holders so nervous, and makes them, for now, hold on to their excess dollars.

Another reason for their nervousness is that the preferred solution of rapidly rising U.S. exports in response to a falling dollar may not be feasible. For one thing, U.S. exports and imports do not always move in tandem with the dollar. More important, however, are the current limits on U.S. manufacturing and service providing capacity for exports. Manufacturing, the biggest part of U.S. trade, now accounts for just 12.7 percent of American GDP—less than health care. Current manufactured exports are about $620 billion while exports of services amount to about $340 billion. To cut the roughly $650 billion trade deficit even in half only by exporting would require more than a 30 percent increase in exports of both manufactures and services. But many of these industries are already running at 80 or 85 percent of capacity. This suggests that when the adjustment comes, it almost surely will be largely through reduced consumption, which very likely means a recession if not worse.

The really significant news is that even if the world can avoid the nightmare scenario, we are all in for a bumpy ride. The forces now altering the global economic future are too strong to be turned back. Since the fall of the Berlin Wall in 1989, three billion new capitalists have joined the world's economy, and we have barely begun to feel their impact. The virtually endless supply of labor, much of it skilled, in China and India, combined with the negation of time and distance by the Internet and global air delivery, will create a new and challenging competitive environment for countries, companies, and individuals. Those who can do things no one else can do will prosper, but those without special skills will face long hours and low pay. The dwindling role of the dollar in international finance will mean a decline in living standards for Americans (for the simple reason that this country won't be able to run chronic trade deficits if other nations don't have to accept dollars as payment). And no industry will be safe from competition. Services, research and development, and basic research, in which the West now leads the world, could all follow manufacturing to Asia.

Whether slowly or quickly, the forces now bringing wealth and power to the East will also bring crisis and painful adjustment to the West. But although the East will regain its historic place as the center of the world, it will also face huge challenges in providing clean air, clean water, and disease control for its huge populations. These are challenges and crises that cannot be avoided, but they can be managed—if we wake up.

CHAPTER 1

Icebergs Ahead

America is in danger of following Europe down the tubes,
and the worst part is that nobody knows it.
They're all in denial, patting themselves on the back
as the *Titanic* heads for the icebergs full speed ahead.
—SECRETARY OF STATE
COLIN POWELL

A s the headlines listed in the prologue attest, many world figures now fear that a crisis scenario may no longer be a fantasy. American leaders are not concerned. None other than former Secretary of State Colin Powell recently told the *Atlantic Monthly* that, "The United States cannot be touched in this generation by anyone in terms of military power, economic power, the strength of our political system, and our values system."

There are good reasons for Powell's confidence. With just 5 percent of the world's population, the United States accounts for over 30 percent of its production and almost 40 percent of its consumption. At $11 trillion, America's gross domestic product is more than twice as big as that of the next largest national economy, and its real per capita income is far above that of any other major country. Its language, American English, is the language of commerce worldwide, and the U.S. dollar is the world's money. Go anywhere in the world and people will tell you how much something costs in dollars and will accept dollars without hesitation. Indeed, Americans have a special privilege in this regard: whereas others must first earn dollars in order to buy oil or wheat or Toyotas on the international market, Americans only need to print more dollars. Of the world's 1,000 largest corporations, 423 are American, and the New

York and Nasdaq stock exchanges account for 44 percent of the value of all the stocks in the world.[1] The United States is home to the world's finest universities and the overwhelming majority of its leading research centers, and it spends more on research and development than the next five countries combined.[2] It is, quite simply, the richest, most powerful nation the world has ever seen.

Americans long ago adopted the view that helping the rest of the world get rich is good for America. And thus, for the past half century, the United States has—through the process of globalization—orchestrated the growing integration of national economies to create an international exchange of goods, services, money, technology, and people. The results have been as intended and expected. This globalization has largely been directed by America, but it has enhanced American wealth and power by enabling others, particularly our allies, to flourish. It was this process, not military threats, that won the Cold War by lifting billions in the free world out of poverty and creating centers of wealth and power around the planet. In Asia, Japan became the world's second largest economy; other countries like Singapore and South Korea flourished so greatly that they became known as "tigers." Across the Atlantic, the European Union grew from six to twenty-five countries and introduced the euro, the first common European currency since Roman times. In Latin America, Mexico has attracted huge foreign investment by becoming a virtual extension of the American economy, and Brazil is flourishing by dint of American and other foreign investment.

Although American corporations initially led globalization, they are no longer the only or even the dominant players. Sony, Nokia, Cemex, and Samsung are just a few of the growing numbers of non-American companies that have become global household names. Of course, American influence has not disappeared. American music, clothing styles, sports stars, and movies are not the only entries, but they set the pace, as have Silicon Valley entrepreneurs and the Nobel Prize winners of great American universities like MIT, Harvard, Stanford, and Caltech. Some people and countries have been uncomfortable with the American flavor of this system and have criticized globalization as a euphemism for Americanization. Yet they have found it hard to resist—one of McDonald's most successful restaurants being on the Champs Elysées in Paris, for example.

In the end everybody seems to want to join, and in fact almost everybody has joined. "Globalization" was an odd term to use during the Cold War because half the world was socialist or communist and not playing. A citizen of the communist bloc who dared to even suggest playing risked being purged (or worse) as a hated "capitalist roader."

Over the past two decades, however, China, India, and the former Soviet Union all decided to leave their respective socialist workers' paradises and drive with their combined 3 billion citizens onto the once despised capitalist road. Although these people are mostly poor, the number having an advanced education and sophisticated skills is larger than the populations of many first world countries. They are arriving on the scene in the context of revolutionary changes. A series of global treaties, concluded largely at American behest, has dramatically lowered trade and investment barriers, making the old rutted capitalist road a lot smoother. With contract manufacturers that can produce anywhere in the world and express delivery companies like FedEx and UPS that can deliver anywhere in the world in thirty-six hours, the road has become a highway. Finally, the global deployment of the Internet negated time and distance for transactions that can be done in bits instead of atoms. Now the highway is a high-speed capitalist raceway, and those 3 billion new people driving on it are, effectively, in your office and living room, and you are in theirs. All of this has generated a whole new wave and model of globalization that is turning the world upside down.

The global economic system was designed during the Cold War to attract these newcomers to capitalism, but no one actually anticipated that they would join or what their absorption into it would mean. Although this new wave of globalization has many potential advantages for everyone, it also poses serious challenges. It comes at a time when a fundamental flaw in the international economic structure has combined with American self-indulgence and Asian mercantilism to stress the system and make it vulnerable. The irony here is that the winners of the Cold War were less prepared for victory than the losers were for defeat. Thus the impact of the new wave, if not handled carefully, could bring the whole system crashing down.

They Can't Move the Snow to India

It was in the winter of 2003 that my oldest son, Chummy, gave me my first glimpse of the powerful forces being unleashed by the new capitalists and how they might interact with the old system and structures. We were skiing on the north side of Lake Tahoe in California, where he lives. On the lift he asked if I would consider coinvesting with him in a local snow-removal company.

"What do you mean by snow removal?" I asked, somewhat surprised because my son is a high-level software developer.

"Well," he explained, "the company has contracts to plow the parking lots and access roads of the hotels and vacation condominiums around here whenever it snows, and that happens pretty frequently between November and May."

"But what on earth are you doing," I exclaimed, "going into something as mundane as snow plowing?"

"Dad," he said, "they can't move the snow to India."

It took a minute for that to sink in. It had never occurred to me that my son had anything to fear from India or anywhere else in terms of his career path. It was I, after all, who had advised him to go into computer science, secure in the knowledge that it would put him in a position to write his own ticket. When I asked if his job was in any danger, he thought it unlikely but noted that "outsourcing" is the new management buzzword.

"You can never be sure," he said, "that some MBA hotshot with little knowledge of the technology but a big need to impress top management with his or her sophistication won't decide to move the whole operation offshore to India or elsewhere."

My son further explained that all the big consulting and service firms like Bearing Point, IBM, Deloitte, and others were making daily pitches to top management on how much they could save by outsourcing to India.

After asking about the snow removal company's financial status and agreeing to put in a few dollars, I decided to add India (where I hadn't been in twenty years) to the countries in Asia I was scheduled to visit over the next four weeks.

At my first stop in Tokyo, discussion centered almost exclusively on China. The tone of the talk was somewhat schizophrenic. Several years ago the Japanese had feared being "hollowed out" as China took over production of steel, machine tools, and electronic components, but now they were talking of China as an opportunity. They even spoke of China possibly replacing America as the world's growth engine and of Japan orienting itself more toward China and less toward America. They were proud of their corporate and national strategy for maintaining a strong manufacturing base that allowed them—unlike the United States, which they said had little to sell—to capitalize on the China boom. Yet in the *hon-ne*, or real truth, of quiet conversation after a few drinks, Japanese corporate and government leaders alike wondered how Japan would be able to compete with China in the future.

In Beijing and Shanghai I was struck again, as I have always been during my visits over the past twenty years, by the rapidity of China's continuing modernization. Stay away from China for six months and you no longer recognize the place when you return. As I took the twelve-minute ride from the airport to downtown on Shanghai's new maglev bullet train, I couldn't help thinking how nice it would be to have something like this in America. That thought recurred over the next few days as I made my rounds of factories, government offices, consulting firms, and think tanks. By now everyone knows that China is the world's location of choice for low-cost commodity manufacturing. But what I kept hearing and seeing was that it is also rapidly becoming the location of choice for high-tech manufacturing and even research and development.

This impression was greatly strengthened by my visit with old friends at Motorola in Beijing. In the 1980s, as the U.S. trade deficit began to soar, Motorola was a prime leader in an effort to ensure continued high-tech production in the United States through a coordinated industry–government program to improve U.S. high-tech competitiveness. Now, I was told, Motorola had just moved a big part of its manufacturing and R&D to China.

I winged on to Singapore, where I was scheduled to meet with the senior minister and father of his country, Lee Kuan Yew. I knew that Lee, having foreseen that China would displace Singapore as a low-cost manufacturing location, had been urging a new high-tech and ser-vice-oriented strategy for the now wealthy and high-cost city-state. How did he view the future? With concern, was the answer. China was moving much faster than even he had anticipated, and India's domina-tion of services was completely unexpected.

In India, after a tour of Delhi, Hyderabad, Chennai, and Bangalore, I realized I was seeing a revolution—a different, more exciting, and more challenging future than I had imagined. In the "accent neutraliza-tion" classes at call center training schools, I listened to English-speak-ing Indian young people learn to sound like people in Kansas or Ot-tawa. Thus, if you're a customer of Dell Computer or United Airlines or some other U.S. company phoning a call center to get tech support or make reservations for a trip, you will think you're talking to some-one across town or in another American city; you won't realize that In-dia is at the other end of your line. In Hyderabad I met with Raju Ra-malinga, the founder of Indian infotech services provider Satyam, and I listened as he explained how in 1972 he had started sending program-mers to U.S. clients for limited software writing contracts. Now, at their request, he has taken over complete management of those clients' back offices all over the world. By doing the work at the Satyam campus outside of town, he cuts client costs by 70 percent. In Bangalore I saw 1800 Indians with Ph.D.s in electrical engineering and computer science designing Intel's latest chips. Again, the cost savings were huge; more importantly, Intel couldn't find the same number of equally qualified people in the United States. In Chennai I visited the new biotech industrial park to be directed by Krishna Ella, a Univer-sity of Michigan Ph.D. who, after several years at the leading edge of biotechnology in the United States, has come home to India, where costs are 20 percent of those in the U.S. market. By the end of my tour, I understood my son's interest in snow removal. I also understood why the notion of outsourcing was sending shivers down the spines of mil-lions of formerly secure upper-middle-class professionals who were beginning to appreciate how blue-collar workers feel about visiting the unemployment office.

I flew home via Frankfurt and Paris. On the Lufthansa flight from Delhi, I read the cover story in *Der Spiegel* about whether, in response to global competition, Europeans could bring themselves to change from their current thirty-five-hour work week to a forty-hour one. After what I had seen over the past three weeks, the question seemed trivial. Can Europe survive? is more appropriate, I thought. But then I remembered that the maglev trains in Shanghai were built in Europe, that Finland has a trade surplus with China, and in Europe my cell phone would work everywhere, instead of only in certain locations, as it does in the United States.

At Charles de Gaulle Airport in Paris, I bought a pile of newspapers and magazines for the flight to Washington Dulles. The *Guardian* of London had a front-page story about how the deficit-ridden British National Health Service was thinking about air-expressing blood samples to India for analysis to save money. Lab results would be returned via e-mail.

As I arrived in Washington, tax time was fast approaching. So I booked a quick appointment with my tax accountant at a medium-size local firm. As we chatted about my expenses, donations, and deductions, I happened to mention that I was just back from India.

"India!" he exclaimed. "We just did a deal to move our whole data processing operation to Bangalore. Your taxes will actually be calculated there." He explained that the move was saving the firm 80 percent on its processing costs. (I wondered why my bill was not being reduced, but that's another book.)

That night I phoned my daughter to let her know I was back and to get caught up on the grandchildren. She lives on the island of Maui and home-schools her two children. Mentioning that I had been in Singapore, I wondered how the kids were doing with the Singapore math curriculum I knew she was using.

"Oh," she responded, "it's great. In fact, they have a new twist now. The kids go online with Singapore and have headphones so they can talk to the teacher there while following the lesson on their computers. They think it's like *Star Wars*. They love it. And they're doing very well."

Incredible, I thought. When I worked for Scott Paper Company back in the 1970s, globalization meant setting up a subsidiary in Brussels. Now it means studying abroad by staying in your own living room.

A few weeks later, back in California to attend a meeting of Intel's policy advisory board, I found its chairman, Andy Grove, lamenting the decline in both U.S. spending on research and development over the past two decades and the number of Americans obtaining degrees in science and engineering. At the same time, Grove pointed out, critical scientific infrastructure spending is being neglected, and the nation's premier research universities are falling into decrepitude. He said, "America is in danger of following Europe down the tubes, and the worst part is that nobody knows it. They're all in denial, patting themselves on the back as the *Titanic* heads for the icebergs full speed ahead."

I had come full circle. My son and Grove were pointing from their different perspectives to the same phenomenon, which I had just observed firsthand while circling the world. I realized that the impact of the 3 billion new capitalists on the old globalization structure would generate difficult questions with enormous historic significance. To understand how historic and how difficult, let's review a bit of the past.

Globalization: The First Wave, 1415–1914

The present system of Americanized globalization is the crest of a Western swell that began to rise in Portugal nearly six hundred years ago. In 1415 China and the area we now call India produced about 75 percent of the global GDP. America was still undiscovered, and the countries of Europe were insignificant and backward. They were aware of the wealth of the East only because Arabs who controlled the overland trade routes deigned from time to time to let a few scraps fall from the table to the Western "infidel" dogs. In Lisbon, King John I's third son, Henry, wondered if it might be possible to get around the Arabs and go directly to the source of the wealth by sea. At Sagres (now Cape St. Vincent, the southwestern tip of Europe) he established history's first national base for exploration and globalization. Think of it as an early version of Florida's Cape Canaveral and Henry's project as a kind of Apollo mission. Except that the prince was aiming not for the moon but to get around Africa. To do so, his shipwrights developed the caravel, a fast, maneuverable ship without which none of the great expeditions, including that of Columbus, would have been possible.[3] The caravel was not large because it was meant to carry a compact but highly valuable cargo—information.

The caravels were the information technology of the day, and Henry sent them as probes along Africa's west coast, charging his captains to "boldly go where no man has gone before." They did, finding ivory, gold, and slaves from which come the names Ivory Coast, Gold Coast, and Slave Coast for parts of Africa. But the real prize wasn't the Africa trade, it was the news that Bartholomeu Dias brought back in 1488 after rounding the southern tip of Africa into the Indian Ocean. That information led to two seminal expeditions. Columbus had hoped that Portugal would fund his scheme of getting to the Indies by going west. When he realized the Portuguese could get there on their own by going around Africa, he turned to Spain for help, with historic consequences. Just as historic was the 1498 expedition of Vasco da Gama, who took a Portuguese flotilla to Calicut on India's west coast.

The sailing, navigational, and naval warfare technology of the Portuguese was superior to anything in Asia. By 1511 Portugal controlled the Straits of Hormuz on the Persian Gulf, had made Goa the capital of its possessions in India, and had taken control of Malacca. It dominated the Indian Ocean and opened sea trade with Siam, the Moluccas or Spice Islands, and China. Spices, drugs, gems, and silks—which for centuries had passed from China and the Indies across the Arabian Sea to the Middle East and then through Venice and Genoa to Europe— were now carried west around Africa on Portuguese ships. The effect was immediate and dramatic. The Egyptian sultans, for example, had kept the price of pepper high by limiting shipments to 210 tons per year.[4] With the Portuguese in the game, pepper prices in Lisbon fell to a fifth of those in Venice. Overnight, Egyptian–Venetian trade was destroyed, shifting the power of Venice to Portugal without a shot being fired. That was the first demonstration of the power of globalization.

This demonstration was not lost on the Spanish, Dutch, English, and French, who quickly adopted and adapted the new Portuguese technology for expeditions of their own. Over the next four hundred years, these five countries (later to be joined by the fledgling United

States and Japan) on the periphery of Europe, comprising less than 2 percent of the earth's surface and less than 20 percent of its population, exploited these advantages to create world-girdling empires that gave the West both economic and geopolitical dominance. The Industrial Revolution cemented this dominance, opening an enormous gap of productivity and wealth between the industrializing countries of the West and the rest. For example, as late as 1830, Latin America, Asia, and Africa accounted for 61 percent of the world's manufactured goods; by 1913 that share was down to 8 percent.

The industrial revolution also tied the world together tighter than ever before. Capital markets became internationalized as the gold standard established a common international medium of exchange that facilitated enormous capital flows. At its peak, for example, Britain's net overseas investment was running at 9 percent of GDP.[5] This was also a period of great movements of people, with annual immigration into places like the United States and Argentina running at rates up to 26 percent of the existing population. Many contemporary observers felt the world economy was becoming so integrated as to make its fracturing and war impossible. Tragically, however, this view proved wrong; World War I, the Great Depression, and World War II put an end to globalization for nearly forty years.

In 1947, with the consequences of aborted globalization vividly in mind, Western leaders prepared for a second round. But it wasn't globalization of the whole world, as Asia accounted for only 8 percent of global output, and half the world's population was in the communist or socialist camp and wasn't playing.

Globalization: The Second Wave, 1947–2000

This second wave of globalization was orchestrated by America, and its purposes, philosophy, and actors were very different from those of the previous wave. Instead of expansion, the objective was to rebuild areas devastated by the war and regain living standards and opportunities for a new generation. There was also the need to construct economies and a trading system that would avoid the pitfalls of the past while providing an attractive alternative to the expanding communist model and defending against the threats of the Cold War. To achieve all this, protectionism and the mercantilist efforts of the past forty years to control critical resources and technologies had to be discarded in favor of open markets and free, nondiscriminatory trade driven by corporations and their key executives.

To put this into practice, the United States—together with its European allies and later with Japan and others—negotiated agreements culminating in the creation of the World Trade Organization, which reduced tariffs, removed barriers, and established nondiscriminatory rules for conducting global trade. As the strongest and richest country and the only one undamaged by war, the United States led the way by reducing its tariffs and opening its markets more than the others.

Gold was the currency of the first wave of globalization; in 1947 the dollar was made the currency of the second. There was some discussion of creating an international currency, but the idea never got off the ground in the face of U.S. opposition. The dollar, however, was linked to gold, so that any country could exchange dollars for U.S. gold reserves at the rate of $35 per ounce. All other currencies (e.g., the British pound, the French franc, and the Japanese yen) were valued at a fixed rate against the U.S. dollar. As part of the war recovery effort, the rates were set to make the dollar strong, thereby making it easier for other countries to export to the United States.

With this free trade, dollar-based system in place, the noncommunist world turned to reconstruction and the transition to peacetime economics. The Marshall Plan in Europe and the Dodge Plan in Japan focused on government programs to set production in motion. In both Europe and Japan, incentives to generate the personal savings necessary for funding investment in new factories were emphasized. Consumer credit was limited, and in Europe retail stores operated on restricted hours and not on weekends. Sales and value-added taxes were levied on consumption, while interest income on savings accounts and stock dividend payments were exempted from taxation. In tandem with this effort to stimulate savings and investment went the provision of various incentives to spur exports. By taking advantage of foreign, principally American demand, exports could justify the large-scale production facilities that would yield the economies of scale necessary to be competitive in world markets. This drive to "catch up" and be competitive was particularly important in Japan. In lieu of the armed forces now banned by the new American written constitution, industrial and technological competitiveness became akin to national security.

In contrast to Europe and Japan, the United States came out of the war as the major producer in almost every industry. It had no concerns about production. But its leaders were haunted by the fear that, absent wartime demand, the economy would lapse back into the depression from which the war had jolted it. America thus adopted a strategy of spurring consumption. Home mortgages were made easier to obtain, with interest being tax deductible. Credit cards were made easily available, and interest on consumer credit purchases was also made tax deductible, while interest and dividends earned on savings accounts and investments were fully taxed. So while Europe and especially Japan focused on saving, investing, producing, and exporting, America's growth policy was one of borrow, spend, and consume.

Initially the results were just what everyone wanted. The twenty-three years from 1950 to 1973 were the golden age of global growth. The U.S. economy boomed as it never had before. Europe and Asia did likewise. Using the latest technology developed as a result of the war effort and achieving unparalleled economies of scale based on history's first mass market, U.S. producers were the low-cost producers even as they paid the highest wages. Productivity rose at record rates, and incomes soared, with per capita U.S. wages hitting a peak in 1973 of $30,713 (in 2002 dollars).[6] The United States was becoming a true consumer's paradise, and Europe and Japan were also getting rich by investing and producing to supply American consumers along with their own increasingly eager shoppers. The action was led by so-called multinational companies as more and more producers found opportunities in foreign markets and strove to stay competitive by expanding abroad. The rising costs of investment in large-scale factories and especially in expensive research and development could increasingly be recovered only by operating in large global markets. Expansion was rapid as names like IBM, Coca Cola, Sony, and Unilever became household words around the world.

The End of Gold

But as early as 1971 a problem emerged that would prove indicative of things to come. All the incentives were working—too well. Americans were consuming like crazy, while the Europeans and especially the Japanese were investing, producing, and exporting like crazy. As a result, U.S. trade and international payment balances began to move into deficit for the first time in nearly a hundred years, and dollars began to pile up in foreign bank coffers. Then, as now, some governments were uneasy about holding all the dollars. Unlike now, however, there was a remedy then, or so the French leader Charles de Gaulle thought. He began exchanging excess dollars for gold bars from the U.S. reserves at Fort Knox. Soon the U.S. reserves were melting like butter in summer. Faced with maintaining the international financial system (which it had largely designed) by adopting austerity measures that would cut consumption in order to balance trade or scrapping the system, Washington unilaterally decided to scrap the system. On March 3, 1971, President Richard Nixon simply halted any further exchange of gold for dollars. Treasury secretary and former Texas governor John Connally commented that "the dollar is our currency, but your [the foreign countries'] problem."[7]

Thus was created the dollar-standard system that has prevailed ever since. All other currencies would float or be fixed against the dollar, and their economies would have to adjust according to the vagaries of U.S. economic policy. The United States, on the other hand, could now buy whatever it wanted with its own money without apparent consequences to itself or obligations to others. Even more than before, it could forget about saving and run continuous trade deficits as long as the rest of the world was prepared to accept dollars or had no other alternative. Whereas other countries had to more or less balance their trade over time and only consume roughly as much as they produced, the United States didn't have to sell anything in order to buy. It could simply print dollars with no link to any value except the "full faith and credit of the United States." Other currencies would bear all the burden of adjusting global trade balances. What a deal! America could now truly be the world's consumer of last resort while also controlling financial markets. In short, it could play the dominant role in globalization regardless of what others desired or did.

Can America Compete

Or could it? In the fall of 1981 I reported for my first day of work as a newly appointed official in the Commerce Department. My new boss, Secretary Malcolm Baldrige, told me my job was to reduce the trade deficit, especially that with Japan, which had reached $14 billion.[8] Without realizing it, I was in on the beginning of the great debate that raged throughout the 1980s over U.S. competitiveness and the viability of the second wave of globalization. Some countries had discovered their central banks could keep the dollar strong and their exports rising by purchasing greenbacks in the foreign exchange markets. Meanwhile, in lieu of any external discipline, Americans continued to consume more than they produced. The resultant soaring trade (technically current account) deficit had to be financed by foreign investors, and some observers feared that the United States was becoming too dependent on a continual inflow of foreign capital.

Meanwhile, U.S. manufacturers were continuing to lose business and jobs. Toyota and Honda were chewing up Detroit. All U.S. television makers went out of business. In a seminal event whose effects (discussed in Chapter 7) are still felt today, Japanese electronics makers took over the video recording business from its inventor, Ampex, and Silicon Valley's semiconductor producers laid off thousands in the face of Japanese competition. Nor was the impact limited to the United States. European manufacturers also increasingly experienced loss of market share to Japanese and other Asian producers. Even more important than the immediate loss of jobs was the fate of manufacturing, which many saw as the source of most research and development, most productivity gains, and the highest wages. It was also seen as very much affected by linkages, meaning that the loss of one industry like video recording could result in the loss of many of the supplier and follow-on industries as well.

The ensuing discussion about what was wrong and what to do

raised several key issues concerning the whole system: the meaning of free trade, the government's role in promoting economic development, the trade deficit, the level playing field. At the core of the debate was the fact that, as de Gaulle had perceived, there was no market discipline on the United States. It could ignore saving, budget deficits, and competitiveness issues as long as it could print dollars and have them accepted by the rest of the world.

In the end, the debate petered out inconclusively. The dollar fell a bit in the wake of a 1986 deal between the United States, Europe, and Japan to orchestrate joint intervention in foreign exchange markets; and tax increases coupled with spending curbs cut the U.S. budget deficits a bit. Then the fall of the Berlin Wall and the collapse of the Soviet Union enabled a dramatic cut in U.S. defense spending, and the U.S. trade deficit was actually balanced in 1991, when foreign donations to help pay for the Gulf War against Saddam Hussein outweighed the U.S. deficit. The rise of the PC turned Microsoft and Intel into the world's leading technology companies, while a semiconductor agreement with Japan guaranteed the U.S. industry about 20 percent of the Japanese market. Americans switched from driving cars to SUVs, vans, and trucks, and thereby bought Detroit a few more years until the Japanese could bring out their own models.

The longest economic expansion in American history began in 1992 and seemed to confirm the view that there was no competitiveness problem. The U.S. economy moved to services and created more jobs than it had in twenty years. Real wages and median family income increased for the first time since 1973. The advent of the Internet and the dot.com mania seemed to confirm the expectation that America and other advanced countries would move on to sophisticated services and innovative high technology as manufacturing moved to developing countries. Then, for the first time in twenty-eight years, the U.S. budget went into surplus.[9] Americans still consumed more than they produced and needed capital inflow from abroad, but the foreigners were only too anxious to invest in the NASDAQ and the dot.coms. Globalization was announced as America's strategy. Through globalization the world would become rich, and thus democratic, and thus stay at peace.

Then the American bubble burst as most of the dot.coms went belly up, the economy went into recession, the budget went back into deficit, and the trade deficit, which had never gone away, exploded. Particularly significant was the fact that the trade deficit exploded even in high-tech goods, while services exports that had been expected to fill the gap failed to do so. Meanwhile, the Japanese and European economies remained stagnant and increasingly dependent for growth on exports to America. All the old questions of the 1980s had come back, but in a new context.

Globalization: The Third Wave

Today a third wave of globalization is washing over the world. Riding its crest, the two giants of Asia—China and India—are coming back into their own after six hundred years of impoverishment and servitude. The key elements of this new wave are the negation of time and distance and the rapid transfer of technology from advanced to developing countries. The already struggling machinery of the American-led globalization of the Cold War will be battered and strained further, perhaps beyond repair, by the impact of the 3 billion new capitalists. The new wave will dramatically change corporate strategy, the balance of power, and the everyday lives of billions of people, from the elite "masters of the universe" to ordinary citizens in America and abroad. It will empower individuals as never before and bring into action talents and players long ignored. One of its defining characteristics is that it will be less driven by countries or corporations and more driven by real people. It will unleash unprecedented creativity, advancement of knowledge, and economic development. But at the same time, it will tend to undermine safety net systems and penalize the unskilled. Nondiscriminatory and already less American and less first world, it will challenge the livelihoods of heretofore secure professionals in Europe, the United States, and Japan. Indeed, it will challenge all the conventional economic wisdom as it shifts wealth and power to Asia.

For example, take immigration. Historically America has attracted immigrants in search of opportunity and work. More recently this has also been true of Europe and even, to a lesser extent, of Japan. Now, however, the flow is going the other way. Some of the work is emigrating to seek the workers, and former immigrants are going home where opportunities now seem better. China has become the location of choice for global manufacturing, while India is becoming the destination for software development and services.

These new players are creating new markets and ways of doing business as well as substantial and badly needed centers of demand in the global economy. China has just displaced America as Japan's biggest trading partner and is supplying the demand for possible Japanese growth. Its enormous appetite for food and primary resources is also spurring development from Indonesia to Brazil. At the same time, the new wave is rapidly raising demand for scarce water, accelerating desertification, and poisoning both the water and the air with pollution. On top of that is the question of energy. The entire world will become more dependent than ever on Persian Gulf oil suppliers, even as the price of oil ratchets ever upward. Both energy and environmental issues will challenge not only the United States but also China and India and the rest of the world (see Chapter 9).

As these developments shift the basic structure of the global economy, they are calling into question assumptions that have long dominated global economic policies. Business executives, economists, and political leaders have resisted rethinking them even when they seemed seriously out of whack with realities. These issues remind me of the flaws in the *Titanic*, since the global system could founder on them, absent new thinking more compatible with the realities of the new wave of globalization:

- The U.S. trade deficit is now over $600 billion, or about 6 percent of GDP annually. As a result, the United States has swung from being a major creditor nation to having the biggest debt—now nearing $3 trillion. These unprecedented amounts, however, have been dismissed as potential problems. They have even been called signs of strength by some who claim they just mean the U.S. economy is growing faster than others. This growth also supposedly makes it easy to finance them because foreigners will want to invest in the fast-growing U.S. economy. More recently, however, leaders like Federal Reserve chairman Alan Greenspan and former chairman Paul Volcker have begun to express concern that the deficits may be unsustainable, while the headlines included in the Prologue testify to the concern of foreign leaders. The United States now needs a fix of over $2 billion a day of foreign money coming in. Without new thinking, there may be a day when it doesn't come.

- Behind the trade deficit lies the zero savings of American households, the federal budget deficit, and the excessive savings rates and mercantilism of a number of other countries. None of these phenomena are sustainable.

- Can, and should, the dollar last as the world's currency? Heretofore there have been no real alternatives; but with the advent of the euro and discussion of an Asian currency unit, that situation is changing. The special role of the dollar as the world's money removes all financial discipline from the United States and enables currency manipulation by other countries. This is the key *Titanic*-like flaw in the current system. It cannot last. But how and when to change are crucial questions not presently being addressed.

- Does manufacturing matter? In the United States, manufacturing has declined from 23 percent of GDP in the 1980s to 12.7 percent today. Europe and Japan have also seen a decline but smaller than in the United States. The conventional wisdom holds that the structure of an economy, what it makes, and the services it provides are not terribly important and should not be the subject of government policy. According to this view, linkages between industries and technologies are unimportant, and technology development is independent of manufacturing and production. This view also seems to be at odds with the realities of the third wave of globalization. Beyond that is the question of balancing the trade deficit, which is mostly in manufactured goods. But the United States does not have enough physical manufacturing capacity to export its way to anything approaching a trade balance even if the dollar goes to zero value. Services exports can surely rise, but it is unlikely they can completely fill in the gap. Without some development in manufacturing, therefore, the only way out of the trade deficit is a significant cut in consumption. Thus the question, Does manufacturing matter?

- Economists have held it as an article of faith that high-tech manufacturing and services are done in advanced countries, while routine, low-value work is done in developing countries (see Chapter 9). But China has more semiconductor plants under construction or about to go into operation than America has. All mobile phone makers have moved most or much of their R&D to China. Nor does India limit itself to mundane software development; it also works at the cutting edge. As for services work, radiology, heart and joint replacement surgery, and pharmaceutical development are regularly outsourced to India. U.S. and European companies emphasize that they do a lot of high-tech work in China and India because they can't get it done as well at home.

- It has long been assumed that as manufacturing jobs disappeared, the service industries would provide secure, high-paying jobs to compensate for the loss of manufacturing. That view, however, is pre-Internet and pre–third wave. It may not be sustainable in the world of 3 billion new capitalists all online.

- The view that the uniquely inventive U.S. economy will always maintain economic leadership by doing the next new thing no longer necessarily holds. U.S. spending on research and development has declined in critical areas, and its technology infrastructure is deteriorating. Other countries are graduating more scientists and engineers, while America graduates fewer and fewer. Most important, the leading U.S. venture capitalists and technology firms are taking R&D and new start-up company development to Asia as fast as possible.

- The MBA and the American business model have had great influence on how business is done worldwide. The success of U.S. business has been largely attributed to its management and its focus on shareholders as opposed to stakeholders. Yet much of the U.S. business success has been due to government support and fortunate circumstances. The change in circumstances and the rise of strong non-American companies with different concepts of their purpose and objectives may require a whole new way of thinking about business.

- Although Western, particularly U.S., business leaders tend to disdain intervention in their affairs by their own governments, they frequently curry favor with authoritarian foreign governments. This practice may make them more subject to the policies of foreign governments than their own. Ironically this situation has been fostered by Western government officials who disdain the whole notion of an economic strategy. None of this thinking may be sustainable in the wake of the third wave of globalization.

- The level playing field concept is much loved by Western political leaders who are quick to call Asian countries trade cheaters while insisting that Western workers can compete with any on "a level playing field." But the truth is they can't. Advanced country workers with the same skills as Chinese or Indian workers will not be able to compete unless they are willing to accept Indian or Chinese wages. Moreover, in a peculiar way, the playing field will tilt toward the two new giants of the global economy. The potential size of their markets, their endless supply of low-cost labor, the unique combination of many highly skilled but low-paid professionals, and the investment incentives offered by their governments will constitute an irresistible package that will attract investment away not only from the first world but from other developing countries as well. China, for example, could be a real problem for Mexico. The only sensible response is massive investment in education and up-skilling of the workforce. Only those who have capabilities no one else has or can work better than anyone else will be secure.

- Americans are likely to find themselves increasingly uncompetitive as individuals. They have never understood the extent to which their high standard of living has been the result of good luck rather than personal virtuosity. In the new world of no time and no distance where education will be at a premium, the poor quality of U.S. secondary education will be even more of a disadvantage than it is now. American students now rank near the bottom of all the comparative international tests. To have any chance of competing on a level playing field, the United States will have to find a way to reverse that situation.

- Unless China and India go totally off the rails, they will become the world's largest economies in the middle of this century. The European Union is already the world's largest economic unit and will remain larger than the United States indefinitely. Despite U.S. military might, the balance of international influence and power is already shifting. As the National Intelligence Council says, the international power situation is more fluid now than at any time in the past half century.[10] The challenge for the United States will be to play its currently powerful cards to shape a new balance of power favorable to its interests in a future when it will be relatively much weaker. Will its pride allow it to recognize that reality?

But these are all subsets of a much larger question. Today's global economy is the most integrated and it offers greater potential opportunities than ever. Yet, in many respects it resembles the *Titanic,* a magnificent machine with serious and largely unrecognized internal flaws heading at full speed for icebergs, armed with knowledge and assumptions significantly at odds with reality. In the pages that follow, I hope to explain the machine's flaws and the true nature of the icebergs so that the third wave of globalization can be even more successful than the second has been.

CHAPTER 2

How the Capitalist Road Turned East

It doesn't matter if a cat is black or white
so long as it catches mice.
— DENG XIAOPING

At approximately 3:30 P.M. on October 10, 1982, Air Force Three banked right and headed northwest. A few moments later the intercom crackled and, as a shiver of excitement coursed through the plane, the pilot announced we had entered Chinese airspace near Shanghai and were on course for Beijing. I was on board as part of a U.S. government delegation led by commerce secretary Malcolm Baldrige, bound for the Chinese capital to negotiate liberalization of the conditions for trade and investment between the two countries.

At this point the American- and European-led movement to regain the pre–1914 level of global economic integration had been under way for about a quarter century. Though this movement had made significant progress, it could only go so far. Nearly half the world's territory and population were controlled by communist and socialist governments, whose ideas about what should be globalized, and by whom, differed from those of the West. Although the Cold War seemed as if it would go on forever, China's leaders had been sending interesting signals suggesting that their Marxist-Leninist ideology would not necessarily prevent them from doing business. Hence our visit.

Few in the group had ever been to China, and all had grown up in an era when China was second only to the Soviet Union in the pantheon of America's enemies. To enter the devil's lair was a bit of a thrill.

Two hours later we landed at Beijing Capital International Airport and pulled to a stop on the tarmac some distance from the terminal building. As I descended the mobile stairs and entered one of the limos that would drive us to the terminal, I was awed. Nine years before, when America first recognized Communist China after twenty years of official relations, I had watched intently as President Nixon descended from Air Force One to be greeted by the legendary Chinese leader Chou En Lai at this same airport. I am struck now by how old and primitive it was, not much more impressive than the cow pasture airfields I visited as an avid model plane builder in high school. How could we have felt so threatened, I wondered, by a country whose capital doesn't even have a real airport?

The thought repeated itself as we drove into Beijing in a caravan of black limos. These copies of the Russian Zis, the official car of Soviet leaders, looked slightly like old Cadillacs, but the wooden passenger seats in back had none of a Cadillac's comfort. The drive into Beijing along a tree-lined, two-lane highway empty of other vehicles took about an hour. At first, I thought the government must have ordered the road cleared for our official entourage. But, as we entered Beijing proper and made our way to the Diaoyutai, the state guest house, it became apparent there simply were no vehicles in this country. Everyone walked or rode bicycles or an occasional donkey.

The state guest house is a village of low-rise apartments and suites set in a large garden of trees, lakes, and bridges, connected by winding trails. We had been traveling for nearly twenty-four hours and went to bed after eating the meal that was waiting for us. Before dawn, I found myself wide awake with jet lag and at 6:00 A.M. gave up on sleeping and went jogging. As I exited the compound onto a broad avenue, I could see only dimly in the dark. Suddenly I heard a soft whoosh and jumped back just in time to avoid being hit by a wave of bicycles, all piloted by figures wearing identical black Mao suits and riding black bicycles. Wow, I thought, whoever makes that bicycle has a whale of a business. Of course it was made by the state-owned bicycle company, which was certainly not making money.

Later that morning, our group got back into the limos for the drive to our first meetings at the fabled Great Hall of the People, where so

much recent Chinese history had occurred. Again, there were almost
no vehicles and no stoplights or even stop signs. The streets were full
of the same Mao-suited bicyclists and pedestrians I had encountered
earlier. Even more striking was the physical aspect of the city. Few
buildings rose above three or four stories, and acres of housing com-
pounds were hidden behind ancient brick walls. The city's drab, aus-
tere mien was broken only by the ochre and gold walls and roofs of the
Forbidden City enclosing the palaces of the former Chinese empire:
the walls made more imposing by their stark contrast to everything
outside them. The Great Hall too was a disappointment, being just
that—a great hall. Our dinner that evening, at a state-run restaurant,
was not so much a delicious, authentic Chinese meal as it was an excellent argument against government control of industry. Nor did sou-
venir shopping at the state run Friendship Store provide much that
would interest my family back home.

In contrast to the sights, cuisine, and souvenirs, the discussions we
conducted and the negotiators we met were most impressive. Many
had studied at leading American universities, and all were well versed
in the fundamentals of market economics and the complexities of international trade. Even more important, they were anxious to learn
more and to increase China's international trade by making it part of
the U.S.-centered system of globalization. We had come to propose
creation of a U.S.-China commission on commerce and trade that
would explore the possibility of future agreements on removing barriers to trade and investment. They were way ahead of us and wanted to
talk now about which barriers to remove first. They were also interested in the minutiae of the international trade rules and procedures
and were particularly keen to discuss how private companies are created and run. They called themselves communists, but they sounded a
lot like capitalists to me. In any case, they were in the middle of a long
march from where they had started.

Nor were the Chinese the only ones on the march. In hindsight,
clearly other developments were under way that would set the stage
for a vastly expanded global economic system and a whole new wave
of globalization. By 1989 the ferment in East Germany and the Soviet
bloc led to the fall of the Berlin Wall and then to the collapse of the So-

viet Union on Christmas Day 1991. That in turn paved the way for India to reconsider socialism. Meanwhile, the rickety old trade system that had been run under a complicated arrangement called the General Agreement on Tariffs and Trade (GATT) was turned into the World Trade Organization, the European Common Market became the European Union, and a number of other agreements like the North American Free Trade Agreement (NAFTA) were concluded. While this was happening, technology in the form of air express and then the Internet was shrinking the globe to a tiny orb by negating distance and time. All of these made it more attractive and easier for 3 billion new capitalists to begin making the global economy truly global.

China: From Workers Paradise to Capitalist Road

Mao Zedong is still treated as a kind of demigod in China, and his embalmed body, displayed in Beijing's Tiananmen Square, continues to draw crowds. However, it is Deng Xiao Ping who will go down in history as the father of modern China. A veteran of the legendary Long March that saved the Chinese Communist Party from destruction and eventually led to its conquest of mainland China in 1949, Deng became general secretary of the Chinese Communist Party in 1956, two years before it proclaimed the Great Leap Forward. In Mao's romantic effort to force-march China into surpassing the production of Great Britain within fifteen years, peasants were famously directed to build backyard furnaces and make steel from their pots, pans, and other metal implements. By 1962, with the economy in a total shambles and the countryside facing famine for want of planting tools and simple cooking utensils, the pragmatically inclined Deng had seen enough of ideology. Saying "it doesn't matter if a cat is black or white so long as it catches mice,"[1] he teamed up with Mao's designated successor, Liu Shaoqi, to restore some semblance of practicality to China's economy.

In 1966, however, Deng became embroiled in the fiasco of Mao's second great revolutionary upheaval—the Cultural Revolution—whose flavor is exemplified by one of its main slogans: "Rather the

grass of socialism than the jewels of capitalism."[2] Clearly that was not
Deng's attitude. Attacked as the "number two capitalist roader" after
number one Liu, Deng was purged and sent to work on the production
line of a tractor factory for seven years. Reinstated as deputy premier
by Prime Minister Zhou Enlai after the latter became seriously ill in
1973, he took over the administration of the government and vigorously pushed Zhou's efforts to modernize agriculture, technology, industry, and the military. But he was not out of trouble yet. After Zhou's
death in 1976, Deng was purged again, only to be resurrected once
more after Mao's death. By 1978, having become the de facto successor to the Great Helmsman, Deng inherited a situation possibly worse
than that after the Great Leap Forward. In the countryside, where four-
fifths of the people lived, a whole family might share a single pair of
trousers and live along with its livestock in a single thatched hut with a
hole in the roof for a chimney.[3] Per capita income, at about $550, was
among the world's lowest.[4]

Fundamental reform followed immediately after Deng came to
power. The pivotal eleventh party congress Central Committee meeting of December 1978 declared the Cultural Revolution a "catastrophe" and adopted Deng's Four Modernizations.[5] By increasing rural
incentives and incomes, encouraging new enterprises, curtailing central direction, and encouraging foreign direct investment (FDI) in
China, Deng aimed to make it a modern industrial nation by means of
a new strategy—the socialist market economy. Deng stressed that
socialism should not condemn people to shared poverty and emphasized that "to get rich is glorious." Thus he led China to take its first
historic step back onto the capitalist road it had left thirty years before. Mao had been right about one thing: Deng was indeed a capitalist roader.

A large package of incentives and liberalization quickly spurred
production. But the step that had the most profound significance for
the long run was the decision to attract foreign investors. For centuries China had tried to keep the "foreign devils" out; now it was trying to get them in. This shift electrified the foreign business community, which continued to nurse its nineteenth-century dream of
supplying the oil for the lamps of China or adding a few inches to

each man's shirt tail. The notion of supplying a market of over a billion people was powerfully attractive. As a senior executive in charge of international marketing with American Can Company in 1979 and 1980, I was fully involved in briefing and planning sessions on China. It became clear very quickly at these meetings that whether or not China ever developed a large domestic market, it was already a very, very inexpensive place to make things for export. Not only were its labor costs less than a tenth those in the United States, but the Chinese were anxious to find ways to help with the problems. Having watched Japan and the Asian tigers get rich by saving, investing, and exporting, Deng figured that what worked for them ought to work for China.

To foster this strategy, a series of measures establishing special economic zones in coastal cities, free trade zones, and special high-tech zones were introduced. Local, provincial, and national government agencies offered investment incentives ranging from tax holidays to outright capital grants that could amount to as much as half the cost of a new manufacturing facility. At the same time, China launched an emergency education effort to make up for the lost years of the Cultural Revolution, when schools had been closed. Not only were schools and universities expanded, but hundreds of thousands of students were sent to the United States and other countries for foreign study. Today China is graduating over 2 million students from college annually.[6]

There has been no letup in domestic liberalization. In 1992 the concept of the "socialist market economy" was incorporated in the constitution. In 1997 the private sector was designated an important component of the socialist market economy, and at the sixteenth party congress in 2001, "red capitalists" were invited to join the party and were even made congress delegates. Finally, in 2003, the "inviolable sanctity of private property" was made a fundamental principle of the constitution.

In response to all this, both foreign investment and exports have soared. From less than $20 billion in 1980, foreign investment in China mounted to $200 billion by 1990[7] and is now well over $500 billion.[8] By the same token, exports have climbed from $18 billion to nearly $600 billion, and China has a trade surplus that has enabled it to accumulate $650 billion of foreign exchange reserves, second only to Japan's $850 billion.

As trade became its primary engine of growth, China applied in 1986 for admission to the General Agreement on Tariffs and Trade, the body that then governed the international move to free trade.[9] The GATT became the World Trade Organization in 1994 at the end of the Uruguay round of negotiations, and China became a formal member in 2001. It was twenty years since Deng's historic decision to open China to the world and exactly one hundred years since U.S. secretary of state John Hay announced China's adherence to the Open Door trade policy, an agreement forced on a weak China by the Western powers and Japan. Now a strong China had decided to open its doors itself and join the global trade game in order to level the playing field. As the world's low-cost manufacturer, China was about to turn globalization into a whole new ball game (see Chapter 4).

India and the Soviets: The Wall Falls on Socialism

Although historians will debate whether it was Ronald Reagan with his Star Wars and Defense Department budget increases who defeated communism, the ultimate cause of the collapse was obvious. The workers paradise was hell. The socialist road was full of potholes and had no traffic signals.

East Germany was the best functioning of the Soviet bloc economies, a testament to the Germans' competence that they could make even communism work. But they really couldn't. Even the Berlin Wall couldn't keep East Germany penned in on November 9, 1989. They tore it down and triggered the fall of the Soviet Union two years later. It was the contrast with the globalized, capitalist European Union that defeated the communist empire and brought its 300 million subjects on to the capitalist road. Almost all the Soviet Union's former satellite countries are in the European Union or soon will be. While Russia will not be, it will probably become a full member of the World Trade Organization soon and thus a full-fledged capitalist roader as well. Impor-

tant as all this change has been, however, the greatest long-term significance of the fall of the Soviet Union my be its impact on India.

When the British finally departed India in 1947, they left large problems and valuable assets. Education has historically been important
to the Hindus, the inventors of zero. Beginning in 1835, the British
East India Company undertook to establish a Western-style education
system with instruction in English. While not universal, the system
provided a practical and science-oriented education for a fairly broad
elite, many of whom eventually took advanced degrees at top British
universities. Thus the British legacy included a large English-speaking
population and a leadership class educated along Western lines. It
also included a basic capitalist system and a reasonably good infrastructure, including railroads and highways joining all of India's major
population centers. During World War II a great number of controls
and regulations were applied to the economy.

When Jawaharlal Nehru became prime minister of the newly independent India, he added to the educational base by founding the Indian Institute of Technology with seven campuses throughout the
country and a world-class engineering curriculum. In time, this institution became one of the world's best universities, in a league with
MIT, Oxford, and Caltech. Nehru also strengthened and enhanceed
wartime controls of the Indian economy to such an extent that IIT
graduates could not find jobs in India commensurate with their quali-
fications. Much of the world saw socialism as the wave of the future,
and India under Nehru and his successors hewed steadfastly to the
socialist path, partly owing to Indian resentment of its colonial experience and to the fact that socialism was seen as anti-imperialist.
However understandable it may have been, this policy made 70 percent of workers government employees and locked India into a low-
growth pattern much like that of Mao's China.[10] One statistic says it
all. In 1938 India's share of world trade was nearly 3 percent; in 1980 it
was 0.5 percent.[11]

Still, there were important differences. India remained a democracy, with rule of law and protection of private property. It also
maintained the institutions of capitalism such as a functioning banking system, courts, and accounting bodies. In addition, it allowed

free movement of its people, of whom many with elite educations went abroad, particularly to a place in the United States called Silicon Valley.

In a perverse way, the system made necessity the mother of invention. India was hostile to foreign investment and insisted that outside companies enter the market only with Indian partners. Tariffs were high and imports highly restricted. For example, companies were allowed to import computers only if they could guarantee to generate export earnings that would more than pay for the imports. Conditions eventually became so difficult that IBM simply shut down its Indian operation, at a time when its name was almost synonymous with computers. Maintaining old IBM computers and developing innovative software to keep them working became a special talent of IIT graduates. When Rajiv Gandhi became prime minister in 1984, the computer-loving former pilot loosened things up by reducing trade barriers and initiating some deregulation. But it took the fall of the Berlin Wall, the first Gulf War, and the collapse of the Soviet system to really break things open.

Prior to 1989, India had a de facto preferential trading relationship with the Soviet bloc rather like Cuba's. To encourage India to lean its way in the international power struggle, the Soviets bought Indian; and by 1989, 18 percent of Indian exports were going to the Soviet bloc. This share fell to 3 percent as the bloc began to disintegrate. India couldn't readily replace these exports because it didn't make anything that anyone else wanted to buy. Also at this time, a significant source of India's foreign currency reserves came from the repatriated earnings of Indians working in the states along the Persian Gulf, especially Kuwait, which hired Indians to run its economy so Kuwaitis didn't have to. When Saddam Hussein invaded in 1990, that source of income dried up overnight, thrusting India into a major crisis.

Domestic subsidies had reached 12 percent of GDP[12] while the government's debt soared to 40 percent of GDP.[13] Just servicing the debt took 30 percent of exports. Now oil prices were heading into the stratosphere while Delhi's foreign exchange holdings fell to $1 billion, barely enough to cover two weeks' worth of imports. Bankruptcy loomed.

At this crucial moment, Prime Minister Narasimha Rao called Man-mohan Singh to the rescue. Part of the Oxford-educated elite, Singh had written his doctoral dissertation on free trade. In a long career as a government bureaucrat, he had come to admire Prime Minister Margaret Thatcher, perhaps as a result of his concern with overregulation and her success in fighting it. Addressing the Indian parliament, Singh firmly declared that for the foreseeable future the business of India would be business. Quoting Victor Hugo, he said, "No power on earth can stop an idea whose time has come."[14] Singh, who is now India's prime minister, proposed to unleash entrepreneurial spirits by slashing tariffs and other trade barriers, deregulating and privatizing, attracting foreign investment, and fostering export-led growth. India's 1 billion people would join China's 1.4 billion and the Soviet bloc's 350 million on the capitalist road. Traffic was getting heavy and a smoother ride was needed.

Globalization Goes Global

The global trade system is a two-tiered structure. At one level is the set of rules and agreements to which all members of the system are party and which form the governance foundation for all international trade. At another level are regional or bilateral arrangements that fit under the rules of the global framework but apply only to a limited number of parties who have agreed among themselves to go beyond the general rules of economic integration. As the new players were coming into the system toward the end of the twentieth century, it was also being redesigned at both levels to respond to rapidly growing and increasingly complex demands.

GATT Goes to the World Trade Organization

When American and European leaders attempted to restart globalization in 1947, they were only partially successful. The initial plan was to create an International Monetary Fund to administer the global monetary and financial system, a World Bank to foster economic growth in developing countries, and an International Trade Organization (ITO) to establish and administer a system of free trade. While the Fund and the Bank were duly inaugurated, the ITO, ironically, foundered on antiglobal American sentiment. At Havana in 1948, the designers of the ITO envisioned an organization that would cover all types of restrictions on international trade, including tariffs, internal taxation, regulation, labor and employment rules, subsidies, state trading, antidumping, antitrust (or competition policy), and free trade areas. Had the ITO been completed and adopted, globalization would have proceeded much more quickly. But because it was negotiated as part of an international treaty, its adoption by the United States was subject to ratification by Congress. Important politicians were afraid the ITO would somehow threaten American sovereignty and reduce U.S. freedom of action in foreign policy. When it became clear that Congress would not ratify, the ITO was abandoned. The other countries participating in the negotiation were prepared to ratify, but without the United States that would have been an empty gesture. The General Agreement on Trade and Tariffs (GATT) section of the ITO, however, was an executive agreement rather than a treaty, and could be adopted without congressional approval. Though only a small part of what had been intended, the GATT became the basis of the international trade rules and all further trade talks.

Over the next fifty years, the member nations tried to broaden GATT into an ITO through a series of "rounds" of negotiations. They chipped away at tariff and other trade barriers, but by the mid-1980s, many important markets remained virtually impermeable to imports. Worse, some countries simply ignored the agreements with impunity because the GATT contained no real enforcement mechanism.

Launched in 1986, the Uruguay round produced agreement in 1994 on compulsory dispute settlement; extensive rules limiting subsidies; the inclusion of agriculture, textiles, and services like banking, accounting, and telecommunications under the trade rules, and creation of the WTO to govern international trade.

Thus nearly half a century after it was rejected by the U.S. Senate, the old ITO was born under a new name. Its impact has been enormous. Compulsory dispute settlement has forced the United States and others to pay attention to long-standing complaints they formerly ignored. The United States has even been compelled to change its corporate tax system to comply with WTO rulings on illegal trade subsidies. Europe and Japan have been forced to open their markets more substantially than ever before. Even more significant, by providing an institution in which all members are on a roughly equal trade footing, the WTO made inclusion of the 3 billion new capitalists in the global system easy and thereby made globalization truly global.

The Making of Europe and North America

Even before World War II ended, a quiet Frenchman named Jean Monnet had begun preaching that the way to a peaceful Europe was through gradual economic union. In the Treaty of Rome (March 1957), Germany, France, Belgium, Luxembourg, The Netherlands, and Italy signed on to make Monnet's dream a reality and created the European Economic Community, which later became simply the European Community (EC).

When I arrived in Brussels in 1972 as head of Scott Paper Company's European marketing operations, the dream of a united continent seemed more like a nightmare. Scott was selling paper towels, toilet tissue, napkins, and facial tissues through a combination of joint ventures and wholly owned operations in all the key European markets. I use the term "markets" advisedly because from my perspective there was no single market. The toilet tissue rolls in Italy were wider than those in Belgium, while the paper in France was a kind of wax paper that made the term "toilet tissue" seem Orwellian—as was the experience of using the stuff. The brand names of the products differed by country, and the grocery stores and wholesalers not only varied by country but were of vastly different types as well. Once a month, I conducted meetings at the Brussels European headquarters. I remember these meetings as among the most difficult of my career. English was supposed to be the language used, but the French refused to speak it, and others simply could not speak it well enough for a serious business discussion. Moreover, if the British said something was white, the Germans were sure to see it as black. I kept arguing that Coca-Cola was a powerful brand in part because it was the same brand everywhere and could get great advertising and marketing efficiencies as well as product recognition. My arguments always elicited at least three hundred reasons why toilet tissue was different from soft drinks and why my idea of a single Scott brand across Europe was merely the nonsense one might expect from a simple-minded American.

Twenty-five years later, I was involved in the establishment of a group called the Trans-Atlantic Business Dialogue. It gathered CEOs and key government officials from both sides of the Atlantic twice a year to discuss how to remove hurdles to greater transatlantic trade and investment. The first meeting was held in Seville, Spain. As the participants were trying to fashion a concluding statement and press release, it was all I could do to keep from laughing out loud. Not because of anything being said or done, but just because of the contrast with the meetings I had held in Brussels long ago. Here the argument was not about why things had to be done differently in one country than in another; rather, it was about how to speed up doing them the same way. Not only was everyone speaking English, they were speaking good English. A French CEO and future finance minister was arguing about where the commas and periods should go in an English-language statement. It was rich, and I loved every moment of it. But the experience bespoke a historic achievement too little appreciated in the world outside Europe. Through endless difficult negotiations and many missed deadlines, the Europeans have achieved an integrated market that has not only made war unthinkable but that has also become a powerful catalyst for reform elsewhere. Today when I travel to Europe, I often think of my first visit there in 1959. The three-hundred-mile trip from Rotterdam to Paris included three passport checks, three changes of money, and three customs inspections, frequently by officials who spoke only one of the languages involved. Today I can take the same trip with no passport checks, no change of currency, and no customs checks. Moreover, the officials all speak at least two languages and most of them speak four (Dutch, Flemish, French, and English) fluently. Nor has this trend to integration ended.

In 2004 the European Union formally inducted ten new member countries and three will follow by 2007. As a maker of more global globalization, Europe has been unsurpassed.

Free trade agreements elsewhere have added to the globalization momentum. When I worked in Mexico in the late 1970s, I discovered that Mexicans were hard-working, conscientious people handicapped by a corrupt one-party quasi-socialist government that operated without the rule of law and provided little in the way of education, entrepreneurial incentives, or essential infrastructure. Yet despite these difficulties, the country's low-cost labor was becoming attractive to U.S. investors, and many U.S. companies like mine were beginning to locate factories in Mexico to supply both Mexican and U.S. customers. But there were numerous bumps in the road, literally and figuratively. The low cost and high quality of Mexican labor was often offset by poor transport facilities, endless waits at the border, and arcane regulations that defied interpretation. By the late 1980s, however, a new generation of U.S.-educated Mexican leaders were in power who concluded that Mexico, like China, needed to reform and get on the capitalist road. They thought the quickest way to do this would be to import the American system into their country in the form of a free trade agreement. In 1989, therefore, they proposed to turn the just concluded U.S.-Canadian Free Trade Agreement into a North American Free Trade Agreement (NAFTA). An intense debate ensued with many Americans concerned about the possibility that the deal could result in a massive flow of U.S. jobs going south of the border.

It seemed to me the argument was otherwise. The jobs were already moving to Taiwan, Korea, Malaysia, Singapore, and China, all of whom had big trade surpluses with the United States. Mexico actually bought more from U.S. suppliers than it sold to them. By shipping components to Mexico for inexpensive final assembly rather than relocating their plants to the Far East, U.S. producers could preserve jobs that otherwise would almost surely go to Asia. My article "NAFTA Why We Hafta" appeared in the *Washington Post* the day before Congress voted on ratification of the deal, which passed by only a few votes. Naturally I take all the credit for its passage.

Other free trade arrangements have followed these and more are on the way. Particularly important have been the Asia Pacific Economic Cooperation forum (APEC), the Association of South East Asian (ASEAN) countries, and the Mercosur treaty, which underpins free trade in the big markets of South America. At the moment, China is talking with ASEAN, Japan has concluded a free trade deal with Mexico, Japan and Korea are talking, and the United States has several new negotiations under way, including a possible extension of NAFTA to include all of the Americas. Thus has globalization spread. With almost everyone now on the capitalist road, the driving has become time-consuming. So some people fly.

The End of Space: Air Express

If you want to see how the traffic is moving, come with me to the FedEx central hub at Memphis International Airport. Things really begin to hum around 11:00 P.M., when 160 airplanes from all over the world begin to converge on this field. If you go to the observation deck at the top of the tower, you get a 360 degree view of the night sky, and you can see points of light coming from all directions. At this hour there is no other air traffic. All the planes are FedEx, and they will land between now and 1:00 A.M. Once on the ground it takes a half hour to unload everything from Dell computers to legal documents to tennis racquets on a big, dumb conveyor that dumps it all into one big bin. The "sort" combines the lowest technology with the highest. At the bin, every package is turned over and sent to the scanner by teams of people who pull and haul all those boxes. Once scanned, the packages go on to smart conveyors that automatically drop them at the right bin for reloading and onward shipment. By 3:00 A.M., all the planes are back in the air and the packages will reach their recipients by 11:00 A.M. If you are anxious about where your package is and wonder whether it will arrive on time, just go to the FedEx website, punch in your code, and track your package to its destination.

You couldn't do this when the GATT was created in 1947. It wasn't until 1953 that UPS offered two-day air service to major cities on East and West Coasts. DHL also sent customs and other documents ahead of shipments by courier on commercial flights, but it was only in 1973 that the modern concept of a dedicated (meaning that's all it did) next-day delivery service was born.

The idea was the 1965 brainchild of Yale undergraduate Fred Smith, who wrote a term paper on the inadequacy of the passenger route systems being used by express shippers at the time. He called for a system that could handle time-sensitive items like medicines and critical electronic parts rapidly and reliably. Following a stint as a marine officer in Vietnam, Smith set up shop in Memphis, and on April 17, 1973, the newly incorporated Federal Express launched 14 small airplanes carrying 186 packages from Memphis International to twenty-five other cities. By 1983 FedEx was a billion-dollar company, but it was still a domestic carrier.

Although DHL had operated internationally from the early 1970s, the FedEx dedicated delivery fleet concept wasn't extended to the international scene until the mid–1980s, and China wasn't fully tied into the network until 1995. Today FedEx, UPS, and others can reach over 5 billion people in more than two hundred countries in one, or at most, two days. With long-range airplanes, it is now possible to fly nonstop from New York halfway round the world to Singapore in about eighteen hours. Using the time difference, it may soon be possible to receive a package in New York before it has been sent from Singapore—that's known as shrinking the globe.

But express delivery is not just about going farther faster. Express companies have begun to take over the whole logistical function from their shipping clients. The Japanese famously invented the *kanban*, or just-in-time delivery sytem, by which components are delivered by suppliers to the manufacturer's assembly line moments before they are needed. This system revolutionized manufacturing, but before the days of express delivery, it required the suppliers to be close to the assembly plants. Today another revolution is occurring as the express companies make it possible to do just-in-time delivery from almost any location on the planet. Their information and delivery networks are becoming an extension of the producer's manufacturing operations because they can dramatically reduce the cost of production by finding low-cost suppliers at long distances. Take the case of Cisco, the world's dominant producer of routers and other equipment for running the Internet faster and better. It doesn't want to have to worry about how to get stuff from here to there. So it gets FedEx or UPS or someone to take care of all that. And the express company does so, even shipping by a competitor if that turns out to be the low-cost route. Increasingly, express delivery is more about rapid transmittal of information than about fast delivery.

The End of Time: The Internet

On October 4, 1957, a new light appeared in the night sky: the Soviet Union had beaten the United States to the punch by launching Sputnik, the first man-made satellite to orbit the earth. I remember running outside that night to catch a glimpse of the satellite as it orbited overhead. I also remember the panic this light caused. Suddenly America was no longer impregnable. There was a public outcry for a response, and one of the steps President Eisenhower took was to create the Advanced Research Projects Agency, better known by its acronym ARPA—later to become DARPA, the Defense Advanced Research Projects Agency. ARPA's mission was to ensure that the United States would never again lag behind an opponent in a key area of defense technology. It proposed to establish a small, elite technical staff in the heart of the Pentagon that would coordinate a network of top American and foreign technologists at universities and research centers around the world. The agency constantly communicated and gathered scientific input, and it had money to fund promising research. Furthermore, it could get this money without going through a lot of red tape. Not surprisingly, scientists began to like talking to ARPA.

After a while, ARPA found talking to scientists a bit of a chore; there were too many of them. Bob Taylor, the head of ARPA's Information Processing Techniques Office, had several different computer terminals in his office, each linked to an ARPA-related university research center. But the different computers and research centers couldn't talk to each other except by old-fashioned fax or telephone.

This meant the researchers often duplicated each other's work while computers remained only partially utilized. Worse, adding new centers and scientists meant more terminals and duplication. Taylor pointed out to his boss, ARPA head Charles Herzfeld, that this could get expensive as well as burdensome. Obviously they needed a way to tie these computers together. After a twenty-minute discussion, Taylor left Herzfeld's office with $1 million to begin developing a computer communications network.

Taylor was not the only one thinking of networks. At RAND (the Air Force think tank R&D), Paul Baran was worried about safe and survivable communication after a nuclear attack. According to his estimates, the AT&T telephone network would fail completely in a Soviet first strike. While AT&T rejected the finding, the air force was more receptive and continued to support Baran's work. Telephone calls at the time were all switched by a central switch and the lines were all dedicated, meaning that if you were talking to me no one else could use that line at the same time. Baran's idea was to fracture messages into packets, or pieces of information, that could be sent over various lines and then reassembled into the full message at the end without necessarily having to go through a central switch. Think of it like moving to a new home with several trucks. You take your dining room table apart, putting the legs in one truck and the top in another. The first truck drives from Washington to San Francisco via Chicago and the second goes via St. Louis, but both eventually arrive in San Francisco, where the table is reassembled in your new dining room. This concept was similar to work being done in London at the National Physics Lab by Donald Davies.

Eventually all of these ideas were incorporated in a design for an ARPANET, and in October 1972, ARPANET had its first public demonstration at a conference in Washington, D.C., where it linked computers from forty different locations. From here, new nets proliferated in the United States, Europe, and Japan.

But it was on the evening of September 23, 1973, that UCLA scientist Len Kleinrock showed what the real potential was. He had just returned from a demonstration of ARPANET at a conference at Sussex University in England. While unpacking, he discovered that he'd left his electric razor in a dorm room at the university. It was not a major item, but Kleinrock wanted it back. He guessed that his friend Larry Roberts was just crazy enough to be working on his computer terminal at the conference in England at 3:00 A.M. A software program at the time allowed Kleinrock to locate anyone currently logged onto the net, and he sent, if not the first e-mail, certainly the most famous one: he wrote a message to Roberts asking him to retrieve the razor and send it along.

Although people could communicate crudely like this with others who were on the same net, they couldn't communicate with people on other networks. That problem was solved when ARPA director Bob Kahn suggested to Professor Vinton Cerf at Stanford that he needed a way to get all the networks to talk to each other with none realizing anything new was going on. By 1974, they demonstrated a way to do this. After extensive development, ARPANET adopted their TCP/IP protocol in 1982 and began linking the proliferating networks together. Thus was born the Internet, and while it had many important applications, Bob Kahn was mostly right when he said, "Everyone really uses it for e-mail."

Over the next ten years, first DARPA and then the U.S. National Science Foundation fostered further development and increased use of the Internet. The number of connected computers climbed dramatically, from 1,000 to 28,000 by the end of the decade. Up until now, development and funding had been driven by the government for purposes of research and education. Commercial use was barred. But two major developments would change all that.

In 1989 Tim Berners-Lee at the European Center for High Energy Physics (CERN) in Geneva was trying to find a way of making research easier by rapid documentation retrieval.[15] He developed a browser/editor program that he called World Wide Web. This revolutionary development vastly multiplied the value of the Internet by making it easy and practical to use. Then Berners-Lee did something even more revolutionary. He released the program free of charge to all comers. Just imagine that Bill Gates had released MS DOS or Windows free of charge. The World Wide Web was followed in 1993 by Mosaic, an improved browser created by Mark Andreeson of the National Center for Supercomputing Applications. Easy to install and backed by twenty-four-hour customer support, it was an immediate hit. By 1994 many thousands of copies had been installed. Mosaic was followed in turn by another improved version labeled Netscape, produced by a start-up company of the same name founded by Andreeson. The initial public offering of stock in the new company was made on August 10, 1995, and started the dot.com boom. At $2 billion, it set a record for offerings up to that time, reflecting the sudden explosion of Internet use. For example, in 1994 there were 3.2 million hosts and 3,000 websites. Within three years the number of hosts hit 20 million and there were well over a million websites.[16]

Then another revolution occurred. The dot.com mania began to drive the U.S. Nasdaq market to stratospheric heights, and talk of the "new economy" dominated dinner party conversations around the world. Investors poured money into anything called Internet, and one of those things was the optical fiber cables that connect all the computers and carry the packets of information as beams of light on glass fibers. Hundreds of thousands if not millions of miles of cable were laid between destinations all over the globe. Among these destinations were, of course, China, India, and the former Soviet bloc countries. All this fiber optic cable lying around provided a glut of communications capacity and the cost of communication began dropping like a stone, which drove international communication use to previously unimaginable levels.

The political implications of the Internet were profound. A totalitarian state in the old twentieth-century sense was no longer possible because no government could control people's access to information. (Thus in a completely unanticipated way, the Internet fulfilled its original purpose of providing a safeguard against the threat of communism.) The economic implications were no less profound. People half a world away became as accessible as those down the street. And these people are notable in a couple of ways. First, there are vast numbers of them. The global economic system has never seen so many new members before. Second, they are all hungry, not so much in the physical sense as in wanting to catch up and be respected. They are eager to learn, willing to work, and anxious to achieve and prove themselves equal to or better than their counterparts in the West. They are not thinking about thirty-five-hour work weeks or whether the value of a Ph.D. in computer science is worth the effort. For them anything less than eighty hours a week is a vacation, and not getting the Ph.D. constitutes a devastating setback. This energy and drive make the third wave of globalization revolutionary and dynamic.

CHAPTER 3

The Global Ballet

It's the death knell for companies
doing their own manufacturing.
—MICHAEL MARKS
CEO, FLEXTRONICS

It is 4:00 P.M. in Shanghai. At Pudong International Airport, the cargo bays of FedEx flight FX 24 are snapped shut as the pilot starts the engines of the four-engine, 315 ton MD 11 freighter in preparation for the daily run to Memphis. This is the penultimate leg of a long journey for the 77 tons of digital cameras, mobile phones, DVDs, and other products packed tightly into the stacked trays of the plane's bays. As the big bird starts its roll, the sun is setting. In seventeen hours FX 24 will be one of those points of light visible in the night sky from the FedEx tower at the Memphis airport. After it lands, all its cargo will go onto the big conveyor with the other 5 million packages being sorted and sent on to their final destination. I should have my new computer by 11:00 A.M.[1]

Getting My New Computer

I helped fill the cargo hold on that particular flight by ordering a new IBM personal computer. To decide on the IBM, I didn't go to a store or talk to a salesperson. I let my fingers do the walking on the keyboard of my old PC, and the websites of the various manufacturers like Dell, HP, and Sony did the talking. After choosing the IBM, I placed my order by following the instructions on the website. To customize the computer, I requested a twenty-two-inch display, an Intel Pentium 735 microprocessor, Microsoft's Windows XP Professional operating system, an IBM embedded security system, a gigabit of memory, an 80 gigabit hard drive, an Intel wireless network connection, a gigabit Ethernet capability, and a CD-RW/DVD-ROM. The final click on my computer mouse not only sent a notice to IBM's sales and accounting offices that an order had been placed but also set in train a myriad of complex interrelated actions all aimed at getting a new PC with the components I specified on a FedEx or UPS truck to my door within three weeks.

Although this computer carries an IBM label and is designed, marketed, and sold by IBM, little of it is made by IBM. For starters the Intel microprocessor and wireless devices and the Microsoft Windows operating system are obviously designed and produced by those two companies. Other companies are involved in designing, producing, marketing, and selling the other components: motherboard, keyboard, touchpad and pointstick, ports, case, and other miscellaneous parts. The production of some components and the gathering and assembling of all the components is sometimes done by IBM itself, but also frequently subcontracted to a company like Flextronics, which has factories in China, Singapore, Mexico, Hungary, and several other countries around the world that specialize in manufacturing and assembly. By locating plants in countries with low labor costs, providing professional management and logistics controls, combining the orders of several customers to get very large production runs, and helping design parts to facilitate easy manufacture, Flextronics and companies like it can manufacture at incredibly low cost. The IBM PC sometimes is assembled at the Flextronics plant in China, and my mouse click becomes part of a production schedule that involves getting suppliers like Intel and Microsoft and logistics management companies like FedEx to arrange for the production, pickup and delivery of all the necessary materials and parts at the Flextronics China plant on a timetable that makes just-in-time deliveries as the computer runs down the plant's production line.

Thus Intel's multibillion-dollar semiconductor fabrication plant in Albuquerque, New Mexico, will take delivery of crystallized silicon from suppliers in Japan and undertake the infinitely complex task of slicing it into wafers and then etching the millions of submicron transistors that comprise the microprocessor onto them. In the course of this process, Intel will use sophisticated equipment from Nikon in Japan, ASML in The Netherlands, and Applied Materials from the United States. At the designated time, these wafers will be picked up in Albuquerque by FedEx, flown to the main hub in Memphis, and then transferred to a flight to Narita, Japan. From there, it is on to Kuala Lumpur International Airport in Malaysia, where they will be unloaded and trucked to Intel's plant in Penang. Each round wafer contains six hundred microprocessors. In this plant the wafers will be cut to produce individual Pentium chips that will be assembled into their protective packages and tested. Then the chips will be trucked back to Kuala Lumpur International and flown by FedEx to China and then trucked to the Flextronics plant for final installation into my computer.

While this is taking place, other components will be following similar routes. The memory chips for the computer may be produced by Samsung of South Korea or they may come from one of several Taiwanese companies. These firms will use Japanese, Dutch, American, and other equipment to produce the etched wafers. They will also use Japanese silicon, but will probably do the cutting, assembly, and testing in their own countries before shipping the chips by air to Shanghai. The disk drive will be designed in Singapore but probably produced in Thailand and then flown to Shanghai. The Windows operating system can be sent directly to Shanghai from Seattle via the Internet, but it may also be supplied from Microsoft's operations in China. I could go on, but you get the picture. Scores if not hundreds of suppliers in many countries contribute to getting that computer on FX 24 and then to me.

Nor is this the end of the process. Once I have the computer, I may need help with installation or understanding the instructions or why it is not working. Fortunately there is a help desk number to call, and the support person's lightly accented speech betrays the fact that the support center is in India. In this case, IBM has subcontracted its customer support for computers to Tata, an Indian firm that is growing exponentially by providing call center and information technology support functions to companies around the world. Naturally it runs its software on IBM workstations.

And let's not forget the Germans. All these suppliers need some idea of what the others are doing and especially of what the overseeing firm, Flextronics, is doing. This involves a lot of talk between computers and various information systems and enabling this talk is the software of SAP, a leading German software corporation headquartered in Walldorf. Just to make the picture complete, Tata also recently listed its shares on the New York Stock Exchange with the aid of American lawyers and investment banks. Why not list on the Bombay market? Of all the world's stock markets, New York's has the best, most transparent, and most predictable regulation, said Tata's chairman, Ratan Tata. Thus the third wave of globalization has made the production and delivery of my computer an immense global ballet orchestrated by sophisticated communications and software that links the most advanced technology with the simplest hand labor in a seamless world-girdling economic web. Essential to this ballet are three key elements: outsourcing, offshoring, and contract manufacturing.

From Doing It Yourself to Outsourcing

The term "outsource" has recently taken on a sinister connotation. "Outsourced" can mean that you lost your job because it was moved overseas, leaving you and your family behind. American executives who have outsourced jobs to low-cost foreign locations have been denounced by some politicians as "Benedict Arnold CEOs." Economists who have tried to defend these measures as beneficial to the country—most notably, President Bush's economic adviser N. Gregory Mankiw—have come under heavy attack. (In one of the milder reactions, Douglas Kiker of CBS News wrote that "Mankiw's assertion illustrates the political ineptitude" of the White House.)[2]

But if you think about it just a little, you realize that outsourcing is plain common sense and without it, all of us would be living back in the Stone Age. I got a haircut last week. I got it at Anne's barber shop in Potomac, Maryland, where I live. Anne is Vietnamese and gives me a great cut plus a head and shoulder massage. For $15, I feel like a million bucks. I could try to shear my own locks or get my wife to do it, but neither of us could do it as well as Anne, and both of us have other things to do with our time. After my haircut, I picked up a suit at the drycleaner, Mindy Lin from Taiwan. She cleans a suit for $8 and sews on missing buttons free. She also is kind enough to play along with my fractured Chinese. I guess I could figure out a way to do my own dry cleaning, but I'm sure the result would be terrible and the cost much higher. So I, like millions of other Americans, outsource my dry cleaning. It is more cost-efficient and convenient to do so. It also creates employment. Thanks to the dry cleaning business, Mindy's two girls have good educations and good jobs.

Although manufacturers have always had outside suppliers, they once preferred to do as much as possible in-house. They believed they could control cost and quality, and protect proprietary technologies and processes by doing everything internally rather than using outside contractors. Henry Ford pushed this logic to the extreme by building the huge River Rouge works near Detroit. Iron ore and coal entered one end of the complex and Ford cars exited from the other, all the steel and other materials having been made and assembled in-between. It was almost complete industrial autonomy. But over the years, the auto companies and other major manufacturers found that contracting the production of at least some of the parts to outside makers was more cost- and quality effective than doing everything in-house.

When I joined Scott Paper Company as a market researcher in 1968, the firm had a full-time medical doctor on the staff and the building was cleaned at night by full-time employees. Although Scott had a small group of full-time lawyers, it also retained outside law firms to assist on unusual issues. Over time, the doctor was replaced by outside clinics and the cleaning was contracted out to companies that specialized in building management. Our market research team had a large budget for retaining outside firms to perform a wide range of market research functions. Since we used them only periodically, it would have been prohibitively expensive to employ them all as full-time staffers. Outsourcing this work was much more cost-effective.

Older readers may remember with some fondness when it was common to call a company and hear a real human operator's voice. Customer service and technical support were handled by full-time company employees at headquarters or in offices and factories scattered around the country. If you called, not only did you hear an authentic human voice, but it spoke unmistakable and understandable English. In the 1970s, however, automatic call distribution technology allowed calls to be allocated to the attendant who had been waiting longest. Continental Airlines used this to cut costs by establishing the first call center in the United States.[3] Others imitated this move, getting call services along with other back-office functions out of expensive headquarters locations. Managers soon realized they could dramatically reduce costs by moving call centers to less expensive parts of the country than the nearby suburbs, and the centers began to move to the Dakotas, southern Texas, West Virginia, and elsewhere. Then somebody figured out that customer service and tech support could be handled by outside contractors just as legal services, building management, and market research were. A whole new industry soon blossomed. With the costs of medical and other benefits rising rapidly, major corporations were anxious to keep non-core support staffs to a minimum. At the same time, call centers were attractive sources of new employment for small towns in rural areas with few industries and declining populations. Since centers caused no pollution and didn't require massive new infrastructure investments, many small towns campaigned aggressively to attract the centers with tax breaks and other incentives.

Just in Time

Meanwhile, beginning in the 1960s, the Japanese perfected their *kanban*, just-in-time system, that took outsourcing of manufacturing to a whole new level. It is structured with a primary manufacturer like Toyota at the center of a series of concentric circles of suppliers. Toyota is wholly responsible for overall design of the car, setting quality requirements, establishing cost targets, and handling assembly, marketing, selling, delivering, and after-sales service. An inner ring of suppliers have Toyota as their major shareholder and supply only Toyota. They work closely with the parent firm and are often responsible for design and development of the parts and components they make. A second and third ring of suppliers, though progressively less controlled and less closely tied into Toyota's operations, are still dependent on and subject to guidance from their primary customer. These companies try to locate their factories close to the Toyota assembly plants because they are expected to deliver the parts to the assembly line a few minutes before they are actually attached to the frame of the car.

The advantages of this model are several. By giving suppliers flexibility to meet general performance requirements however they think best, it enhances simplicity and speed of manufacture and assembly. In the early 1980s, Japanese producers were turning out cars with less than half the worker-hours per car of their American and European competitors. The system also reduces parts inventories to virtually zero. This dramatically cuts the cost of carrying inventory even as it creates pressure to maintain high levels of quality and efficiency because, in the event of error, there is no alternative but to stop the whole line, a very costly step. Beyond this, the suppliers are under enormous and unceasing pressure to reduce costs and improve quality and manufacturability. The wages and benefits paid to the supplier workforce are significantly less than those paid to the main manufacturer workforce, and the former can more easily be laid off because many of them are temporary rather than permanent employees. The system has been so effective that it has forced all major global producers to adopt it in one version or another.

I'll Take the Factory Off Your Hands

It wasn't until the early 1970s, however, that anyone thought of contracting out all the manufacturing and logistics. This was the brain child of Olin King, who had founded Space Craft Incorporated (SCI) as a twenty-seven-year old rocket scientist in Huntsville, Alabama, in 1961. King had been building rockets for NASA and knew they were in constant need of small quantities of special parts that were difficult to obtain on the open market. With two associates he opened a shop in his basement making parts as a subcontractor for NASA. The company quickly became a major subcontractor building components for the Saturn V moon rocket and then making subsystems for military and commercial aircraft. In the 1970s, as the Apollo program and the Vietnam War both wound down, King had to look to the business world for new opportunities. He persuaded IBM in 1976 to give him a contract to make some of its computer terminals. These dumb terminals were in no way central to IBM's business, and King figured he could make them a lot cheaper than IBM could do, with its high overhead and high-wage workforce. By 1981, he was making the new IBM PCs, and the business expanded from there.

Solectron is another pioneer that owes a lot to IBM. Founded as an assembly shop in 1977 by Atari dropout Roy Kusumoto, it handled the peak-period overload of some large Silicon Valley companies in order to fund its real objective of getting into the solar power business. After struggling for several years, Kusumoto sold former IBM physicist Winston Chen a 50 percent ownership stake and made him CEO. Until then, contract manufacturing had been plagued with a sweatshop reputation. Chen's idea was to set Solectron apart by taking it upscale. He introduced strict quality control, intensive workforce training, and advanced automated equipment. He sought to blend the best Japanese management methods with American entrepreneurship and innovation. It worked. Manufacturers began to subcontract for more of their production and for more sophisticated products.

This trend was accelerated by the 1988 arrival of Ko Nishimura, also a former IBMer and a devotee of *shibui*, the Japanese concept of the perfect balance between too much and not enough. As chief operating officer and eventually chairman, Nishimura focused on winning the U.S. Commerce Department's Malcolm Baldrige National Quality Award for the country's outstanding manufacturer. In 1991 Solectron became the first contract manufacturer to win. Then a breakthrough came in 1992. Solectron bought IBM plants in Charlotte, North Carolina, and Bordeaux, France, and simply took over the IBM manufacturing workforce in those areas as its own. A wave of imitation followed, as other big producers like Hewlett-Packard and Dutch electronics gi-

ant Philips, and others made similar deals to shuck manufacturing by
turning whole plants and divisions over to contractors and outsourcing manufacturing to them.

As the long boom of the 1990s turned into the Internet bubble, outsourcing of manufacturing became almost a requirement for good
management. Business schools and management journals alike urged
companies to focus on core competency and outsource everything
else. Solectron boomed. From sales of $93 million and 1,500 employ-
ees in 1993 it grew to become a world-girdling giant with thirty facilities scattered over twenty countries, sales of nearly $20 billion, and
65,000 employees.[4] Although largely unknown to the public, it was
larger than Silicon Valley icons like Apple, Oracle, and Sun Microsys-
tems.[5] Nor was Solectron alone. Its competitors, like SCI, Flextronics,
and Jabil, grew so rapidly that the entire industry went from revenue
of $59 billion in 1996 to $178 billion in 2001.

This explosive growth drew on significant advantages. The contract
manufacturers don't have fancy offices or elaborate R&D facilities.
The *shibui* concept emphasizes the elegance that derives from the
Spartan approach. Overhead is kept extremely low. Because contractors combine the production runs of many client companies, their
economies of scale are greater. They procure parts and materials in
enormous volumes at rock-bottom prices. Because manufacturing and
assembly are their business, they put the best brains to work figuring
out how to do things faster, cheaper, and better. They work closely
with clients, often suggesting design changes that won't affect a product's performance but will make it easier or cheaper to produce. Increasingly, contract manufacturers are becoming contract designers
as well, taking over the design function along with manufacturing
from their clients, who then focus on distribution and marketing.

Sitting in the modest San Jose building where Singapore's Flextronics Corp. has its main office, CEO Michael Marks explains graphically
how manufacturing is being revolutionized and why contractors are
trying to become designers too. According to Marks, the only profit is
in the intellectual component that goes on a piece of silicon. Costs and
prices are being driven down at exponential rates. It took ten years for
the price of the VCR to fall from $1,000 to $100 but only eighteen

months for the DVD to do the same. Five years ago a cell phone cost $500 and had 1,500 parts. Now it costs $50 and has 50 parts. All products, continues Marks, are being commoditized at light speed. Take an inkjet printer. The manufacturing value added in the product is $5. Logistics is $15 and the design, distribution, and marketing is $50 to $200. To survive, a manufacturer has to operate a global manufacturing grid and optimize globally. Gross margins are only around 5 percent. That's about what supermarkets do. So if costs shift much in Mexico, Flextronics must be able to switch production instantly and seamlessly to China or Hungary. This is the death knell of this chapter's epigraph for companies trying to hold on to their own manufacturing. And even for the Solectrons and Flextronics of the world, it's a jungle out there.

For example, between 1997 and 2001, outsourcing enabled telecommunication equipment makers to drive total supply chain costs down from nearly 12 percent of revenue to 6 percent.[6] Indeed, contract manufacturers have enabled some companies to get rid of factories altogether. Cisco Systems became the dominant company in telecommunications equipment and briefly the most valuable company in the world without doing much manufacturing at all. The contractors allow it to stick to design and marketing without ever getting its hands dirty. Or take the case of Handspring, a Silicon Valley start-up that introduced its Visor PDA product only fifteen months after the company was founded—an impossibility if Handspring actually had had to build its own factory to make the product.

This would have been impossible before the advent of the Internet and broadband communications. To see why, glance at the Flextronics computer system. A single terminal shows all plant locations. A manager can see instantly what a parts buyer is paying in Mexico and, after comparing that price to Singapore's, maybe leverage the information into a better price at one of those locations. Or she may see that Singapore has an oversupply of the parts needed in Mexico and make adjustments internally. This kind of global information base is also a powerful tool in moving up the chain from manufacturing to design. Many contractors have moved from making to taking over the entire design function, a development that raises a red flag for some executives who worry that without control of design they will not be able to differentiate their products and will lose competitive power in the long run. Nevertheless, because doing your own manufacturing is a kind of death wish, most major U.S, European, and even Japanese companies are making outsourcing an integral part of their production strategies.

From Outsourcing to Offshoring

Establishing plants in foreign countries is nothing new. The multinational manufacturer is nearly as old as manufacturing. By 1911, Ford Motor Company had production plants in England and Japan while Daimler Motor Works made cars in the United States. But these efforts were aimed at supplying overseas markets locally. Although the production of overseas plants often displaced exports to these markets from the United States, such production was rarely exported back to the U.S. market to displace domestically made products.

The notion of locating production facilities offshore to supply the home market was another response to the impact of the Japanese on world markets in the 1960s, as well as to the rising power of consumerism in the United States. The combination of an undervalued yen and the efficiencies of the Japanese production system allowed companies like Teijin, Sony, Matsushita, and Hitachi to make massive inroads into the American and, to a lesser extent, European markets. By the early 1960s, Japanese textile makers had taken such a large share of the U.S. market that the U.S. government begged the Japanese government for relief for American workers through a "voluntary export restraint" agreement. Consequently Japanese makers formed a kind of cartel to establish maximum export quantities to the United States and allocate shares under this ceiling. The Japanese assault on the U.S. market for black-and-white television sets, which gave them a market share of 98 percent by the mid-1970s,[7] was repeated in living color as the Japanese share of U.S. color TV sales rose to 45 percent by 1976. Producers of everything from autos to semiconductors suffered similar experiences during this time.

In Europe the situation was different only by degree. The Japanese took longer to conquer the more protected European markets, but they eventually dominated consumer electronics and other markets there as well.

One of the reasons for this rapid conquest of key U.S. markets was that U.S. producers and distributors applied the old adage, If you can't lick 'em, join 'em. Remember that the American strategy was to grow by stimulating consumption. Political leaders, business executives, and academic economists all emphasized getting good deals for consumers as the main goal. Accordingly, mass merchandisers like Sears Roebuck established buying centers in Japan and elsewhere in Asia to get directly to the source and import the best and least expensive goods for American consumers. They also subcontracted to Japanese producers for the manufacture of their store brands, like Sears Kenmore. They even joined the Japanese cartels. Sears was eventually fined millions of dollars by the U.S. government for customs fraud related to its dealings with the Japanese electronics makers.[8] Key U.S. manufacturers also got into the act. RCA, the company that more than any other made television a fixture in the American living room, moved its manufacturing to Taiwan and Mexico while subcontracting VCR production to Hitachi. At a Harvard Business School symposium in 1983, I heard then RCA chairman Thornton Bradshaw explain that the RCA brand was so powerful that RCA could sell VCRs made by Hitachi more profitably than Hitachi. Three years later RCA ceased to exist as an independent company. The RCA brand, however, is still being kept alive by its latest owner, Thomson SA of France.

To offset the Japanese cost advantage, many producers—particularly the U.S. and European semiconductor makers who were rapidly losing market share to Japanese producers—began looking for production sites in other Asian countries that had lower labor costs than Japan. Several U.S. manufacturers, like Motorola, Intel, and Texas Instruments, had been experimenting with operations in Malaysia, Singapore, and Taiwan for several years. They now began to transfer the labor-intensive part of the semiconductor manufacturing process to factories in these countries.

But it wasn't just the low labor costs that drew them. Unlike the United States, these small Asian countries could not focus on domestic consumption as the driver of economic growth because their home markets were too small to justify investment in facilities costing hundreds of millions of dollars. So they focused on investment and production to supply others, especially the giant U.S. market, and offered enticing financial incentives to tempt manufacturers into locating facilities inside their borders. On a selective basis, they might offer tax exemptions for ten or twenty years, worker training grants, infrastructure construction grants, and even large grants to cover as much as 50 percent of the capital cost of a new plant. This combination of low labor costs, financial incentives, and a pro-business policy environment proved irresistible.

If you live among wild animals, you need all the help you can get. That's where offshoring and investment incentives come in. Flextronics may be headquartered in San Jose and look like an American company, but it's incorporated in Singapore because taxes are lower there. It and the other contract producers have campuses in Mexico, China, Hungary, and elsewhere and do most of their production there. They have the advantage of low-cost workforces and typically benefit from tax holidays and other financial incentives so that capital costs are reduced and the tax burden is low. In effect, it is tax holidays in developing countries that are keeping the contractors alive and driving costs down.

By the early 1990s, tiny Singapore, with a population of just over 3 million people, was one of the world's major exporters of electronics products. In disk drives, for example, it accounted for nearly half of global production. Malaysia was becoming a major location of semiconductor production, and Thailand was also moving into disk drives in a big way. By the late 1990s, nearly 80 percent of all laptop computers and 50 percent of all computer motherboards were being made in Taiwan.

Look, Mom—No Factory

Taiwan also originated a whole new approach to semiconductor manufacturing. Between 1970 and 1990, production of semiconductors evolved into a prohibitively capital-intensive business, with the cost of a plant rising from $10 million to $2 billion. This became a major barrier to entry, and it began to look as if what was once an entrepreneurial industry funded by venture capital would become too expensive for start-ups. That was before Morris Chang entered the picture. After his family escaped the communist takeover of mainland China in 1949 and moved to America, Chang got his B.S. and M.S. degrees in mechanical engineering from MIT and a Ph.D. in electrical engineering from Stanford University. He eventually wound up working for Texas Instruments in Dallas, where I met him in the early 1980s. TI, like all the other U.S. semiconductor makers, was desperately trying to figure out how to compete with the Japanese. Chang realized that the capital cost issue was a major one. At the time, Japanese companies were enjoying virtually free capital, owing to implicit government guarantees ensuring their business. Their capital did not come from the stock market but from banks in their industrial groups that lent on the basis of long-term relationships rather than balance sheets and cash flow. One idea for overcoming the Japanese advantage was that of establishing a semiconductor foundry, one big plant that could produce multiple products for different companies. In addition to major economies of scale, this concept could potentially solve a lot of problems. Semiconductor companies would no longer have to burden themselves with huge investment costs and could concentrate their resources on designing new and better chips; and the foundry concept would help dampen the ups and downs of a cyclical business. Without big plants and investments of their own, the semiconductor companies would weather downturns better while the foundry would spread its risk by supplying more than one company in more than one sector of the technology industry.

It was a brilliant scheme that called for a huge investment. But Chang knew just where to go—the Taiwanese government. Jealously watching Japan and Korea move up the value-added scale in electronics, the Taiwanese government was seeking a way to move its workers out of labor-intensive activities into more sophisticated and higher-paying jobs. Semiconductor manufacture seemed to offer that in spades. So when Chang came calling, the Taiwanese government responded by establishing Hsinchu as a high-tech industrial park. Here the new company would receive a package of incentives that would cut both the initial investment and the long-term production costs. It all worked like a charm. Initially companies assigned only their lower-tech products for production by the foundry. But gradually they gave it more and more of their production until eventually many companies simply abandoned their own production to the foundry.

By the late 1990s, only three or four very large semiconductor makers were still investing in their own plants. This created a new, unexpected dynamic. Maintaining a leading-edge position in the semiconductor industry depends on working closely with the makers of the production equipment and on being the first recipient of the latest equipment. For example, Intel, as the biggest producer of leading-edge chips, has always been a favored customer of the equipment makers. Initially the foundries were at the back of the line. But as they have risen in both volume of production and level of technology, their status has changed dramatically. They have become favored customers, and they are increasingly in a position to dictate the direction of design and technological development.

What was true for chips had also by the mid-1990s become true for other manufactured goods. As manufacturing, with technology development and design following behind, moved to Asia and to a lesser extent to Mexico and Eastern Europe, one of the new drivers on the capitalist freeway could be heard shifting into high gear and pulling into the passing lane.

CHAPTER 4

Made in China

Look, China is the most exciting place in
the world right now to be a manufacturer.

—MARK WALL
PRESIDENT, GE PLASTICS CHINA

If you are in Shanghai, the place to dine is M on the Bund, although some say the really chic spot is 3 on the Bund, a combination restaurant, art gallery, and spa replete with canals of Evian Water. Either way, try to get a window or, better yet, a veranda seat. Don't mind the prices; the view is worth it. From high up, you look down on the bustling Huangpoo River and the embankment where clipper ships docked in the mid-nineteenth century as Shanghai was aborning. Next door is the old HSBC building with its golden dome, and along the embankment as far as the eye can see are high-rise buildings topped by glowing neon signs advertising Motorola, Panasonic, Samsung, and many more of the world's great companies. Now look directly across the river at the area known as Pudong. The Shangri-la Hotel, with its name in script across the top, is easy to spot to your right. To the left is the eighty-eight-story Hyatt Hotel and further to the left a kind of space needle structure that looks poised to lift off at any moment. Beyond are blocks and blocks of high-rise offices, hotels, and apartment buildings. Old-timers in Shanghai are always amazed by this view because ten years ago it wasn't there. There were the rice paddies and small farms that had been for centuries.

For most of recorded history, China was the world's largest economy. Until the end of the fifteenth century it was by far the leader in technology and had the highest per capita GDP on the planet. While Europeans were hacking at each other with broadswords, the Chinese were scaring their enemies to death with fireworks. Europe overtook China in per capita GDP by about 1500, but China remained the world's biggest economy until well into the nineteenth century. As late as 1820, the Middle Kingdom accounted for nearly a third of global GDP.[1] By 1950, however, that had shrunk to less than 5 percent and China's per capita GDP was one of the lowest in the world.

Getting Rich Is Glorious

The transformation of China began slowly and cautiously, with certain cities or areas being designated as special development zones and given the right to liberalize regulations and offer investment incentives, while the rest of the country remained strictly on the socialist track. The 1982 trade mission that took me to Beijing with the secretary of commerce concluded with an agreement to open several U.S. foreign commercial service offices around the country. They provided information and assistance to U.S. businessmen interested in getting in on the ground floor of the new China.

China was interesting for two reasons—one was, of course, endless cheap labor to produce low-cost products for export, but it also had the potential to become the world's largest market. An early pioneer interested in China for the first reason was Joseph Ha, senior vice president of the sport shoe manufacturer Nike. He followed me to China to test whether Nike could lower costs by setting up factories that used inexpensive labor to produce and export to the United States and other global markets. The going was rough at first. The Chinese government insisted on joint ventures with inexperienced, untrained Chinese firms. Although labor was cheap, logistics were a nightmare, as was the regulatory maze. Nike typically arranges with outsource contractors to operate and even own the factories that produce its branded products. In this case, its contractor was the Taiwanese Feng Tai group. Gradually Feng Tai established several factories to produce inexpensive commodity shoes. By the end of the decade, these ventures had proven that China could be an unbeatable export platform, and Nike laid plans to expand and make high-quality shoes there.

Another pioneer was Motorola chairman and CEO Robert Galvin, who took his first look at China in late 1984. As he related it to me, Galvin was skeptical about investing in a place that had long been hostile to the United States and to the market system. "Why should we do business with them was my going-in attitude," he said. After two weeks on the ground, however, Galvin realized the Chinese leadership was serious about changing, and he converted to the view that Motorola had to get into China as fast as possible. But not on the terms the Chinese were proposing, which entailed joint ventures and many bureaucratic conditions. In meetings with Deng Xiao Ping, Jiang Zemin, and other top leaders, he threw down the gauntlet by predicting they would fail if they insisted on doing things their way. Motorola was ready to invest $100 million in world-class facilities for high-tech production, Galvin told them, but only if it fully owned and controlled the company. By late 1988 the Chinese had agreed, and Motorola prepared to begin production in China. Expectations were especially high because the Chinese people had already introduced innovations in the use of Motorola pagers. They developed standard codes so that, for example, 234 meant "I want to order a Tsingdao beer" and so forth. The pager thus became a kind of primitive forerunner to the mobile phone. As a result of pager sales, Motorola's revenue in China hit $100 million four years ahead of schedule. The company's executives were eager to accelerate the momentum.

By the end of the 1980s, China was really beginning to move. Its exports had doubled from $30 billion in 1981 to over $60 billion, and many other U.S., European, Taiwanese, and Japanese companies were preparing to follow Nike's and Motorola's lead. Then the democracy movement and the repression of the demonstrations in Tiananmen Square in June 1989 brought everything to a screeching halt. For two years, businessmen around the world held their breath as well as the investment dollars they had earmarked for China. Hundreds of millions of Chinese also watched and waited. No one knew whether the Tiananmen Square incident was a hiccup along the way to further liberalization or the signal of a new cultural revolution. Finally, in January 1992, the aging maximum leader, Deng Xiao Ping, embarked on what was later called his southern inspection tour. In Shenzhen, a fishing village bordering Hong Kong that became the first special economic zone, he rubbed the Jade tree and hailed the progress being made. But he also urged bolder action and faster reform. "Reform is liberation of productive forces, and taking the socialist road is none other than bringing about the common prosperity," he said.

This was the signal everyone had been waiting for. Deng's words were "like the collapse of the Berlin Wall," and they set off a renewed wave of investment, construction, and growth.[2] Motorola announced a $240 million investment for a new factory in Tianjin to produce semiconductors and telecommunications equipment, by far the biggest foreign investment in China at the time. It was also remarkable for being aimed at producing high-tech rather than commodity products. Nike moved aggressively to establish a network of facilities dedicated to producing shoes for export to the United States and other global markets. These trailblazers were soon followed by others from all over the world.

Whereas foreign direct investment in China had totaled only $20 billion for the whole decade of the 1980s, it soared to $200 billion[3] by the end of the century and then more than doubled to $450 billion in the next three years.[4] In 2003 China passed the United States as the number one recipient of foreign direct investment, $53 billion to $40 billion.

Despite official resistance and restrictions, Taiwanese investors were the leaders, putting over $100 billion into mainland China operations. The Taiwanese government was forced by its own businessmen to remove its ban on transfer of semiconductor technology across the straits to the mainland as the Taiwanese foundries sought to establish factories there. But if the foreigners were investing, it was only because the Chinese were investing more. Companies like Haier in appliances, Legend in personal computers, TCL in television sets, and Huawei in telecommunications equipment came out of nowhere to challenge the world leaders in their fields. It was not consumption that gave China its miraculous growth rate but investment, which reached an astounding 44 percent of GDP.[5] To understand this transformation, you need to tour a few factories.

From Beaverton, Oregon, to Shanghai: Nike

An hour south of Shanghai, Nike's Harry Johnson factory complex sprawls over an industrial zone that includes dormitories for the workers, medical facilities, a gym, recreational areas, and cafeterias as well as the production lines. As I arrive in May 2004, I am greeted by John Chang Chien, the plant general manager, and several of his key staff members. The factory was built in 1996, he explains, as part of a major expansion of Nike production in China. Because this is an area slated by the government for development, Nike was able to obtain a very favorable development package at low cost. It owns the buildings but leases them to the Feng Tai Group. Thus John is a Feng Tai employee, as are two other key managers. John has a wife and children in Taiwan but spends about three weeks of each month at the factory, which has living quarters for him on the top floor of the administrative building. It is good that he is enthusiastic about his work because in this isolated area there is not much to do. The fourth week finds him back in Taiwan with his family and attending management meetings at headquarters.

The production of a Nike shoe begins at company headquarters in Beaverton, Oregon. There the marketing research team reviews consumer data and identifies possible new kinds of shoes or new features that might attract consumers. The new product development team takes those concepts and tries to mold them into a concrete sample of a new shoe or shoe feature that is then market tested. If the new product tests well, prototypes are sent to Feng Tai in Taiwan, where they are produced initially on a pilot line to identify problems as well as the best way of manufacturing them. From there the product becomes an official Nike item and is assigned for manufacture, perhaps to this Shanghai plant.

Feng Tai leases the buildings from Nike and installs its own equipment, which is largely imported from Italy, Taiwan, Japan, and Germany. Some stitching machines are procured from Chinese makers, and in the future more of the equipment will undoubtedly be sourced domestically. But for now, it is mostly of foreign origin and is the same equipment found in the most modern factories of Europe, Japan, or the United States. Because shoemaking is a dying industry in those countries, this factory is probably more modern than theirs. At the same time, some functions that might be automated abroad are done by hand here because the low cost of labor makes certain expensive investments in automation unnecessary. This is not true across the board. Where automation gives much higher productivity, processes are automated. But the low cost of labor changes the cost of capital versus cost of labor ratios here. Thus Feng Tai gets a twofer. It has inexpensive labor to begin with, and that enables a less costly capital investment as well.

The plant's 4,652 workers (3,476 women and 1,186 men) are hired by Feng Tai and are Feng Tai employees. John laments that Shanghai workers are becoming too expensive; local people are too well off and are turning up their noses at shoemaking. But he has a ready solution. He is now hiring about two-thirds of the workforce from nearby rural provinces, where millions of workers are ready to do whatever it takes to get a good shoemaking job. These outsiders live in the dormitories on the factory premises. Most are young women who send the bulk of their earnings back to their families in the countryside. They work eight hours a day with an hour for lunch five days a week. But since most of them, like John, live here, the factory and Feng Tai and Nike pretty much become a way of life. Conditions are not unpleasant. Food is provided along with dormitory rooms, and the factory is inspected annually by former U.S. Ambassador to the U.N. Andrew Young to ensure that there is no abuse and no exploitation.

At the same time, there are no unions, and John explains that managing the workforce is easy because the work ethic is excellent, much better than in some other Asian countries where he has worked. The pay scale has six ranges. Ordinary line workers get anywhere from $165 to $250 a month. For first line supervisors, the range is $300 to $500 a month. For directors it is $750 to $1,250, and for senior managers and monitors, from $1,250 to $2,000. John is paid about $3,000 a month or $36,000 per year to manage a factory that produces 344,000 pairs of walking shoes per month for shipment primarily to the U.S. market. A similar job in the United States would pay $80,000 and in Japan it would be about $55,000. As inexpensive as this all sounds,

John is quick to point out that the cost of labor here is actually higher than in Vietnam and parts of Thailand. But then he emphasizes the essential point. Because of the work ethic, the skill of the workers, the proximity to the world-class airports and ports of Shanghai, and the availability of world-class telecommunications and the broadband Internet, productivity here is much higher. This high productivity coupled with low-cost labor makes China the best place to make shoes, with costs 20–30 percent below those of any other manufacturing location.

The Silk Road

Three hours south of Shanghai lies Hangzhou, perhaps China's loveliest city. A graceful, temple-filled, tree-lined town by a lake, Hangzhou is where President Richard Nixon and Chinese President Mao Zedong forged the historic rapprochement between their two countries in 1972. I have been invited to visit the headquarters and main factory of Hempel, a fast-rising Chinese silk textile producer. As my car pulls up in front of the main building, the limo of the founder and CEO, Ko Chi Wai, also pulls up. He has just put his daughter on a plane for Los Angeles, where she is a UCLA student. As we enter the main lobby, Ko's cell phone rings insistently, and I study the architecture while he talks. This place is like no textile company building I have ever visited. It looks like the headquarters of a successful Silicon Valley start-up, where everyone, including the receptionist, is a millionaire from cashing in stock options. As we walk to Ko's conference room, we pass the completely outfitted gym and the indoor tennis courts. Who is this guy Ko Chi Wai, I wonder, and how did he get here?

During breaks in the steady stream of calls to his two cell phones, the forty-six-year-old Ko explains that his route was unlikely and circuitous. He started thirty years ago as a line worker in a state-owned enterprise (SOE) that made housewares and textiles. Over twenty years, he gradually worked his way up into management ranks. There he made contacts in foreign companies like Wal-Mart that were coming to China in search of low-cost suppliers whose products could be sold back in the U.S. market. By 1991 he realized the SOEs had a limited future. He had seen bold entrepreneurs make quick fortunes by producing inexpensive textiles under contract for U.S. mass merchandisers and U.S. fashion design houses. He decided to have a go himself and founded the Huili Company with a $400,000 investment by two friends in the textile business in Hong Kong. The money was used primarily to obtain sewing machines for the local housewives Ko hired to work as seamstresses at a warehouse he rented as his factory. His first order was from a Hong Kong trading company for eight hundred pairs of men's undershorts destined for U.S. retail shelves. With workers making about $60 a month and the ability to piggyback on the sophisticated logistics and trading networks of Hong Hong, Huili was a very low-cost producer with costs less than half those of Korea, Taiwan, and Hong Kong.

For a while in the early 1990s, Wal-Mart closed its China buying office under the impact of Sam Walton's drive to sell products made in America. After Walton's death in 1992, however, Wal-Mart's commitment to "everyday low prices" once again trumped its commitment to made in America, and the company returned to China with a vengeance.

Ko rewarmed his old contacts and business soared when Huili became a contract supplier for Wal-Mart. In contrast, at this time his old SOE employer went bankrupt.

Although doing extremely well, Ko began to hanker for more independence and better margins than those of a straight contract manufacturer always under the lash of demands for price reductions. He moved toward fashion silk apparel and changed the name of the company to Hempel, meaning the finest silk. He became a major contractor for the Liz Claiborne label and began to develop his own brand too. By bringing in Italian, American, and Japanese designers, he has created a Hempel line that now sells in China and accounts for 10 percent of his sales. This percentage may seem small, but for most houses like Ko's, exports constitute the entire business. The next step will be to buy an established but perhaps lesser known U.S. brand and make it into a global player by marrying it to his high quality and lower costs. Says Ko, "The fashion industry is the most likely of Chinese industries to establish a global branded presence."

That may seem ambitious. But to the Italians, the world's premier silk and fine cashmere apparel makers, it is only too realistic. Dominant players in the world of high fashion silk since Marco Polo's return from ancient Cathay, the Italian industry is now in its death throes as a result of competition from companies like Hempel. In the past three years, China's exports of silk apparel and cloth have been soaring. Although Hempel has doubled wages over the past ten years to $120 per month, that is far below the $1,800 per month paid in Italy.[6] "The second shock has begun," says Michele Canepa, president of the International Silk Association.[7] In Como, the center of Italian silk production, about 80 percent of the region's business has left since the mid-1990s. "We have lost almost everything," says Guido Tettamanti, head of the silk section of the industrial union.[8] In Hangzhou, Ko is thinking of buying up famous Italian brands and turning them into Hempel brands.

From "Made in America" to Everyday Low Prices

In the fifty years since its founding, Wal-Mart has become the world's largest corporation by focusing relentlessly on cutting costs in order to fulfill its self-proclaimed mission of giving consumers "everyday low prices." So stingy is Wal-Mart that truckers making deliveries are sometimes made to unload their own trucks into the Wal-Mart warehouses. The temperature of all stores is controlled centrally from Bentonville, Arkansas: 73 degrees in summer, 70 in winter. And the example is set from the top. CEO H. Lee Scott Jr., who made $18 million last year, empties his own trash and shares budget hotel rooms when traveling.[9] Like everyone else in the company, he always flies coach.

Inevitably the search for lower costs drove Wal-Mart buyers abroad. They were among the first to visit China after its initial opening, and by the mid-1980s, they were already buying in significant quantities. Then in 1985, Sam Walton launched his *Bring It Home to the U.S.A.* program. "Wal-Mart believes American workers can make a difference," he proclaimed and offered to pay as much as 5 percent more for products made in America. He later claimed that this program had saved 100,000 U.S. jobs.[10] But the need to maintain the lowest prices in town soon overwhelmed that program. The truth was that products made in Asia, especially in China, were underpricing U.S. products not by 5 percent but by 50 percent. By the mid-1990s, Wal-Mart was not only back in China but had formed a kind of ultimate joint venture with it.[11] The world's largest retailer linked itself intimately with the world's most populous country in a common mission to supply goods at the lowest possible cost to the world's consumers, especially Americans, who consumed more than any others. Wal-Mart provided the logistical and distribution know-how and China, the world's greatest promoter of capitalist production, provided tax-free zones, business-friendly regulation, endless cheap labor, a ban on all but party-run unions, and a stable currency pegged to the dollar.

To watch this combination at work, let's visit the Shenzhen Baoan Fenda Industrial Company in Shenzhen, just across from Hong Kong. Here 2,100 workers labor amid deafening machinery and clouds of sawdust to turn out 360,000 stereo sets for Wal-Mart each month. No one wears ear plugs or protective goggles as screeching band saws carve wood for the stereo cabinets. Many of the women stuffing circuit boards have bandaged hands, but few wear gloves. Most of these workers migrated to Shenzhen from the countryside in search of these jobs, which pay about $120 per month. Because they frequently work long days, six days a week, this comes out to $0.50 or $0.60 per hour. But should they become dissatisfied, a sign on the wall reminds them of their circumstances: "If you don't work hard today, tomorrow you'll have to try hard to look for a job."

Harsh conditions for the workers is, however, good news for Western consumers. Wal-Mart pays $30–$40 for these stereo sets and sells them for $50 in its U.S. stores.[12] Multiply that by the approximately 5,000 Wal-Mart contractor factories in China, and you have some idea of the impact of this joint venture on both China and the rest of the world. Wal-Mart estimates that in 2003 it spent $15 billion on Chinese-made goods that were exported mostly to the United States, with some going to Canada and Europe.

Wal-Mart's role goes far beyond buying low-cost Chinese goods. It is encouraging other U.S. producers to outsource more of their production to China. For example, Lakewood Engineering & Manufacturing, of Chicago, makes box fans sold by Wal-Mart. Ten years ago the fan carried a price of $20, but Wal-Mart said that was too high. Lakewood CEO Carl Krauss redoubled his cost-cutting efforts. Automation reduced the required number of workers from twenty-two to seven, and Krauss got his suppliers to cut the prices of their parts. But that still wasn't cheap enough. Finally, three years ago, Krauss opened a factory in Shenzhen, where the workers were paid $0.25 per hour as opposed to $13 in Chicago. Now 40 percent of his products are made in China, including the key parts of his box fan, which now retails at Wal-Mart for $10.[13] Some complain that these kinds of prices are precisely what is driving the U.S. trade deficit to unprecedented and perhaps unsustainable heights.

You can get a good idea of Wal-Mart's impact by looking at what's happening in other developed countries. In 2002 Wal-Mart imported about $12 billion of merchandise from China into the United States. This grew to $15 billion in 2003, or about 15 percent of the U.S. trade deficit with China. If Wal-Mart were an independent country (some people think it is and some foreign countries send ambassadors to Bentonville), it would rank ahead of Germany and Britain as an importer from China. Another interesting comparison is with the activity of European mass merchandisers. Carrefour of France, for example, imported $1.6 billion from China in 2002 and $2 billion in 2003. For B&Q in Great Britain, the figures were $1 billion and $1.3 billion for each year; for Auchan of France, around $300 million for each year; and for Ito-Yokado of Japan, $1.5 billion each year (includes Hong Kong and Taiwan).[14] Based on relative population proportions, these numbers would be about double what they are if European mass merchandisers were having the same impact Wal-Mart is having in the United States.

On the other hand, European and Japanese consumption patterns often lag behind those of the United States by a few years. Still, the European and Japanese numbers are already large and growing, and may soon more closely resemble the U.S. figures.

And perhaps that will be true of the overall balance of trade as well. This Wal-Mart–China joint venture has been a significant contributor to the rising U.S. trade deficit with China. Wal-Mart's procurement in China accounts, all by itself, for over 10 percent of the bilateral trade deficit. As the deficit has grown, so have demands for the U.S. government to pressure China to revalue its currency and impose some restrictions on imports from China. But Wal-Mart's Asia president Joe Hatfield knows whose side Wal-Mart is on. "That would be a travesty to do to the consumer in the United States."[15]

From Sweat Shops to Clean Rooms

Back in the Pudong, a world away from the sweatshops that feed Wal-Mart, looms the gleaming white facade of Shanghai's most significant new factory. This is the $1.8 billion main fabrication plant of the Semiconductor Manufacturing International Corp. (SMIC), the first semiconductor foundry in mainland China. CEO Richard Chang greets me at the entrance, and we prepare for the plant tour by donning shoe covers, hair nets, and white jackets before entering the clean room facility. (Semiconductors are usually manufactured in rooms in which a steady downdraft keeps the air almost free of dust particles.) Chang is emblematic of the powerful trends driving business to China today. Born in Nanjing in 1949, he grew up in Kaoshiung on Taiwan, where his parents fled after the communist takeover of mainland China. After graduating from National Taiwan University and completing his military service, he studied at the State University of New York in Buffalo, from which he graduated in 1977 with a master's degree in engineering science. A job offer from Texas Instruments (TI) took him to Dallas, where he worked on developing a speech synthesizer for the air force that eventually became the TI Speak N Spell toy for kids. Chang soon became part of a group at TI led by the legendary Jack Kilby, coinventor of the integrated circuit. This group was responsible for continuing development of the product then at the heart of the company—dynamic random access memory or DRAM. As Chang acquired expertise in the production of this key device, he was sent to oversee construction of plants TI was building in Singapore, Italy, and Japan. In 1997, although he had become an American citizen, he moved back to Taiwan to help found Worldwide Semiconductor Manufacturing Company, one of the major semiconductor foundry operations. When this group merged with another leading Taiwanese foundry a few years later, Chang objected to planned workforce reductions and left the company. A group of investors and former customers put up $1.6 billion as initial funding for a new foundry, and Chang went looking for possible plant locations. He happened to begin his search just as China launched a high-level program to attract semiconductor manufacturers to its shores.

Although China is the world's largest producer of such items as DVDs, microwave ovens, and television sets, it imports over 80 percent of the semiconductor chips that are the brains of these devices. In 2000, for example, China produced only $900 million worth of semiconductors compared with $11 billion for Taiwan and $12.4 billion for Korea.[16] Chinese factories have been unable to meet the rapidly growing demand, and both government officials and business executives have increasingly come to focus on development of a domestic semiconductor industry as essential to the further development of the whole industrial base. As Yu Zhongyu, president of the China Semiconductor Industry Association, says, "Semiconductors are the key to the information technology industry. If we want to develop further, we need to have this skill."[17] Xu Xiaotian, in the Ministry of Information Industry, adds that "we already make many of the world's computers and cellular phones. This will be true in semiconductors as well."[18]

But to develop this industry, China needed foreign capital and especially foreign talent and technology. Project 909 was launched as a five-year plan to build chip plants and develop technical expertise. Barriers to foreign investors were lowered, and special high-tech zones were created offering free land, favorable utility rates, tax holidays, and capital grants. To induce factories to use domestic chips in place of imports, a 17 percent sales tax was imposed on imported chips, while the tax on domestic chips was set at 3 percent. This was illegal under WTO rules, but at the time China was not a WTO member.[19] Combined with China's low labor rates, this was a deal made in heaven. Chang, a devout Christian, decided to take it and set up his new factory in Shanghai. Although Hong Kong had been his first choice because of its better educated workforce, more transparent legal system, absence of corruption, and cosmopolitan environment, the

Hong Kong authorities were unable or unwilling to match Shanghai's tax incentives. No U.S., European, or Japanese site was even considered. Costs are too high and financial incentives too few.

Because a foundry is running nearly all the time and produces a large variety of different chips for different customers, it is more engineering intensive than the usual dedicated company plant. China is short on experienced semiconductor engineers, and consequently Chang scoured the globe to assemble a team of designers, engineers, and production experts. He offered the classic Silicon Valley deal: a ground floor opportunity with lots of stock options. He also offered housing near the factory as well as a bilingual school. The team he gathered with these inducements includes 560 Taiwanese engineers, 300 Americans, 40 Koreans, 15 Japanese, and 80 from Singapore, Malaysia, and Europe. He also employs 400 mainland Chinese engineers. All are paid on the same salary scale, which is about one-third the U.S. level and about one-half that of Taiwan. This discrepancy is somewhat balanced by the fact that living costs in Shanghai are lower and China has no capital gains tax. But Chang has other motivations as well. As a Christian, he says an important reason for his selecting mainland China as the plant location was an opportunity to "share God's love" at this critical moment in China's transition from communism to a liberal, market-oriented society.

Roger Lee, the forty-three-year-old head of memory technology development whom Chang lured from Micron Technology of Boise, Idaho, was also born in China and educated in the United States. He says he saw an opportunity to help his native country become a world center for chip manufacturing. Shou Gouping, who heads the firm's design service department, fled Beijing to the United States two years after the 1989 Tiananmen Square incident, expecting never to see his homeland again. After getting advanced degrees in electrical engineering, he and his Chinese wife, a physicist, worked in Silicon Valley for ten years. A few years ago, they returned to China to see Shou's aging mother and realized how good it felt to be surrounded by the family, culture, and language of their childhood. As Christians, the two shared Chang's sense of China's need for a new spiritual life. Said Shou, "I had a feeling that my life should be in China, serving people and God."[20]

Today the company is a resounding success; it went public on the New York Stock Exchange in March 2000. One reason for the success is that SMIC operates at the cutting edge of technology. It recently bought Motorola's giant chip factory in Tianjin in an equity swap that made Motorola the second largest shareholder in SMIC. More important, the deal brought Motorola's technology into SMIC. Now, in a new plant coming on line in Beijing, SMIC is using the most advanced technology available to make semiconductors on 300 millimeter wafers with circuits as fine as 0.10 microns, or one thousandth the width of a human hair. With this capacity, SMIC can begin to satisfy China's seemingly unquenchable thirst for sophisticated chips.

The other part of the success is the company's low costs. For example, although Taiwan and Korea are generally considered the low-cost locations for producing DRAM memory chips, SMIC's costs are 10 percent below theirs. There are several reasons for this. To begin with, the price of land for the factory in Shanghai was 95 percent less than comparable land elsewhere. Indeed, it was virtually free. In addition, the Shanghai authorities guarantee water and electrical supplies without interruption and at better quality and better prices than elsewhere. Then there is the cost of labor. A machine operator with a high school diploma, who, for instance, costs SMIC about $250 per month, would in Taiwan cost six times as much and about twelve times as much in Japan, Europe, or the United States. Since each plant needs about 1,000 operators, SMIC's labor cost saving is substantial. The argument that the cost of labor is relatively insignificant in the whole cost mix, since semiconductor production is capital intensive rather than labor intensive, ignores the impact of low labor costs on final capital costs. Because labor is so inexpensive, it is sometimes not cost-effective in China to invest in the automated equipment of standard semiconductor fabrication facilities elsewhere. Thus a clean room in China costs 40 percent less than it would anywhere else, making the total capital investment necessary to construct a leading-edge semiconductor plant in China substantially less than in Taiwan or Korea, let alone in Japan or Europe or the United States. The combination of low labor costs, low capital costs, leading-edge technology, and large tax and financial incentives makes SMIC an unbeatable competitor. Perhaps this explains Richard Chang's confident tone as he addresses the weekly meeting of his management team in the company language—English.

SMIC's success has not been lost on the rest of the semiconductor industry. "Everybody is making a dash into China," says Kirk Pond, CEO of Fairchild Semiconductor International, which has built a $200 million facility in Shanghai. A number of Japanese chip makers have also announced new investments. In Taiwan the government for years barred its chip makers from doing business on the mainland. It feared that transfer of chip making technology to the mainland would hollow out its own economy and give China additional leverage in the long-running political struggle between Taipei and Beijing. But Morris Chang and the other heads of the big Taiwanese foundries feared losing competitiveness to mainland-based facilities, and this eventually outweighed the political concerns. In 2002 heavy lobbying by the foundry executives forced the government to ease its restrictions. The result was a rush by Taiwanese business to set up new semiconductor plants on the mainland. Just down the road from SMIC is the new Grace Semiconductor plant, cofounded by the son of former Chinese President Jiang Zemin and the scion of Taiwan's giant Formosa Plastics Group, whose owners have long been militantly anticommunist. Also under construction nearby is the new lab of Morris Chang's Taiwan Semiconductor Manufacturing Company, the world's biggest producer of custom-made chips. That the Taiwanese have been forced to move factories and important technology to mainland China constitutes a very big statement. China will be able to compete with the best in just about anything.

The Real Great Leap Forward

Today a true great leap forward is under way in China, powered by investment in manufacturing. At over 40 percent of GDP, China has one of the world's highest savings rates. The heavy flow of foreign investment into China pales next to the investment the Chinese themselves are making. Indeed there is evidence that some of the "foreign" investment is really of domestic origin. Because foreign investment sometimes receives special benefits, canny Chinese send money to Hong

Kong or Taiwan and then bring it back in. Depending on the extent of that practice, domestic investment is anywhere from 42 to 45 percent of GDP, to which must be added the foreign investment. In total, domestic plus foreign investment equals close to half of China's GDP, and nearly all of it goes into building new infrastructure and manufacturing plants. To put this figure in context, U.S. investment is 19 percent of GDP. Japan's is 24.2 percent, and the EU's is 19.9 percent.[21]

The result has been an explosion of production that is bringing China back to its historic position as the world's largest economy. Over the past decade, China has generated more than 30 percent of world GDP growth while more than doubling the size of its own economy.[22] Today, depending on whether you convert the yuan into dollars at the market rate or in terms of its domestic purchasing power, it is either the world's seventh largest economy or the second largest. The International Monetary Fund believes China can easily maintain a 7–8 percent annual growth rate for another decade and perhaps longer. At that rate, China's GDP by the most conservative measure would pass Japan around 2016 and could be approaching the size of the United States as soon as 2040.[23] If you look at this in terms of China's domestic purchasing power, however, its GDP could be effectively as large as America's by 2025.

This growth is being powered by China's rise as the world's premier manufacturing and industrial power. China already produces two-thirds of the world's photo copiers, shoes, toys, and microwave ovens; half of its DVD players, digital cameras, cement, and textiles; a third of its DVD-ROM drives and desktop computers; and a fourth of its mobile phones, TV sets, PDAs, steel, and car stereos.[24] Much of this production is of exports, which have increased eightfold to $400 billion since 1990.[25] Last year, China shipped over 30 percent of Asia's exports of electronic goods and slipped past Germany to become the world's second largest exporter, just behind the United States.[26] Much of its production is also for a rapidly growing domestic market that is now the world's largest for over one hundred products, including mobile phones, machine tools, cement, steel, and television sets.[27] China has become the second largest national market for personal computers and will certainly pass the United States in this category in the not too distant future.[28]

Underlying this dynamism is the simple but powerful equation we saw at work in the Nike, SMIC, and Hempel plants in Shanghai and Hangzhou. While labor is surely inexpensive, that is not the only factor. Labor is cheaper in Vietnam, Africa, and parts of Latin America. But Chinese labor is well disciplined and largely literate with the ability to learn skills quickly. A significant portion of the Chinese factory work- force is as skilled as U.S. production line workers. But while Americans earn $15–$30 per hour, in China they are paid $0.25—$1.00 per hour. This labor force is effectively nonunion with little ability to strike, com- plain, or take legal action against the employer. It is accustomed to grindingly long hours and prepared to work under difficult conditions. Furthermore, for all practical purposes, the Chinese labor supply is endless. When Japan, Korea, and Taiwan became industrialized, their growth created labor shortages that resulted in the bidding up of wages. This eventually negated some of the initial competitive advantage. But China is another story. While salaries for managerial positions have risen sharply because of a shortage of experienced people, wage rates for production line workers have not moved much at all despite the ex- plosive growth. The reason is that there are still 800 million poor people in the countryside just aching for a shot at a factory job in the city.

When this labor force is combined with modern production technol- ogy and techniques, good transportation and communications infra- structure, a currency managed to remain weak against the dollar, and substantial tax and financial incentives, the total manufacturing pack- age is extremely powerful. To this must also be added the potential economies of scale and long-term market opportunities of operating in what already is or shortly will be the world's largest market for your products. Put it all together and it is a nearly unbeatable combination that is rapidly creating a phalanx of Chinese manufacturers who are rising to challenge the current global leaders.

Chinese Champions "Straitjacket" the West

Take Haier as an example. When Zhang Ruimin, a minor bureaucrat in the eastern city of Qingdao, took over a loss-making refrigerator com- pany in 1984, the workers were so undisciplined they got drunk and

urinated on the factory floor. Twenty years later, Haier is China's leading maker of refrigerators, air conditioners, washing machines, and
other appliances with sales of over $10 billion. Haier has just passed
GE to become the world's fourth largest white goods maker, just behind Whirlpool, Electrolux, and Bosch Siemens. It now controls 30
percent of the U.S. market for small refrigerators and half the market
for wine coolers. In Europe, it already claims 10 percent of the market
for air conditioners and is opening sales offices in 165 countries.[29]
Then there is Huawei. Founded in 1988 by a former People's Liberation Army sergeant as a distributor of switchboards, Huawei now employs 22,000 people and dominates China's market for high-speed
switches and routers. More than that, it is giving Cisco fits in international markets. Last year it beat out all the top world suppliers to build
a third-generation wireless phone network for the United Arab Emi-
rates.[30] I could go on, but you get the idea. There is a new force of nature at work.

Increasingly, American, and also Japanese and European, companies are finding China's low costs irresistible. According to Jim Hemmerling of the Boston Consulting Group, going offshore, especially to
China, will save a manufacturer 20–50 percent of the landed cost of
making and shipping the goods. China holds a fifteen- to thirtyfold advantage in labor cost. Beyond that, however, is the matter of capital investment. Building and equipping factories in China can cost as much
as 70 percent less than in the developed countries. Thus a $50 million
factory in the United States might be available in China for as little as
$15 million. Another element of capital cost savings arises from re-
design of the manufacturing process. In the first world, extensive use
is made of robotics and automation to save on the cost of expensive labor. In China, however, low-cost labor can be substituted for expensive equipment. Thus one leading manufacturer of household appliances has eliminated conveyor belts in its Chinese factories.[31] The
enormous Chinese market offers opportunities to manufacturers for
great economies of scale that greatly lower costs. Moreover, many
firms report saving as much as 20–30 percent on materials and components. Finally, government financial incentives are a significant source
of cost savings. So generous are tax and other financial offerings from

China's central and provincial governments that some firms claim to have built factories cost free.[32]

The final factor forcing the issue for Western manufacturers is the Chinese domestic market. It is or will be the biggest in the world. In the debate over trade and jobs Americans speak as though China is the place where the world's companies *choose* to take advantage of low-cost manufacturing. The assumption is that the companies and the consumers of their goods have choices. In fact, however, China is "straitjacketing the choices of American as well as of European, Japanese, and other global companies."[33] Its size and favorable cost situation not only make low-cost manufacturing possible, they compel it. Increasingly, it is what China chooses that will determine the West's economic future, not the other way around.

Let's go back to Motorola as a good example of what I mean. We saw earlier how then chairman Bob Galvin made the dramatic decision to invest big in China in the early 1990s because he saw a potentially huge new market for Motorola to serve. He was right. With 300 million subscribers and rising, China's is by far the biggest mobile phone market on the planet. It is also the most competitive. In addition to Motorola, major European producers are also now big investors in China. But 40 percent of the market is now controlled by Chinese makers like Ningbo Bird, which is poised to enter the ranks of the world's top ten mobile phone producers.[34] Though business can be tough in China, Motorola has concluded it can't remain competitive in world markets without moving more and more of its manufacturing and even R&D to China.[35] GE Plastics has reached the same conclusion. Says its China region president Mark Wall, "Look, China is the most exciting place in the world right now to be a manufacturer."[36] That sentiment is luring U.S. manufacturers to China. Whether it is toy maker Mattel, wood furniture manufacturer Bassett, electronics producer Hewlett-Packard, or shoemaker Nike, all and many more feel compelled to switch their production heavily to China.

Nor is it only the Americans. Japan's NEC has moved its hard drive production from the Philippines to Shanghai; Toshiba has put its PC production in Hangzhou, joining thirty-three other plants it has scattered around China; and Pioneer has 3,550 workers turning out DVDs around the clock in its plant south of Shanghai. Japanese companies have plowed $9 billion in new investment into Shanghai in the past five years.[37] Meanwhile Finland's Nokia, like its competitor Motorola, has moved much of its mobile phone production to China, and Siemens has moved half of its R&D there as well. For Volkswagen, China is the most important market and production base outside of Germany.

Ironically, the largest exporter from China in 2002 was the Taiwanese firm Hon Hai Electronics. With 40,000 companies and over $100 billion of investment, Taiwan is the leader in outsourcing to mainland China. Its companies have over 50 percent of the world markets for keyboards, motherboards, monitors, and laptop computers, and production is all being moved to the mainland. Not to be outdone, Korea's Samsung has made China the main base for production of its PCs and flat-panel displays, while Hyundai is building capacity for production of a million autos in China by 2007. The move by the Japanese is perhaps the most significant because they have long resisted moving production offshore. Pioneer Shanghai chairman Hiroyuki Mineta explains the current sentiment: "We hesitated in the past, but we cannot say that anymore. We have to overcome our fear or we won't be able to survive in the market."[38]

With so much of the world's manufacturing moving to China, an obvious question is what the rest of the world's workers are going to do, particularly those in developed countries whose manufacturing is disappearing rapidly. Over the years that question has been answered with one word—services.

CHAPTER 5

Serviced in India

India is beginning to do in services what China
has been doing in manufacturing.
—AZIM PREMJI, WIPRO CHAIRMAN

When I arrive at the Wipro Spectramind building on the outskirts of Delhi during a follow-up trip in November 2004, it is about midnight and the action is really getting hot. If I didn't know better, I'd think I had come to a nightclub. The area is brilliantly illuminated by spotlights as vehicles and people continuously come and go. Inside there is a kind of college clubhouse atmosphere. Women in brightly colored saris and sandals and men in slacks, casual shirts, and tennis shoes create a din of ceaseless chatter. Most are in their twenties and no one is over thirty-five. The walls are hung with slogans: "We Have the Right Stuff," "We're on a Mission," "Migrate High Speed or Low Cost," "I Am Confident," "I Add Value to Calls."

I am in the call center area of a multiproduct service provider. I strike up a conversation with Nishat, who works at a telephone in the AOL Retention Center. She is an attractive woman of about twenty-five dressed in a gold sari and blue-banded sandals. Like 200 million other Indians she speaks English, and like maybe 40 million of them she speaks it as her first language with only a hint of the usual Indian enunciation. She explains that she was majoring in English literature at a local college, when she took a break from her studies and had a chance to work here. This center handles calls from the United States. Because of the time difference, her working "day" begins at about 10:00 P.M. and ends at 5:00 or 6:00 in the morning. Despite, or perhaps because of, the crazy hours, Nishat says she now loves this job so much she is not sure when she will return to finish her degree. Her job is to handle your call if you dial the 800 number to cancel your AOL account. Her task is to persuade you not only that you don't want to cancel, but that you really want to renew for another couple of years. As we're talking, her phone bleeps, and I listen in as she answers using her screen name, "Megan." It's Bob calling from Camden, New Jersey, where I once lived. He's really had it with AOL. Here's how the conversation proceeds:

> Bob: Hello, are you the cancellation desk? I'm in Camden and I don't want another minute of AOL. I want to get out of it right now. Please just cancel me immediately.
>
> Megan (in a soothing tone): Bob, my name is Megan, and I know how upset you are. I'll cancel you if you want me to, but I just wonder if you would tell me a little bit about how you use your computer. For instance, do you do instant messaging?
>
> Bob: What's that?
>
> Megan: Well, it's our service that lets you contact all your friends who are online immediately instead of waiting for the normal e-mail to go through. You know that can sometimes take a while. But with instant messaging you can carry on a real-time conversation.
>
> Bob: That sounds useful, but how come nobody ever told me about it before?
>
> Megan: I'm not sure, but I can give you a break on the subscription if you want to renew your subscription.
>
> Bob: I don't know. I wonder if I'd use it that much.
>
> Megan: Bob, *trust me, believe me*. You'll love it. Just give it a try. You can always call me back.
>
> Bob: Okay, if I can call you back, I'll give it a try for another six months.

So Megan/Nishat notched another win for tonight. Her average success rate is 80 percent, well above the office average of about 70 percent. I was really impressed with the *trust me, believe me* line—authentically American with just the right intonation. I asked her where she picked that up. "Oh, those are the power words they teach us in the accent neutralization classes," she replied. Wow, I thought. Here I am ten and a half time zones away from Bob, but Nishat might as well be in his living room.

For AOL, on the other hand, she is definitely offshore, where her $300 a month salary is a fraction of the $3,000–$5,000 a month a stateside counterpart would be paid. Yet her earnings are considered so good here that conservative Hindu parents waive many taboos so their daughters can come home in the wee hours of the morning after spending the night talking to foreigners. Without the Nishats of India, already troubled AOL might not survive.

My guide, a tall, thirtyish call center veteran named Manish, takes me through the rest of the building. As we pass the cafeteria and fully outfitted gym, where an aerobics class is in progress, he explains that young people love it here not just for the money but also for the camaraderie and the upscale facilities the company provides. It's a whole different lifestyle with unimaginable opportunities for young people, he emphasizes.

As we continue the tour, we come to the Dell help center floor. If you call the 800 number to get help setting up your new Dell computer, this is where the call comes. Maybe a hundred young people are patiently explaining what keys to push to callers in Pittsburgh, Mobile, Chicago, and elsewhere.

Next is the Fingerhut corner. I am startled because when I worked for American Can Company back in the 1970s, I had a lot to do with the Fingerhut division. Logistics and order fulfillment had been a problem then. Now it is apparently being solved by having the orders fulfilled from India. Then I realize I shouldn't think that way. It's not really from India. It's really just next door.

In another part of the building about 2,500 recent university graduates are processing insurance claims on the daytime schedule of a major U.S. company. Their colleagues who worked the Indian day shift completed tasks that were on the desks of the U.S. executives when they arrived at their offices in the morning. Wipro uses the time difference between India and the U.S. East Coast to provide next-day delivery at a cost that is 60 percent under the U.S. price. At the other end of the building, a team of scientists with doctorates in molecular biology are reviewing and summarizing research papers for several U.S. and European pharmaceutical companies. These results would also be delivered either in real time or the next day for a fraction of the U.S. or European cost.

As I leave the building and walk back into the spotlights to get my cab, I think of how I'd once thought of India as determinedly backward. Now I am witnessing a revolution—for India and for the world. A lot of the service jobs traditionally tied to particular locations and times have just been untied. From now on they will float, just as manufacturing jobs have been doing for the past thirty years. I have glimpsed a new way of doing business, and it appears to work very well. Where, I wondered, did all this come from?

From North Dallas to South India

Texas is the answer. You may remember Ross Perot as the 1992 third party presidential candidate who ran in opposition to NAFTA, which he said would create a "giant sucking sound" as all the jobs left America for Mexico. Ironically for those who fear jobs moving to India, it was Perot who invented information technology (IT) service outsourcing. A star salesman at IBM, Perot met his sales quota for calendar 1962 by the end of January. But he was already looking beyond sales to something potentially much bigger. He realized the customers often weren't able to get the most out of the hardware IBM was selling them. So he proposed offering computer services along with the hardware. When IBM rejected the idea, Perot quit and with $1,000 of his own savings founded Electronic Data Systems (EDS) on June 27, 1962, his thirty-second birthday.

Seven months later he signed a landmark deal to take over and operate Frito-Lay's entire computer facility. The first long-term, fixed-price agreement for computer services, it was a five-year deal with a contract value of $5,128. This arrangement had something for everybody. Frito-Lay was able to forget about a part of its organization that was not central to its business but generated unexpected headaches and costs. Moreover, it got rid of this problem at a fixed cost known in advance. EDS got a steady revenue stream and the opportunity to make additional money by cutting its costs far below the contract amount. This deal became the model for many future EDS contracts.

But if the Frito-Lay arrangement ensured EDS's stability and survival, it was the U.S. government and the state of Texas that made the company rich. In 1965 Congress passed legislation creating the Medicare and Medicaid Title 17 programs. In response, EDS designed a system to process insurance claims and payments for the new state Medicare program managed by Texas Blue Cross and Blue Shield. Two years later, EDS concluded a contract to manage data processing for the Texas Medicaid program and then made a similar deal with the state of Kansas. The rest is history. EDS grew into a world-girdling company with hundreds of thousands of employees and billions of dollars in revenues.

In founding his company, Perot also founded an industry. Think of EDS as the software and IT services analog to contract manufacturers like Solectron and Flextronics. Just as Solectron got its start by taking over and running some IBM factories, EDS began by running Frito-Lay's computer operations and taking over medical claims processing from Texas and Kansas. Just as Solectron progressed in some instances from running factories to running the whole supply chain, so processing medical claims and running computer operations led EDS to new fields as well. If you could process medical claims you could process other insurance claims, and maybe you could do payrolls and credit card billings and lots more. The twin forces of globalization and automation multiplied at a geometric rate the things that needed to be processed, monitored, and supported. And developing systems for and handling this work became a gold mine for companies like Oracle, SAP, EDS, IBM, Bearing Point, Accenture, and others. At first this work was done either at the client's site or at the consulting or software firm's offices. But that was before names like Wipro, Tata Consulting, Infosys, and Satyam became known.

It was another Texan, Mark Shepherd, who first thought of bringing all this to India. I got to know Shepherd in the early 1980s, when he was chairman of semiconductor giant Texas Instruments and I was negotiating semiconductor issues with Japan. A big, intimidating man, he was more visionary than manager. Some feel he nearly ruined Texas

Instruments with his bad sense of business timing and his sometimes brutal treatment of subordinates. Nevertheless, he probably saved not only TI but the whole U.S. semiconductor industry in the late 1980s. He, more than any other business leader, persuaded the U.S. government to stop the Japanese dumping of memory chips that was playing havoc with the U.S. industry at the time.

In addition to being chairman of a leading technology company, Shepherd fancied himself a prophet with a long-term view of the world that he expounded in detail at the company's annual planning meetings and in its annual reports. In the early 1980s, this view included a vision of China and India as major economies and world-class technological powers. This was not a common perception at the time, and some wondered if Shepherd had entered an early dotage. But while many winked knowingly, Shepherd insisted that Texas Instruments set up a software development center in India. To many at TI, this seemed quixotic. Sure, India was cheap, but it was also eleven time zones and a twenty-hour flight from Dallas; and it was dirt poor. There was no demand there for the stuff TI made. How exactly was this offshore software development center supposed to be anything but another drag on a company that was barely clearing the treetops as it was?

Is India Smarter than IBM?

What Shepherd apparently saw and others didn't was a lot of very talented people doing interesting things amid the socialist lethargy, dust, and backwardness of India. The talented people came from both a long tradition of Indian learning and the IIT campuses Jawaharlal Nehru had established. The interesting activity, however, was sparked by America's decision to stop supplying India with critical electronics equipment during its 1965 war with U.S. ally Pakistan. In response, the Indian government launched an effort to become self-sufficient in small and medium-size computers within ten years. Presciently, the government's Electronics Commission also recognized that a computer system is only as versatile as the software that comes with it. Software is strategic. Software is business.[1]

Because the military needed access to advanced equipment, the government initially allowed IBM and Britain's International Computers (ICL) to operate freely in India. By the early 1970s IBM controlled nearly 75 percent of the market. Then a new policy was adopted that sought to limit foreign investment and compel IBM and ICL to transfer trade secrets and technology to Indian companies. In the tense negotiations that followed, Prime Minister Morarj Desai challenged an IBM executive by asking, "Is IBM smarter or is India smarter?" His answer was not recorded, but the company's response was very clear. IBM closed its doors and left India. Its decision had unexpected consequences for everyone.

The immediate effect was to severely handicap the whole Indian economy. But the difficulties also created opportunities. Some of IBM India's former staffers set up companies to service the old computers and develop software. With IBM and its proprietary operating systems out of the picture, the Unix operating system, first developed by AT&T and made freely available by U.S. anti-trust law to all comers, became India's system of choice. The significance of this cannot be overemphasized. Unix supported a host of derivative systems, like DOS, Mac OS, and Windows NT, along with such programming languages as Java. Thus Indian programmers, already well educated and fluent in English, became proficient in exactly the systems American and European companies were rushing to embrace. Moreover, the Indian government, having targeted software as a potential export industry, was taking halting steps toward promoting software exports as a way of covering its pressing foreign exchange needs.

It wasn't exactly Silicon Valley, but the door had opened a crack, and a lot of entrepreneurs went for it. Tata Consulting Services had been struggling to make a go of it since 1968, when the government identified software as a key industry. It now got its first big export assignment in 1974 when it did a stores and inventory control system for an electric company in Iran. It followed that the next year with development of a hospital information system in the United Kingdom.

Wipro, short for West Indian Vegetable Processing Company, was another pioneer. Founded in 1945 by the father of its present chairman, Wipro originally produced cooking oil. In 1966 Azim Premji, now

India's richest man, dropped out of Stanford to take over the company when his father died. The business made good money, but Premji was bored. When IBM was booted out, he and Wipro jumped in to develop replacement computers along with a spreadsheet and word processing package.

A short time later, seven young Bombay-based programmers dreamed of building an Indian software company that would compete with the best in the world. Under the leadership of Narayana Murthy and Nandan M. Nilekani, they pooled their savings of $250 in 1981 and founded Infosys. As Murthy later explained, "Right from day one we were externally focused. There was really no market for software in India at that time. All of us who founded the company had had experience of working or studying outside of India, and we realized that's where the whole action was. We said, look, if we want to experience the good things that go with being on the leading edge of technology, we have to be globally competitive. We have to be externally oriented."[2]

In attacking the U.S. and other foreign markets, Murthy saw India as having several advantages: a pool of English-speaking, educated, low-cost professionals and a geographic location twelve hours away from the United States, which enabled a twenty-four-hour working day for combined U.S.-India operations. Said Murthy, "The gambit was, how can you lose when you offer your customers top-quality service on a low-cost round-the-clock basis?"[3]

It was also around this time that Raju Ramalinga thought India was ready for personal computers and began planning a retail chain that has since morphed into Satyam Computer Services. Recently Ramalinga explained that a chain of stores seemed like a natural extension. (His farmer father had turned a grape orchard into a bloc of real estate holdings.) As things turned out, the idea was way ahead of its time.

End of the Permit "Raj"

In 1984, however, two seminal events dramatically moved the business forward: Rajiv Gandhi became prime minister of India and Mark Shepherd forced TI to invest in India. Elected after the assassination of his mother, Prime Minister Indira Gandhi, Rajiv had previously been a pilot for Air India. This experience not only gave him an opportunity to travel widely but also turned him into a technology enthusiast. As prime minister he immediately liberalized the software and computer industry. In those early days, according to Murthy, the industry faced enormous difficulties: "It used to take us about 12 to 24 months and about 50 visits to Delhi to import a computer worth $1,500." Owing to what Indians called the "permit raj," even ordinary business actions required a license or stamp of approval. As Murthy explained, "The kind of inhibition these permit laws brought into play, the kind of friction to business that these policies cost, is something that can only be experienced. You can't explain it."[4] All this was targeted for reform by Rajiv and his "computer boys."

Rajiv's government set the goal of becoming to software in the 1990s what Taiwan and South Korea were to hardware in the 1980s. The strategy was to begin with high-volume, low-value-added exports and then move up the value chain. At this critical moment, Texas Instruments became the first foreign company to establish a software development facility in Bangalore. It began by doing relatively simple software applications support work. To facilitate communication with Dallas, it applied for permission to install an earth station for satellite data link services. Despite the new policy, getting the station in operation took two years and the creative evasion of twenty-five government rules. But ultimately, by demonstrating the feasibility of offshore software support operations, it sparked a huge wave of interest in India's software and IT potential. Ramalinga abandoned his computer retail stores and turned Satyam into a software and IT services firm as Wipro, Infosys, and Tata Consulting also began building their capabilities. By the end of the 1980s, this activity had quadrupled India's software revenues from about $40 million to $160 million, with nearly half coming from exports. The groundwork had been laid for a quantum leap forward.

From Body Shopping to Shopping for Bodies

Indians had been going to the United States for higher education and staying on for employment since the U.S. restrictions on immigration were relaxed in 1965. Although they represented only 3–4 percent of all immigrants, they accounted for over 20 percent of those with professional and technical skills.[5] In the U.S. biotech, software, and electronics industries they achieved success as scientists, executives, and entrepreneurs. As Murthy had anticipated, when the Indian software and IT services companies came calling with their highly educated talent available at a third or less of the prevailing costs in the U.S. and European markets, it was an offer few could refuse.[6]

When Indian software programmers initially went to U.S. and European sites to do relatively routine work on limited-time contracts, they received Indian salaries and lived in hotels or temporary quarters near the project site. Known as body shopping, this practice became a booming business in the mid-1990s because of the difference between American and Indian salaries. In 1999, for example, an Indian systems analyst was paid $20,500 annually while an American analyst made $58,300; an Indian test engineer earned $11,700, compared to an American's $57,100.[7] With savings of that magnitude available, it did not take long for clients to extend the scope of the Indian contract work to more sophisticated areas. Indian companies soon went beyond contracting to partnering with their client companies. As one U.S. CEO told me, "At first I hired them because they were cheap, but then I continued to retain them because they were also better." Once this kind of confidence was established, there was a further temptation, in view of the TI experience and the satellite data links, to seek even greater cost advantages by offshoring parts of the work to India. Then new U.S. visa restrictions on temporary workers, enacted after 9/11, tended perversely to drive the work offshore.

Going offshore, however, involved issues of confidential communication and security. The Satyam experience is a good example of how offshoring arrangements got started. In June 1991 Satyam signed up Deere & Co. as its first Fortune 500 client for a software project. The work went well and the relationship expanded. In January 1992 Satyam installed its first 64 kbps satellite link, paving the way for on-line access to global clients. Obviously Deere stood to make large savings by shifting much of its project work to India via satellite, but there were uncertainties. As a kind of pilot project, Ramalinga explained to me, Satyam created "India Land" near Deere headquarters in Moline, Illinois, a replica of a Satyam office in India, complete with a staff of three hundred Indians who moved to Moline for the duration of the test. The simulation was set up to work just as it would if the project were farmed out to Hyderabad. A communications link like the one that would exist between Moline and India was established between Deere Moline and India Land Moline. The staff of India Land kept Indian hours, working all night and sleeping during the day. Although they were only a few hundred yards apart, there was no physical contact between Deere headquarters and India Land. Everything was done by data links. Only after running successfully in this mode for several months did Satyam and Deere shift the work to India, where the system eventually came to perform just as smoothly as it had in Moline, and much more cheaply. Experiments like these began the trend to offshoring software and IT service work even before the Internet came into wide use. With increasing commercial development of the Internet and the introduction of the Netscape browser in 1994, the revenue of the Indian firms and the proportion of the work done in India leaped still further.

Gold in the Back Office

But software and IT services are only part of the Indian story. Let's go back to where we started, Wipro Spectramind, and listen to Raman Roy tell us about the other part—back office processing.

A well-spoken, nonstop executive whose two cell phones ring incessantly until he kindly turns them off, Roy is the genius and the sparkplug behind the industry of which this company is a leader. Born in Lahore in what is now Pakistan, he was transplanted to Delhi when his family fled the violence that broke out during the partition of India and Pakistan. He grew up poor and focused on accounting as the road to a better future. With thirty-three accounting degrees and certifications to his credit, he signed on with an American Express accounting office in India in the late 1980s. He remembers opportunity presenting itself when one of the company's top executives visited India on a tour that was ostensibly for business but really for pleasure. After visiting the Taj Mahal and other attractions, the executive stopped by the office. Initially condescending, he became interested and ultimately exclaimed in obvious surprise, "Hey, this work is good." It was so good that six months later, when Amex decided to reduce its global accounting centers from forty to three, India was one of the three on the strength of the plan Roy presented to the management committee.

Roy clearly remembers Amex Controller John McDonald's comment at the conclusion of the meeting: "Okay kid. You've got it. Now go and deliver."

But delivering was not so easy. This was 1991. There was lots of opposition inside American Express, where few had confidence in the Indians. And there wasn't even a satellite dish in Delhi that Amex could use for data transmission. Trying to get a dish became a Herculean task of enduring one bureaucratic delay after another. Finally Roy had a cable link installed. But soon after it began to work all systems suddenly and mysteriously went down. It turned out that someone had dug up the cable to get the copper wire. The electrical supply was unreliable, so Roy imported generators and Amex India generated its own electricity. Another problem arose when some Indian bureaucrats suspected Roy and his team of being a CIA operation because of the large amount of data they were processing. Through it all, however, one thing held up—the quality of the Indian accounting work. Roy's team cut Amex accounting and processing costs in half. Like the prospectors of an earlier century, they had struggled with adversity and now they had struck gold.

Jack Welch's Secret Weapon

As word of Roy's operation at Amex got around, he received a call from a company that was still prospecting. Like Mark Shepherd, the GE chairman and CEO, Jack Welch, seemed to be aware of India's talent and potential and began visiting in the late 1980s. After the government's market liberalization in 1991, GE invested in four joint ventures, expecting explosive growth. By late 1995, however, bureaucratic delay, crumbling infrastructure, and unreceptive markets had resulted in no growth. That's when Scott Bayman, GE's chief in India, realized that the money was not in the joint ventures but in GE itself. GE was writing a lot of its own software. Why not do it in India at a quarter of the cost? The same with engineering. Welch was a big promoter. Says Bayman, "Jack just kept squeezing budgets. When managers complained, he had a standard answer. Have you been to India? Don't talk to me until you've been there."

One of those who went was GE Capital head Gary Wendt, and it was he who persuaded Roy to join GE in late 1995. There he proceeded to organize the same cost reductions in accounting and back office processing for GE that he had achieved for Amex. At the same time, he requested $250,000 to experiment with doing call support from India. "Impossible," said some of the heavyweights at headquarters. "You can't possibly rely on foreign voices halfway around the world. Nobody will understand them, and even if they do the sound delay and potential for downtime are too great." But the experiment proved it could be done, with "accent neutralization" and sufficient backup facilities. Soon GE Capital was finding more gold in its call centers and back office than anyone had imagined could exist.

Then Roy had another idea that he popped on Welch in a presentation. "We're a cost center. Why not become a profit center by selling this as a service to other companies?" Welch's response was revealing and also helped Roy make a difficult decision. "No way," said Welch. "You guys are my secret weapon. Do you want to make Whirlpool cheaper than GE?" It was a logical response. But it left unfulfilled the need for a third party player.

To try to meet that need Roy left GE, found some venture capital, and founded Spectramind. He was convinced that "geography is history": distance is no longer an impediment to doing business anywhere you can find customers. That conviction was sorely tested in the beginning, however, as potential U.S. customers responded to sales presentations by saying, "Are you crazy. You think you can do that from India?" Then, after signing up a few intrepid clients, there was the problem of who would answer the calls. About half the staff are young women, and Roy recalls spending a lot of time explaining to worried mothers that their daughters would be perfectly safe and that no stigma should attach to their coming home in the early morning hours. But eventually it all worked. Spectramind was acquired by Wipro a couple of years ago and now has a staff of over 14,000. The only limit on growth seems to be the physical capacity to hire and train the many new people who want to sign on. Roy notes that while his operation will "cut the MBA premium" in the West, there is lots of available talent in India and he is feeling no wage pressure. For the moment the sky seems to be the limit.

The same seems to be true at GE. Bayman notes that "the back room became the front room" as GE discovered it could do the work with fewer people and get a better-quality product. As a result, GE now employs 15,000 Indians in its call center and back office processing operations. It also has one of its biggest research and technology centers in Bangalore, employing several thousand Ph.D. scientists and engineers who work at the cutting edge on the whole range of GE projects. And the GE seal of approval led other global firms to give India a look. They found the high-quality, low-cost, sophisticated work proposition just as seductive as Murthy had said it would be. The fever for India became contagious.

Three additional forces made it an epidemic. One was the Y2K scare of the late 1990s. Computer programmers in the 1950s, anxious to conserve precious memory, dropped the first two digits from the four-digit year by which they kept track of computer time; thus, 1962 became merely 62 and so forth. The danger at the turn of the century was that when their internal clocks turned to 00, the computers would read the time as 1900 and consequently generate trillions of costly miscalculations. A massive effort to reprogram the world's installed computer base was launched to ward off catastrophe, whose name, Y2K, was tech speak for the year 2000. (K stands for 1,000 in mathematical lingo.) This problem, which resided mainly in older computers, created a demand for programmers who knew old computer languages and codes. And who had the most and most knowledgeable programmers of old languages? India, thanks to IBM's exit from the country and the consequent need for Indian programmers to baby old machines along. Thus in the last two years of the twentieth century, it became nearly impossible to book a flight out of India because the planes were full of programmers fluent in arcane computer languages.

The second factor was the U.S. investment bubble at the end of the twentieth century. What the Federal Reserve chairman, Alan Greenspan, had called "irrational exuberance" in 1996 left many industries with massive excess capacity and a pressing need to cut costs drastically when the bubble collapsed in 2000.

One way was to outsource software and IT services to India. This occurred in dramatic fashion because of the third force—the high-speed Internet. Until 1999, data links to India carried information at the relatively slow rate of 64 kbps—the speed of dial-up domestic Internet service. As any reader who has become accustomed to broadband service knows, 64 kbps is maddeningly slow. Then in 1999, high-speed optical fiber undersea cables connected India to the world. Connected at 2 megabits per second, it only took 2 seconds to get a message from the United States to Bangalore. Business went from $5.6 billion to $8.4 billion in one year. As Murthy had predicted twenty years earlier, Indian software and IT services were an offer no one could refuse.

Shining India

India's service-providing capabilities are both world class and extraordinarily broad, encompassing not only information technology but also biotech, a range of medical treatments that have given rise to medical tourism, combinations of technology, finance, and more. Following India's lead, other countries with similar English-language capability and highly educated elites have begun to follow suite and virtually all of the world's multinational companies are getting into the game.

Info Tech

India is a big country, and to see the full extent of the revolution you have to travel around a bit. In Hyderabad, I stop for breakfast with Satyam CEO Ramalinga. Jubilee Hill, where he lives, was once a quasi-slum, but his father bought a lot of the property and developed it into a comfortable upscale neighborhood. As his wife graciously serves breakfast, he outlines Satyam's origins, operations, and ambitions as well as his views of the future development of the IT services industry. He explains that Satyam has come a long way from that first experiment in Moline. Today the company straddles the entire IT space, offering services ranging from consulting to direct implementation of IT solutions for clients. Its strengths include software development, engineering, system integration, customer relationship management, supply chain management, e-commerce, and outsourcing consulting. It has excellent competence in the auto, banking and finance, insurance, and health care industries. Its network spans 45 countries on 6 continents, and its 15,000 employees serve 325 global companies, including over a hundred Fortune 500 firms.

Ramalinga, whose net worth is reportedly north of $1 billion, emphasizes that the sky is the limit for Satyam, India, and Asia into the foreseeable future. The world's e-business focus, he maintains, will gradually shift from the United States to Asia. "If you take the cell phone, Asia is already way ahead in both usage and technology," he says. He also notes the new direction of student movement. "In the past, most of our top students were trying to get out of the country to improve their career prospects in the United States or UK. But now they're coming back."

After breakfast, we drive to the Satyam headquarters on the outskirts of Hyderabad. Its lovely campus puts me in mind of Stanford University with its neatly trimmed grass, tall palm trees, and colorful flowers. The staff is strikingly young and energetic. A large number have degrees from leading U.S. universities and graduate schools. The company is growing at about 30 percent annually, and recruiting is a major activity. The year 2003 saw a 45 percent increase in employees. The leader of the campus tour noted that the company is particularly strong in doing application outsourcing on SAP and Oracle platforms; although 75 percent of its business comes from the United States, it is expecting to obtain several sizable contracts from large clients in Europe. As I walk the spotless halls and watch the flawless Power Point presentations in the campus auditorium, I can't help thinking of Perot's old company, EDS. It is struggling now, shedding employees and moving work offshore. Part of its problems resulted from poor management decisions. But ultimately these Indian guys are very good, and they cost less than a third of the prevailing rates in the U.S., European, and Japanese markets. That's tough competition for EDS or anyone, and why the balance of power in IT is shifting to Asia.

Biotech

After leaving Satyam, I have a late dinner with Dr. Krishna M. Ella and learn about a new dimension of the Indian offshore story. Ella, a molecular biologist, grew up in India but did his university and graduate study at the University of Wisconsin–Madison and University of Hawaii–Honolulu. After graduation he worked for five years at the Medical University of South Carolina–Charleston, becoming known internationally as a leader in his field before returning to India. Ella is not exceptional in making this return. Many of the world's top biotech experts are Indians who have taken a similar path. Just as it has sought to capitalize on its people's software and IT skills, the Indian government has also promoted development of a biotech and pharmaceutical industry. India has already built the world's fourth largest pharmaceutical industry by making itself a major producer of generic drugs.

Nine years ago, Ella saw the opportunity to found what could become a major company and to do something for his native country in the process. With his own money and assistance from a group of investors, along with the national and local governments, he founded Bharat Biotech. Bharat's spanking new laboratories and production line are located in Genome valley, a half hour drive through the countryside outside of Hyderabad. Ella tells me a story much like what I heard in China. This modern drug development and production facility, which meets GMP (good medical practice) standards, was built at a cost of $4 million. In the United States it would have cost $25 million. Just as in China, labor and the required investment cost far less. As we take the tour, Ella proudly explains that one of the lab's major products is a hepatitis B vaccine produced using Bharat's proprietary technology that dispenses with the use of cesium chloride, thus making the vaccine affordable for developing countries. Bharat is the only company in the world that can make the vaccine in this manner.

In addition to Ella, I am accompanied by several of the company's key directors, all of whom trained and worked in the United States before coming back to India. The company is working on a typhoid vaccine and has an arrangement with Wyeth Laboratories of Mumbai to manufacture hepatitis vaccine that Wyeth then supplies to other Asian markets. Ella emphasizes that although the product is made and sold in Asia, because it is sold under the label of a U.S. company it must meet American FDA standards. It's as good as anything in the States.

Bharat is also collaborating with the Centers for Disease Control in Atlanta and the U.S. National Institutes of Health on development of a roto virus vaccine. The clinical trials have all been done in India, which, Ella explains, is ideal for such trials because of its diverse population and because it is far easier and cheaper to persuade people to participate in the trials here than in the developed world. He expects that in the future most clinical trials by the world's drug makers will be done in India.

After the tour, Ella tells me about his latest project over lunch. Bharat has received a grant from the William and Melinda Gates Foundation to develop a malaria vaccine. Because malaria is a tropical disease mainly afflicting the world's poorest people, most people in the developed world are only vaguely aware of it. The big global pharmaceutical companies have invested far less in fighting it than in developing drugs for male erectile dysfunction. But year in and year out, malaria is one of the world's biggest killers. Still, of all the world's pharmaceutical companies, why did the Gates Foundation choose Bharat to find a cure? Ella explains that there were three reasons. Working on malaria in a tropical region made sense. The development costs in India are far lower than anywhere else, and Bharat has world-class capabilities.

Medical Tourism

An hour southeast of Hyderabad by plane lies Chennai and the Apollo Hospital. It is one of thirty-seven such facilities in the Apollo

Hospitals Enterprises chain founded by Prathap C. Reddy in 1983. The son of a wealthy mango and sugarcane plantation owner, Reddy studied medicine in India and moved to the United States in the 1960s.[8] He worked in a Boston hospital and then moved to Springfield, Missouri, where he established a successful internal medicine practice. But homesickness got the better of him, and he returned to India. In 1979 he advised a patient who needed a coronary bypass to get treatment in Houston because the necessary equipment was not available in India. When the patient, who couldn't afford the airfare, died, Reddy vowed to devote his life to establishing modern medical facilities in India.

He founded Apollo in 1983, but it struggled for years under the "permit raj" system. Then the same 1991 economic liberalization that spurred software development gave wing to Apollo. Reddy attracted investment from Citigroup, Goldman Sachs Group, and Schroders PLC as well as from investors in the Bombay Stock Exchange to import the latest equipment from anywhere in the world. His initial target was the 250 million middle-class Indians who can afford to forgo the free but mediocre treatment offered at state-owned hospitals in favor of the $90–$100 checkups available at Apollo. But it wasn't long before he discovered medical tourism.

Take the case of Terry Salo, a resident of British Columbia who was a commercial fisherman until being sidelined by a bad hip. Canada's National Health Service would provide a new hip free of charge but the wait was at least a year. He could also have gone to a private hospital in Canada or the United States, but the cost was prohibitive—about $20,000. After doing some research, Salo found he could get the same treatment at the Apollo Hospital for only $4,500. Even with the $3,000 airfare to India, this was less than half the other alternatives. Since 2000, more than 60,000 foreign patients like Salo have taken advantage of Apollo's top-notch care at Indian prices.[9]

Apollo doesn't just do patient care. Visit the hospital at night, and you'll find the same beehive of activity I witnessed at Wipro in Delhi. Hundreds of data processors do billing and process insurance claims for U.S. hospitals and insurance companies. A score of doctors and technicians are reading and interpreting X rays and CAT scans that

U.S. clinics have e-mailed for evaluation. Apollo also conducts clinical trials for foreign drug companies like Pfizer and Eli Lilly.[10]

To attract more business, Apollo is setting up marketing offices in cities like London and Dubai with the encouragement of the Indian government, which sees health care as a growth industry and is helping train over 20,000 new doctors a year. The prices are hard to beat. Apollo does cardiac surgery for $4,000, compared with $30,000 for the same procedure in the United States; orthopedic operations go for $4,500, less than a fourth the U.S. price. Remember, this is for truly world-class care. Apollo patients are greeted at the airport and taken in limos to the hospital, where they stay in private rooms with one-on-one nursing care. When sufficiently recovered, they can also visit a resort as part of their package. The consulting firm McKinsey & Co. estimates that medical tourism could become a $2 billion a year business for India by 2012.[11] But that's just a guess. The category is so new it can't really be measured.

Everything Technology

It's just a short flight from Chennai to Bangalore, India's answer to Silicon Valley. Like the valley, it is renowned for its pleasant climate and good universities. It is also the heart of the Indian high-tech industry for the same reasons the valley is the center of U.S. high-tech action: it's a nice place to live and has a lot of talented people.

I arrive in the evening, but it seems like morning. As the tropical sun sets in a blaze, the roads are choked with minibuses taking young people to work. It's 7:00 P.M. here but that's 9:00 A.M. on the U.S. East Coast, and these kids have to slip quickly into their telephone cubicles, don their American accents and identities, and start helping people in Boston, Philadelphia, and Washington with their plane reservations, Internet service, computer glitches, and credit card bills.

Not everyone works at night in Bangalore. It is interesting and informative to cruise the bars around Mahatma Gandhi Road and Church Street in Bangalore's Shivaji Nagar district. If software writing is Bangalore's favorite activity, right behind it ranks pubbing. Here in the bars, the hotshots of India's software industry gather to drink beer, listen to music, and talk software. It is mostly a young male crowd, since mixing of the sexes is still not done in India. They nurse their beers a long time. Beer here costs about $1 a bottle, and since the typical software programmer's starting salary is around $300 a month, they can't do this every night unless they make the bottles last. What really lasts is the talk, or what they call the "Church Street buzz," about rising salaries at Infosys or new hiring at IBM and whether that will create a backlash against outsourcing in the United States. It's amazing how many of these kids know more about the United States than Americans do. They watch us closely because our futures are intimately linked, and they know it even if we don't.[12]

A morning drive through Bangalore shows what people mean when they talk about the Indian technology "miracle." The ten-acre Infosys campus with its gym, library, grasslands, and video conference center is just outside town. Near the airport is the Wipro office, and not far away is the Texas Instruments research center where young engineers are designing third-generation mobile phone chips. The GE John F. Welch Technology Center sits on a leafy fifty-acre campus complete with open-air cafeteria and cricket grounds.

I am on my way to Intel's India headquarters, where I receive a warm welcome from Intel India president, Ketan Sampat. Here, as everywhere, Intel has forgone luxury for utility. From Chairman Andy Grove to the lowliest new hire, everyone at Intel gets a cubicle. And so it is in Bangalore.

Established only six years ago, the operation here employs 1,800 Ph.D. electrical engineers and computer scientists. This team is designing Intel's next generation of microprocessors. It is linked to a similar team at Intel's installation in Folsom, Oregon, so that when Folsom sleeps, Bangalore is at work, and Intel never stops. Sampat notes that some things are still best done in the United States because of a lack of experience in India, but in time the two installations will be equal in capability. Bangalore is run for about a third of what Folsom costs. But that's not the main reason for Intel's commitment to India. It's the talent: Intel hires only the best. Because it can use more Ph.D. engineers than the U.S. supplies, the real driver here is the global search for the world's smartest, best-educated technologists. This is the reason Intel and other high-tech companies cannot afford not to be here.

Hi Fi

My last stop is the Morgan Stanley offices in Bombay. Morgan Stanley long ago moved its back office operations to India to take advantage of the time difference and Indian salaries. Recently, however, it has moved about fifty of its analysts to India as well. Analysts are MBAs who do research and analysis of corporate financial statements, business plans, and execution in order to make investment recommendations on various stocks and bonds. This is not data entry: it's a major part of the core business of investment banking, and the guys who do it earn $80,000 a year and up in New York or San Francisco. The people I met at Morgan Stanley Bombay were every bit as impressive as those I know in America and they knew the U.S. scene intimately. Their American managers told me they also work harder and make fewer errors while earning only $20,000 a year.

As I leave Bombay, I pick up an article that further confirms the power of the Indian high quality–low cost offer: Reuters has announced that it is moving more work to Bangalore. The London-based news service and data company is trying to reduce costs by $782 million by the end of 2006. It moved its back office to India years ago. Now it's switching up to fifty members of its editorial staff to India as well. CEO Tom Glocer says, "The amazing thing—and this is the dirty little secret about outsourcing that people need to talk about publicly a bit more—not only is the cost reduction amazing at four, five, and even six to one, but the quality and productivity is better too."[13]

Everybody Does It

The Reuters announcement was also a reminder that outsourcing to India is not unique to American companies. British Airways was a pioneer in outsourcing data processing and call center work to India in the late 1980s. In recent years, Germany's SAP has established software labs in India that employ over 1,300 engineers and computer scientists. The Dutch electronics giant Philips has cut 22,000 jobs in North America and western Europe, while building up its staff in India, China, and Eastern Europe. Says CEO Gerard Kleisterlie about Europe's declining competitiveness, "In a rapidly and radically changing world, Europe is more preoccupied with maintaining the existing economic order than with building another future."[14] In Paris, Valtech CEO Dan DeVille emphasizes that "the reality of the market today is simple. To remain competitive you have to spend less on information technology systems."[15] In London, the big British insurer Norwich Union is in the process of moving 3,700 back office and customer service positions to India. Its customer service director, Simon Machelle, says, "It will cut the cost in half."

Nor is India the only offshore location. A number of French companies are moving call centers to French-speaking former colonies like Morocco, Mauritius, and Senegal. Some say the Senegalese have the best French accents. The Japanese are going to their former colony in northern China, where the city of Dalian has maintained its Japanese-speaking capability and become the location of choice for many Japanese support centers as well as Japanese manufacturers. Meanwhile, German Industry and Trade Association President Martin Wansleben notes that high-value management and R&D jobs are also starting to move out of Europe. Chris Gentle, Deloitte's EU research director, agrees: "If you compete with Citicorp, and they grow revenue by three times their costs by outsourcing, you don't have a choice. You have to outsource. It's going to change the whole operating model of European institutions." This is a view that Wipro's founder, Azim Premji, wholeheartedly shares: "India is beginning to do in services what China has been doing in manufacturing."[16]

The Last "Tiger"

For the world, the implications of this development are as immense as those of Chinese development. Like China, India is a big, poor country.

Its total GDP is about $600 billion. Its roughly 1.1 billion people have a per capita income of about $1.50 a day, barely above the official international poverty level of $1.00 a day. But like China it has recognized its assets and has begun to use them. By 2010 India may be the largest English-speaking country in the world, with more English speakers than the United States. As many as 50–75 million of them—or the equivalent of a large European country—are well educated. In addition, as many as 20 million belong to a diaspora that has reached the top levels of business, medicine, and technology in the United States, Europe, and elsewhere.

After years of grinding poverty and stagnation, India has taken off in what seems to many like a miracle. But the reality is solid. India is now producing 3 million college graduates a year, and that number will climb to 6 million over the next five years. This compares to 1.3 million in the United States and 2.9 million in Europe, with 2.4 million in China. In engineering and science India now produces about 250,000 graduates, rising to 500,000 annually, who earn a starting salary of $5,000–$6,000 a year.[17] Even the 3,000 annual graduates of the elite Indian Institute of Technology will receive starting salaries of only about $10,000–$12,000 per year. These figures compare to 400,000 science and engineering graduates annually in the United States and to $50,000 and up starting salaries. Already, there appear to be more IT engineers in Bangalore (150,000) than in Silicon Valley (130,000), and the number of IT engineers in all of India is expected to grow from the present 400,000 to over 1 million by 2008.[18]

Keep in mind that we are talking about all these engineers for an economy of half a trillion dollars versus a U.S. economy of $11 trillion. So the talent per dollar of GDP ratio is extremely high and growing in India. At the same time, the salary-to-talent ratio is very low compared to almost anywhere else. Whereas a programmer's salary in the United States is typically around $80,000, in India it is about $11,000. So it is easy to see how GE calculates that it is saving about $350 million a year on the work of its 17,000 Indian employees, and why Morgan Stanley and Norwich Union and others say that much of their work can be done in India for a third to a half the cost of doing it in the United States or Europe or Japan.

This combination of skills, low cost, quality work, and instant communication means that few aspects of your life will remain untouched by the outsourcing of services to India. You may not be aware of it, but whether it is your yellow pages, the interactive websites of companies like Boeing or Morgan Stanley, or the report on the X rays you had yesterday, the skilled hands and brains of Indians are present. Just as China has become the location of choice for global manufacturing, so India has become the location of choice for global software and info tech services. No corporation can ignore it. Says consulting firm IT's Bangalore-based managing partner, Avinash Vashistha, "It is getting to a state where companies are literally desperate" to get something going in India.[19]

That desperation is transforming India into the newest Asian tiger and putting it on the path to riches. In 2000 Indian software exports were about $6 billion. By the end of 2004 they were estimated to have hit $16 billion.[20] The big accounting and consulting firm Deloitte forecast last year that within five years, the world's largest financial firms will have shifted $356 billion and 2 million jobs offshore, mostly to India. SurePrep notes that while 25,000 U.S. tax returns were done in India in 2004, the number is expected to multiply nearly tenfold to 200,000 in 2005. In a joint study, India's NASSCOM and consulting firm McKinsey & Co. forecast that India's IT services industry will hit revenues of $57 billion, employ 4.4 million people, and constitute 7 percent of GDP by 2008.[21] Separately, McKinsey has also forecast that India's software industry will record sales of $87 billion and employ 2.2 million people by 2010.[22]

According to Goldman Sachs, all of this means that India's economy can sustain 7–8 percent annual GDP growth for the indefinite future. In the past two years it has grown faster than China, and some believe that with its legacy of capitalist institutions, rule of law, and democratic processes it may well outstrip China over the long term. At those rates of growth India would have a GDP of over $2 trillion at nominal exchange rates by 2025. On the basis of purchasing power parity, that would be about $8 trillion, making India the world's third largest economy and perhaps on the way to becoming the biggest. The surest sign of this is the fact that cell phone sales are skyrocketing.

From about 20 million phones in 2003, sales are already nearing 50 million and are projected to hit nearly 200 million by 2008.[23]

This historic development is lifting hundreds of millions of people out of abject poverty. Consider the remote village of Tihi and its 2,500 inhabitants; 72 percent of India's people live in remote villages like this, having virtually no contact with the outside world since most businesses don't bother with towns of less than 5,000. Tihi's inhabitants are mainly farmers. They have no phones or power lines and only dirt tracks connect them to the outside world. But they have something that many farm families in America still don't have—full global Internet access. So when Ravi Sham Choudry turns on the village computer in his front room and goes to the Chicago Board of Trade website, everyone in town knows the soybean futures prices as well as local prices, weather forecasts, soil testing techniques, and other expert information.

Choudry is the leader of the local e-*choupal* organized by ITC, a vegetable oil processor that buys a large part of the soybean crop. *Choupal* is the Hindi word for village square. ITC dreamed up the concept as part of its strategy to get around middleman soybean trading companies and go directly to the growers. ITC donated a computer, satellite links, and solar panels and selected a leader in each village to run the computer and Internet link on behalf of the village. Via the e-*choupals* the villagers get better prices and ITC has been able to reduce its transaction costs and get better-quality soybeans. ITC is also thinking beyond soybeans as it plans to sell tractors and other items on the e-*choupals* and perhaps become the Wal-Mart of India.[24]

At the other end of the scale is the new generation of young people just emerging from India's universities to enter an exciting new global industry that promises personal freedom, riches, and power. Deepa Paranjpe is a good representative of this generation. The twenty-four-year-old daughter of a former railroad worker, she has just completed a master's degree at the elite Indian Institute of Technology in Bombay. She speaks English, Hindi, and Marathi, and she is fluent in nine computer languages, like Java and C++. She is planning to work in India for a Silicon Valley high-tech company at a starting salary of about $10,000, but her real ambition is to do her own start-up. "Good Indian engineers can do good design work, but we need a venture industry," she says.[25] The icons for this generation are people like Desh Deshpande, founder of Sycamore Networks and Cascade Communications, and Vinod Khosla, a top venture capitalist at Silicon Valley's famed Kleiner Perkins Caulfield & Byers. But the goal for Deepa and her friends is to top these pioneers by doing it in India. She expects to have a traditional arranged marriage, but she insists that whoever the lucky guy is, he'll have to be an entrepreneur and a tech whiz "so we can have a common platform."[26] Right now the world is definitely her, and India's, oyster.

CHAPTER 6

High Tech I:
America's Baby

In five hundred years of Western history
there has always been something new.
Always, always, always, always, always.
— MARC ANDREESEN
NETSCAPE DEVELOPER

Most Americans are convinced that high technology is America's special preserve—the marvels of computers, memory chips, the Internet, miracle drugs, Mars exploration, and much between. Many believe not only as Marc Andreesen says in the chapter epigraph that there will always be something new, but that because of an innate pioneering spirit and a uniquely entrepreneurial system it will always be the United States that produces that next new thing.[1]

There is good reason for this confident faith. America spends more on research and development than any other country. Its leading universities, such as MIT, Caltech, Stanford, and the University of Michigan, are unquestionably the best in the world. The whole notion of venture capital–funded start-up companies, of highly trained professionals chucking status and security to go for the gold with a chancy new company, of mere children or old geezers who have failed two or three times being given big money to try or try again, is definitely American. And it has paid off big-time, both for those who took the chance and for the global economy. Companies like Intel, Apple, Microsoft, Cisco, Dell, and Google exemplify the protean nature of the system and the extraordinary value it has produced. They are also the

basis for the U.S. dominance of global technology, and their leaders—
people like Andreesen, Steve Jobs, Bill Gates, Andy Grove, and
Michael Dell—have iconic status around the world.

Yet all is not necessarily well in Silicon Valley or elsewhere in the
U.S. high-tech establishment. The media focus on charismatic business leaders and hot new companies means that most people don't understand the real sources of technological leadership, particularly the
entrepreneurial role of the U.S. government and the extent to which
present U.S. tech leadership is the result of past government efforts.
Nor do people understand that technological advance usually does not
come from a flash of insight but is rather the fruit of an ecosystem of
interrelated companies, universities, government institutions, bankers,
and, yes, lawyers. Even leading economists don't understand that if
you don't have a camcorder industry you probably won't make digital
cameras either. Most of their econometric models don't account for
the fact that it was easy to go into the semiconductor business when
$10 million could buy you a new plant but nearly impossible now that
you need $3 or $4 billion. Economists don't fully realize that if you
don't think you can get a job as a software developer, you probably
won't take a degree in computer science. With some exceptions, both
industry and government have been eating their seed corn and not saving it to invest in future technology development.

Uncle Sam Ventures LTD.

To help you understand the hidden role of the U.S. government, let me
ask if you know why Bill Gates is the world's richest man. I'll bet you
think he invented Windows or had a fabulous idea for a new kind of
software company that would get a virtual monopoly on the heart of
the personal computer and thereby force computer users to buy his
software. Good guesses, but they're wrong. Gates and most of the U.S.
technology industries owe their leadership as much to U.S. victory in
World War II, U.S. defense policy, and overall U.S. industrial primacy
as to entrepreneurial virtuosity. Victory in the war meant extreme
weakening of the competition just when certain fundamental tech-

nologies like computing were being established and standards set. Americans tended to set the standards because nobody else was in the game. Let's look at computing to see how this all worked.

Preliminary development of computers took place during the war as part of the effort to break the German and Japanese codes and to calculate artillery firing sequences. The first modern computer was demonstrated on February 15, 1946, shortly after the war ended, although if you saw it today, you wouldn't call it modern. Dubbed ENIAC (electronic numerical integrator and calculator), it covered 1,800 square feet, contained 18,000 vacuum tubes, and consumed 174 kilowatts of electricity. When it ran, the room temperature rose to 120 degrees.[2] It was a long way from your laptop, but it worked in much the same way.

After the war, however, there wasn't a lot of interest in monsters like this. Great Britain had the interest but not the money as it, along with the rest of Europe, dug out of the war rubble. In the United States, the smart guys at GE, RCA, and other major companies anticipated a commercial market, but it would take time to develop. IBM CEO Tom Watson said, "I think there is a world market for maybe five computers." No one was interested in developing it without government backing. The U.S. government was the only entity on earth with both an interest in and the resources to pursue computer development. Not only did the army, the navy, and the National Bureau of Standards see the computer's potential—they also poured in the bucks.

IBM, then a maker of office and data processing equipment, successfully bid against companies like Burroughs, Honeywell, and RCA to get a big share of the money. More than half of IBM's total revenue from domestic electronic data processing activities in the 1950s came from government contracts for the B–52 guidance system and the North American air defense system. Through the 1950s and early 1960s, the U.S. government paid for well over half of IBM's R&D expenses. Based on this, IBM developed its revolutionary System 360 mainframe computer. Introduced in 1964, the 360 represented a quantum leap in both computing technology and its adaptation to practical business needs. The 360 made the computer indispensable to corporate America, which in turn made IBM. By the early 1980s, IBM controlled over 70 percent of the global computing market, and its system had become the standard for computer data processing.[3]

Then a small cloud appeared on IBM's horizon in the form of the Apple II personal computer developed by Steve Jobs and Steve Wozniak in their Palo Alto garage. IBM initially dismissed the Apple II as a toy, but when it developed an enthusiastic following, the word went out from IBM headquarters that something had to be done to put the upstart in its place—fast. The need for speed was critical to what happened next.

Up to this time, IBM had always produced its own components and software, thereby maintaining proprietary control over the sources of the technology that created the unique IBM package on which computer use was standardized, and which gave IBM control of the market. Now IBM's top executives wanted to get a personal computer into the market in a year and a half. Given IBM's internal sluggishness, they had no confidence they could meet that timetable through the normal development process. Consequently they opted for a skunk works operation detached from IBM that would use parts and software made by others and already on the market.

IBM's Management Committee (MC) convened in early August 1980. Seated at the point of the V-shaped MC table, Chairman Frank Cary could survey an empire not unlike that of nineteenth-century Britain: the sun never set on IBM's factories and offices sprawled around the globe, and decisions made at this table could rock governments and affect millions of people.[4] But the decision made on this day would eventually rock IBM itself. PC skunk works head Bill Lowe made the presentation and asked for a go-ahead on his program. He got it after only a little discussion about whether using outsider-supplied parts and software would mean losing control of the market's direction. Ultimately, doing so wasn't seen as potentially dangerous enough to warrant a lot of consideration. Said one committee member, "The general attitude was that you don't have big problems in small markets, and we thought the personal computer was a very small market."[5]

Lowe had actually started in early July when one of his executives, Jack Sams, talked software with Bill Gates, a twenty-four-year-old college dropout in Bellevue, Washington, and his number two, Steve

Ballmer. When the discussion got around to the operating system, Gates said he did not have one to sell, but Gary Kildall of Digital Research Intergalactic (DRI) had one. Known as CP/M (control program/monitor), it had sold about 600,000 copies and was the leading program of its type for personal computers. Gates arranged for Sams to see Kildall the next day in Pacific Grove, California, but Kildall never showed. He decided to fly his airplane that day and left his wife to deal with the white collars from IBM. She wanted no part of IBM's paperwork and nondisclosure deals. Sams eventually went back to Gates and told him he had to find an operating system or write one himself; otherwise, any deal with Microsoft on other software was off. Through his partner, Paul Allen, Gates approached Tim Patterson, a Seattle programmer who had developed a system he called QDOS—quick and dirty operating system—that was similar to Kildall's CP/M system. After clearing it with Sams, Gates bought the QDOS system from Patterson for $75,000 and then arranged to license it to IBM for use in the new PC. IBM agreed to pay Microsoft a fixed fee of $80,000 and no royalties and agreed that it could not restrict Microsoft from licensing to other firms. (IBM struck a similar deal with Intel for use of its 8088 microprocessor.)

To IBM that seemed like a very good deal. That anyone would be able to duplicate the IBM PC or that the arrangement would give Gates the power to control a new technology standard was unimaginable.[6] At first IBM seemed vindicated in its new approach. PC sales hit the first year's forecast in about a month and went up from there. By 1985 IBM had an 80 percent market share in the personal computer market. Apple had been put in its place and IBM was back on top. Or so it seemed. Compaq was the first clone in 1993 and was followed by hundreds of others. Bill Gates, who collected royalties on them all, was on his way to becoming the world's richest man, as IBM's market share gradually fell to about 10 percent.

The point is not how good a negotiator Gates was, or how myopic and arrogant IBM was, although Gates was really good and IBM was really blind. The point is that the U.S. government created the world's dominant computer industry. If IBM had not moved boldly and shrewdly to seize leadership, another American company would have been the industry leader. There was never a chance that it would be a European or an Asian company. By the same token, once IBM set the standard in personal computers, whoever controlled that standard was bound to become immensely rich. It could have been Gary Kildall or even IBM. It just turned out to be Bill Gates.

Intel was struck by the same lightning when IBM chose its 8088 microprocessor to be the engine, along with DOS, of the new PC. At the time, Intel was locked in a life-and-death struggle with Japanese producers for the market in memory chips that Intel had invented. So desperate was the battle that IBM invested close to $400 million in Intel to help it withstand the Japanese onslaught while the U.S. government took legal action on behalf of Intel and the other U.S. chip makers. People at Intel remember that on the day the 8088 was adopted by IBM, the sale was seen as a nice piece of work, but there was no dancing in the hallways. No one recognized at the time that the PC was destined to do for Intel exactly what it did for Microsoft. But by concluding a nonexclusive deal with IBM, Intel captured the microprocessor standard for PCs from IBM and went on to become the world's dominant chip maker.

Uncle Sam's Portfolio

The U.S. electronics, aerospace, and telephone industries are equally in the government's debt. RCA was literally created by the U.S. government when President Woodrow Wilson recognized the significance of radio communications at the Versailles Conference in 1919. He directed his assistant secretary of the navy, Franklin D. Roosevelt, to use navy funds, contracts, and influence to create a new corporation designed to achieve American leadership in radio. With the navy as the founding shareholder, Roosevelt did what he was told. Subsequently RCA not only took leadership in radio but pioneered television and founded the global consumer electronics industry.

The U.S. aerospace industry likewise owes its dominance to a powerful and generous government. Although the Wright brothers invented the airplane, American aircraft manufacturers were lagging seriously behind their European competitors by 1915. To reverse this situation, Congress established the National Advisory Committee for Aeronautics (NACA) and gave it the mission of ensuring U.S. aeronautics leadership by developing and freely disseminating aerospace technology to U.S. industry. Boeing was launched in 1916 with a $575,000 navy contract for fifty trainer seaplanes, and it prospered for the next forty years mainly on defense contracts for bombers like the B-17, B-29, B-47, and B-52. The Boeing 707 that gained fame as the first American commercial jet was just a version of the KC-135 air force tanker.

Finally there is the example of AT&T and its Bell Laboratories. Early telephone was hampered by incompatible standards. To overcome this discrepancy, the U.S. government agreed to make AT&T a regulated monopoly on the condition that it provide universal service and make its technology available to all at a reasonable royalty rate. As a result, Bell Labs became a unique national asset. If you were a scientist working there, all they asked you to do was whatever research you wanted. For over fifty years the labs regularly turned out new inventions and Nobel Prize winners. Silicon Valley actually got started here. After inventing the semiconductor along with John Bardeen and Walter Brattain, William Shockley returned from the labs to his native Palo Alto to establish Shockley Semiconductor Laboratories. Most of the American semiconductor industry traces its lineage to this lab.

My point is twofold. First, the apparently effortless technological supremacy Americans assume as a birthright is significantly based on special, transient circumstances. The two World Wars and the Cold War stimulated a massive and, for Americans, unnatural collaboration between government and industry to develop technological superiority. U.S. domination of these industries had nothing to do with market forces and everything to do with targeted policy decisions. Additionally America was the world's first mass market. Americans had the best technology and the lowest costs. U.S. manufacturers used government grants to expand their plants during the war in order to fulfill government war materiel contracts. After the war, these essentially free plants turned to satisfying a continental market in which long pent-up demand was suddenly unleashed. In the 1950s, for example, General Motors regularly produced a million units of the same Chevrolet sedan. These economies of scale pushed costs down even as wages rose dramatically. A virtuous circle was created in which new technology led to new products that could be produced in America at far lower cost than anywhere else, even as American workers were paid far more than anyone else.

Second, these industries and technologies were all tied up with manufacturing. Manufacturing in 1948 accounted for about 28 percent of U.S. GDP. It paid nearly 8 percent more than the general wage level and, along with the government, funded virtually all R&D. It was the source of enormous wealth and technological progress, and the great momentum of that time is still felt today. Yet early harbingers of changes to come were also present.

The Hare Goes to Sleep

American technological supremacy bred a carelessness about its nurture along with overconfidence that led to missed opportunities. Japan recovered quickly from the war and developed a voracious appetite for new technologies that were frequently ignored by Americans. At the same time, the collaboration between U.S. industry and government began to give way on the one hand to mutual suspicion and on the other to a new economic trend toward laissez-faire. Linkages between one industry and another and the role of manufacturing were increasingly deemphasized while asymmetries between countries in international economic practices were ignored. Finally, research and education expenditures began to be cut as spending on consumption increased.

From America's Ampex to Japan's Sony

In 1944, Russian immigrant Alexander M. Poniatoff founded Ampex Corporation (its name from his initials plus ex for excellence) to make electric motors for the navy. Business was initially good, but demand collapsed at the war's end, and the company had to find something else to make. At about this time Masaru Ibuka, an engineer who had spent the war making electrical parts for the Japanese navy, and his friend Akio Morita had just formed Tokyo Telecommunications Engineering Corporation (later known as Sony). They too were looking for something to make.

What both companies were looking for was actually in Germany. During the war, U.S. soldiers were sometimes astonished to hear the Munich

Philharmonic Symphony Orchestra playing at 3:00 A.M. The music was faultless, but what were these people doing giving concerts at that hour of the morning? In fact they weren't. To make people think Hitler was speaking at one place when he was actually elsewhere, the Germans had developed the magnetophon, a magnetic tape recorder that could duplicate sound and retain it far better than any other device of the time. Once the war was over, Signal Corps officer Jack Mullin recovered a couple of these from a German radio station and brought them home to San Francisco.[7] When Poniatoff happened to see a demonstration, he knew immediately that he had found what he was seeking. It was powered by three electric motors similar to those Ampex was already producing.

He worked out a deal with Mullin, and the two cloned the German machine. After experts from General Electric and Stanford Research Institute advised that the device had no future, the two showed it to Bing Crosby. He loved it. Because the sound quality was so good, he could record his shows instead of doing them live and consequently could spend more time on the golf course. With Bing's backing, the recorder and Ampex took off. The product line was quickly extended to include precision recorders for a variety of military, scientific, and industrial applications. Everything Ampex touched turned to gold. By 1956 the company's annual revenue had grown from $1 million to $10 million.

Meanwhile, in Tokyo, Ibuka saw a version of the new machine and was inspired to develop a clone for Japan. The Japanese market was then protected by high tariffs and tough restrictions on investment by foreigners. Thus Ampex could not produce or sell there, and Sony's new recorder quickly dominated the Japanese market. Then, on one of his trips to the United States, Ibuka made another discovery—the transistor, which had just been invented at AT&T's Bell Labs. With this device AT&T could have controlled the future of the entire electronics industry. But as a regulated monopoly under U.S. law it was required to license the technology to all comers, foreign or domestic. Ibuka bought a license for $25,000. While American competitors like RCA, Motorola, and Emerson slept, Sony introduced the first transistor radio in 1955. It immediately became a huge hit, especially in the open American market, where competitors were self-satisfied, tariffs low, and customers willing.

Television, pioneered by RCA, became the big new thing in the 1950s, but time-delay broadcasts (the same show three hours later) for the West Coast were expensive, complicated, and unreliable. RCA chairman David Sarnoff put up $50 million and called on his engineers to develop within five years a video recorder, or "videograph," that would make it possible to show the same broadcast at different times as if it were a live show. Poniatoff also sensed the potential of video recording and gave his engineers $15,000 to try to beat RCA. It worked, and when the annual convention of the National Association of Radio and Television Broadcasters met in Chicago on April 14, 1956, it was the upstart Ampex rather than the giant RCA that stunned the audience with a perfect video playback. In the next four days, Ampex took orders for one hundred machines even before it had a production line. Ampex had exclusive ownership of the key patent rights and, at this moment, controlled the destiny of video recording. Sales zoomed from $10 million in 1956 to $70 million in 1960 and Ampex became one of the era's darling growth stocks.

Sony, meanwhile, was not asleep. As part of a consortium organized and funded by the Japanese government, it was able to produce a near copy of the Ampex machine within a few months. Although other Japanese companies soon followed, all faced the problem of infringing the Ampex patents. Ampex, however, faced problems of its own. Not only did it need transistor technology to enable further miniaturization, but it also was barred by Japanese government policy from entering the growing Japanese market without a Japanese partner. Here differences in attitudes and government policy had a huge impact. The U.S. government at this time focused on developing things like Minuteman missiles. No one in government or industry saw any strategic value in a video recorder, but the Japanese did. On top of that, the United States viewed Japan's trade barriers as hurting only Japan by preventing Japanese consumers from buying superior U.S. products. But the barriers also badly hurt U.S. companies like Ampex by preventing them from exploiting their advantages in the Japanese market and by forcing them to transfer their technology in order to gain market entrance.

In this case a Sony-Ampex joint venture and cross-licensing deal was concluded in 1958 as a way of solving the problems of each side. It is important to understand that Sony got this deal not because Ampex wanted it, but because it was the only way for Ampex to get into the Japanese market. However, after a financial hiccup, Ampex named Bell & Howell's Bill Roberts as its new CEO. He unilaterally canceled the deal in 1960 because of suspicion that Sony was misappropriating Ampex intellectual property. Sony sued for breach of contract and won a fully paid-up license for the Ampex technology. The race was on.

None of this dampened Wall Street's enthusiasm for Ampex. It had established a foothold in most of the key markets of the dawning information age. Ampex set the standard for commercial audiotape recorders, broadcast (as in television) videotape recorders, instrumentation recorders for defense use, recorders for data storage, magnetic tape, and core memories that were the new storage medium for computers.

All this put Ampex among a select group of favored technology stocks, along with Texas Instruments, Polaroid, and Hewlett-Packard, and there was great pressure on Ampex to match them in growth and profitability. Unsure of his company's ability to keep up with the rest of the glamour fraternity simply by growing its core business, Roberts turned to other strategies. The conglomeration boom of the time was supported (or at least rationalized by) new business theories arguing that the linkages between a company's various products and technologies were of small importance, and that products should be managed like a portfolio of stocks. The theory classed products as stars, cash cows, dogs, and question marks. The idea was to get rid of the dogs, milk the cows to invest in the stars, and carefully select a few question marks for future development. Though Roberts didn't get rid of many dogs, he went on an acquisition binge for stars, buying an instrument maker and a ferrite core memory producer while also getting into the prerecorded music business and taking a fling at backing a Broadway play called *Purlie*. Wall Street loved it, but none of it advanced Ampex's main video recording technology.

Meanwhile, in Tokyo, Sony and the other Japanese makers were sticking to their knitting. They kept bringing out improved versions of their Ampex clones and products they developed to get around the Ampex patents. They also began aggressively developing recorders based on the so-called helical scan technology that Ampex had licensed to them at a time when it was desperate to raise money to keep its conglomerate strategy alive. In particular, the Japanese began to use this technology to develop products aimed at a potential consumer market. By the late 1960s, Sony was the leader in Japan and had made significant inroads in the U.S. market as well.

To fight back, Roberts brought in Richard Elkus Jr. to work as his direct assistant. A former employee whose father, Richard J. Elkus Sr., was a member of the board of directors and headed its executive committee, the younger Elkus was charged with developing a killer VTR for home use. Many companies had already failed in this attempt and many others were still trying. Because all were in one form or another licensees of Ampex, Elkus had a unique view of what others thought the new markets might be. Although the market for "instantaneous response" (the recording of events for immediate playback) had the greatest immediate potential for growth, it was not being served by the Japanese or anyone else. It required reliability, portability, ease of operation, and inexpensive machines that could be used by unskilled operators, as well as ease of manufacture and distribution.

In late 1968 Elkus presented his study with an outline of how the market for consumer video recording would progress and recommended product development ideas to parallel the market demand up to and including the confluence of videotapes made by consumers and prerecorded videos produced by Hollywood. Roberts bought the idea and a team was assembled that presented an "Instavideo" prototype to the board in early 1969. The board members were stunned by the performance of this new device, thinking Ampex had performed another technological miracle. The company truly had the world in its hands. It still controlled the key patents for videorecording, and now Elkus had stolen a march by developing the first version of a product that would become the biggest consumer electronics product of its time. It set the stage for a dramatic advance of the information age and rocked the foundations of the Soviet empire by undermining the Communist Party's control of information.

Elkus was directed to carry the project forward to commercialization and, after clearing many hurdles, stood before three hundred reporters at the Americana Hotel in New York on September 6, 1970, to formally unveil the new Instavideo recorder. It was a smash hit. Weighing less than sixteen pounds with batteries, it offered slow-motion, stop-action playback, and monochrome or color capability, all for $1,500. One industry representative asked if he could place an order for 10,000 units on the spot.[8] A commentator wrote that "while it had long appeared that U.S. industry was abdicating the cassette to the Japanese, Ampex was now bringing it home." The Instavideo was featured as the centerfold in *Life* magazine's next issue on the coming revolution in video and television.[9] Heroic Ampex seemed once again to have used its entrepreneurial and technological virtuosity to throw a hail Mary over the goal line and beat the big guys in the last minute of play. Ampex stock price jumped 50 percent in two days. Elkus became an overnight media celebrity. The sky appeared to be the limit both for him and Ampex.

Then it all fell apart. The stars of conglomeration had turned out to be dogs. The diversification divisions were all hemorrhaging red ink. Ampex was strapped for cash. Indeed, the company's top executives had skipped the Instavideo unveiling in favor of *Purlie*'s Broadway opening because they hoped to plug the cash drain with revenue from the show's music rights. Instavideo should have been manufactured in Chicago close to the R&D team to minimize communications glitches. Toshiba, however, was willing to fund a new plant if the product was produced in a joint venture in Japan. Elkus urged Roberts to produce it jointly with Motorola or Magnavox, both of which were interested and had essential expertise. But Roberts, fearing they might copy the product and with little regard for possible competition from Toshiba, said he didn't need any more U.S. competitors and opted for the Toshiba deal. As Elkus had feared, this became a disaster of misunderstanding and mismanagement. But as things turned out, it was the least of Ampex's problems.

Elkus now discovered that the company's celebrated financial statements were a mirage. While sales and profits appeared to be climbing nicely, the truth was that Ampex was a kind of prelude to Enron. In a desperate effort to maintain its glamorous facade, the company concluded deals with customers who agreed to accept an invoice on the condition that Ampex wouldn't ship the product and they wouldn't pay. By this "shipping in place," the company could record revenue even as cash flow fell like a rock. When an increasingly suspicious Elkus made his concerns about these and other unusual arrangements known to the senior Elkus and to Roberts, he was told to let the company's financial officers mind the business. Shortly thereafter, Roberts, Elkus Jr., and Elkus Sr. parted company.[10] By the end of fiscal 1971, however, the charade could no longer be maintained, and the company reported a $12 million loss that later grew to $90 million. Roberts resigned, but, as Enron's Ken Lay was later to do, managed to sell his shares before public announcement of the debacle. This situation eventually triggered a historic reaction—the first class action lawsuit.

Nearly two years later, with cash mostly gone, Elkus Sr., now Chairman of the Board, announced cancellation of the Instavideo project. Three years later Sony launched its Beta Max product as the first commercial consumer VCR, and in 1976 JVC launched its VCR using the VHS format. This was quickly adopted by Matsushita and became the industry standard. Over the next fifteen years, the VCR became the biggest consumer product ever. While Ampex struggled to survive on royalties from the licensing of its old patents, Sony became a $50 billion company with dominant positions in a wide variety of electronics and consumer products and with capabilities in a broad range of technologies that made it a formidable challenger, even to the most powerful American technology companies. The VCR became a Japanese monopoly and the United States was out of the business altogether.

Ampex was not the first U.S. company to fall victim to inappropriate U.S. trade policies and its own poor management. By 1972 the textile and steel industries were failing to compete with the Japanese and losing market share. RCA and the rest of the U.S. television industry had pretty much given up on black-and-white television and within four years the Japanese (Sony, Hitachi, Matsushita, Toshiba, Mitsubishi Electric) had 50 percent of the color market, on their way to 100 percent. Radio production had long since moved to Japan, and stereo sets would soon follow. The pattern kept repeating itself. A U.S. company would introduce a new product that would enjoy success in the U.S. market until a Japanese competitor introduced an improved model at half the price. Then the Americans would get out of the business.

Ampex represented a milestone in that the VCR business was the first major business from which the Americans were excluded from the beginning. In the past they had always developed a market, only to lose it later to the Japanese. Now the Japanese were beating them to the punch. This story also highlights the crucial difference in attitude between the U.S. and Japanese governments and their respective corporations as well as a shift in U.S. thinking. Past American presidents had been concerned about catching up in industries like aircraft and radio. Now it was the Japanese government that paid attention to these issues while the U.S. government believed them to be unimportant and not the proper business of government. Ampex executives, seeing the company's mission as one of raising earnings for shareholders, tended to be pressured by the short-term expectations of Wall Street and guided by the fluctuating management consulting fads of the day. Ibuka and Morita, on the other hand, saw Sony as a national institution with a long-term mission of strengthening society.

Finally, this story illustrates the dynamics of linkages and their long-range implications. Although you may think that the development and manufacture of products are independent and separable operations, that is not necessarily the case. As Elkus recalls, Sony president Akio Morita insisted to him again and again that any technology pushed to its logical extreme is related to many other technologies. For example, anyone who is not involved in the VCR business will find it difficult to get involved in what arises from the VCR. Because of this dynamic and the huge size of the market, the Japanese dominance of the VCR contributed greatly to a shift in the technology balance of power that is still going forward. The VCR drove development of flat-panel display, battery, and materials technology to new heights and to the Asian shores of the Pacific. For example, the VCR was known as a semiconductor "hog" because of the large number of chips incorporated in each device. As one of the important linkages, it was the VCR that put the Japanese in the semiconductor business, where they waged one of the epic industrial battles of the century with the denizens of Silicon Valley.

Winners and Losers

The 1980s saw continuous trade conflict between Japan on the one hand and the United States and, to a lesser extent, Europe, on the other as Western manufacturers fought to survive the flood of high-quality, low-cost exports streaming out of Japan. The Japanese challenge, formidable in its own right, was heightened by the budget deficits and rising dollar of the Reagan administration. The Big Three automakers closed one factory after another while the U.S. government negotiated a deal under which Japan agreed to voluntarily limit its car exports to the American market. Although the steel industry had a "trigger price" arrangement that put a floor under U.S. steel prices, the U.S. industry continued to lose market share. Motorcycles, machine tools, auto parts, lawn mowers. You name it. Anything that was made in a factory was mostly made in Japan, as U.S. companies laid off their workers and closed up shop. Eventually everything seemed to come down to the semiconductor industry.

It became my problem in the fall of 1981 after I took up my duties as counselor to commerce secretary Malcolm Baldridge. He told me my job was to reduce the burgeoning U.S. trade deficit with Japan (especially the deficit with Japan that was widely said to be economically and politically unsupportable). Semiconductor technology was one in which the U.S. industry was indisputably the leader, with companies like Intel, Texas Instruments, and Motorola at its cutting edge. Nevertheless, the U.S. makers were closing plants and laying off workers while seeming to be completely incapable either of penetrating the Japanese market or meeting Japanese prices in the U.S. market. As a result, between 1984 and 1986 the U.S. industry lost $4 billion and laid off 50,000 workers. What was going on?

In a word, dumping—the practice of selling in a foreign market below the price at home. It is the international equivalent of discriminatory pricing by a monopoly. The dumper can make a big profit in the protected or monopolized home market and use the money to gain market share abroad by selling at a loss. As with VCRs, the Japanese government had early identified the semiconductor as an economically strategic product that Japanese companies had to dominate. It therefore imposed prohibitive tariffs on semiconductor imports, prohibited foreign investment except in joint ventures in which Japanese companies acquired technology inexpensively, organized and funded industry consortia to do collaborative "catch-up" R&D, and directed Japanese companies to "buy Japanese" as much as possible. This effort had results. Japanese companies launched forays into the relatively open U.S. and European markets from their protected home base. Memory chips were the main semiconductor product at the time, and by the early 1980s the Japanese producers had gained 60 percent of the global market for the dominant 64k chip. They were also pricing the newly introduced 256k chip very aggressively. One internal Japanese company memo directed its sales staff to sell at any price that would get the sale.[11] In other words, "dump the chips on the market."

The plight of the semiconductor industry raised a serious issue about America's future, as well as its economic philosophies and policies. As the auto, steel, and other rust belt industries had shut factories and laid off workers, people had been told that their future lay in high technology. But if a quintessentially high-tech American industry like semiconductors couldn't succeed, what future was there? While academic economists and some pundits objected on grounds of free trade, a cry went up from Congress and elsewhere to help the industry. Dumping is illegal under both U.S. and international law because it effectively exports unemployment. The dumper typically has a protected home market in which prices and profits are high. By using those profits to underwrite an artificially low price abroad, the dumper expands volume and keeps his workers on the job while undercutting foreign employers, which may have to lay off their workers.

A dumping legal action can be brought by petition to the Commerce Department from an affected industry or directly by the secretary of commerce. Although no secretary had ever done so before, Baldrige decided to initiate an action. But first he felt it necessary to consult the White House and his cabinet colleagues and a meeting was arranged in the Roosevelt Room. The following conversational notes convey the flavor of the discussion:

Secretary of commerce: I have incontrovertible evidence of massive illegal dumping of semiconductor memory chips by several Japanese producers and would like to have your support in initiating an antidumping investigation.

National security adviser: Well, we have to be careful here. We want the Japanese to work with the Pentagon on new elec-

tronics and things and we wouldn't want to do anything to an-
tagonize them. Besides, I believe our industry is way ahead of
them.

Me: If we are so way ahead, why do they have an 80 percent market share? (I got no response.)

Undersecretary of state: But dumping is good for the consumer.
The user gets inexpensive chips and makes inexpensive computers that we all benefit from. Why would we want to stop
that?

U.S. trade representative: But you are forgetting about the 50,000
people who just lost their jobs in Silicon Valley.

Undersecretary of state: Well, we have a booming services economy and they can easily get jobs at McDonald's or someplace
like that.

Deputy Treasury secretary: Why do we want a semiconductor industry? If our guys can't hack it, let 'em go. We don't want
some kind of industrial policy here where we pick winners and
losers.

Secretary of commerce: Okay. Which of you will accompany me
to the hill to tell the Congress that this administration is not
going to enforce U.S. and international trade law?

All: Oh, if you put it that way, Mac, of course, we support you.

After Baldrige initiated the case, a negotiation ensued in which
Japan agreed to prevent further dumping and ensure that foreign producers would gain at least a 20 percent share of the Japanese market.
This helped staunch the bleeding but hardly ensured a healthy
industry.

The key to semiconductor technology leadership is not so much in
the chips themselves as in the equipment that makes them. Here again
the linkages that Elkus and Morita emphasized were playing a critical
role. Because the U.S. chip industry was sick, it wasn't investing, and
because it wasn't investing, the U.S. equipment makers were in big
trouble, and because they were in trouble the U.S. chip makers were in
danger of falling behind. To solve this problem the administration
formed SEMATECH, a joint government–industry company, to stimu-

late research and development of semiconductor equipment and production processes. The National Advisory Commission on Semiconductors (NACS) was also appointed and it issued a number of ringing recommendations to save what it called *A Strategic Industry at Risk.*

The NACS report was part of the broader competitiveness debate of the time. Another important report was that of Hewlett-Packard CEO John Young, who headed the Presidential Commission on Competitiveness. These and other reports sounded an alarm that the United States was losing important manufacturing capabilities. Because of strategic linkages between manufacturing and technology, this loss was undermining the country's long-term technological potential. When the Reagan administration paid no attention to its own commission chairman, Young founded the independent Council on Competitiveness.

The Council and other groups made a number of creative proposals. The NACS, recognizing (as Elkus and Morita had) the significance of consumer electronics to the development of other technologies, suggested creation of a consumer electronics capital corporation as a pool of patient capital that would fund the resurrection of the U.S. consumer electronics industry. Then DARPA head Craig Fields proposed that the government pull a repeat of President Wilson's RCA trick by helping start up a company to achieve leadership in high-definition television, a field the Japanese were then emphasizing. Yet another idea was for the users and makers of memory chips to pool resources to create U.S. Memory as a producer from which all would commit to buy. Later the Defense Department got into the act. DOD used a lot of flat-panel displays and found itself increasingly dependent on the Asian suppliers who made most of them. It formed an intergovernmental task force aimed at creating an American flat-panel display industry that would be globally competitive. Then the Clinton administration came up with the idea for a national information infrastructure. None of these ideas went anywhere for four reasons—industrial policy, the rise of the personal computer, the bursting of the Japanese bubble economy, and the expansion of the U.S. Internet bubble economy.

Economic thinking in America had changed dramatically from the early days of the twentieth century, when President Wilson could just order up an RCA. Now it was firmly believed that government should not, indeed could not, conduct an industrial policy of "picking winners and losers." Fields was forced out of DARPA for daring to challenge this orthodoxy, and the other proposals were all slammed in the press and the think tanks for smacking too much of that dread industrial policy. In any case, the dramatic rise of the PC changed the landscape. With control of the PC's heart and head, Microsoft and Intel were transformed into the most important technology companies in the world. After struggling to beat back the Japanese in the memory market for much of the 1980s, Intel ceased making the DRAM chips it had invented in favor of the microprocessors in which it had a virtual monopoly. As new companies like Dell came to the fore, America looked to be back in the technology driver's seat.

Then the air went out of the Japanese bubble. Companies for which capital had essentially been free suddenly found themselves burdened with bad debt as the banking system ground to a virtual halt. The Japanese economy went from high growth in the 1980s to no growth in the 1990s, and many in America and Europe began to wonder why they had ever feared the Japanese. This sense of superiority turned to euphoria as dot.com mania spread in the late 1990s. Cisco, Juniper Networks, Sun, Netscape, and Yahoo were among the hot companies whose stock market values sometimes topped long-established performers like GE. Then there was biotech, which U.S. industry dominated absolutely, since the U.S. government through the National Institutes of Health (NIH) spent more on biotech R&D than the rest of the world combined. There was also an apparent resurgence of high-tech manufacturing. The Internet was hot, and everyone wanted the high-speed capacity provided by optical fiber communication links. Corning Glass more than doubled production of fiber and added new plants. The contract manufacturers like Flextronics took over manufacturing for the likes of IBM, Cisco, Lucent, and others and ramped up production to meet the seemingly endless demand of what *Business Week* chief economist Mike Mandel called the new economy, characterized by endless growth and rising productivity. It seemingly had broken free of the business cycle to prove that nobody could touch America in development, use, and manufacture of technology.

Is Manufacturing Un-American?

Like the Japanese bubble before it, the U.S. bubble of the late '90s had to burst, and it did in 2000 with the fall of the NASDAQ stock average from over 5,000 to an eventual low of 1108. A lot of smart and important people lost their shirts. Cisco Systems, once the most valuable company in the world, saw its stock plunge by nearly 90 percent. It survived and eventually came back strong, but many didn't make it. Some people lost their reputations and jobs as hard questions were asked about the basis of forecasts and analyses that had been so wrong. The American economy also came in for a closer look, and the picture that emerged was not nearly as rosy as many had previously assumed.

For one thing, the manufacturing renaissance was illusory. To survive in the postbubble environment, the contract manufacturers closed the plants they had taken over from IBM, Cisco, Lucent, and others and decamped to Asia, Mexico, and Hungary in search of lower costs. They scoured the world for cheap labor, free land, capital grants, and tax holidays. Flextronics, for example, established ninety-one factories in thirty-five foreign locations, anchored by two enormous industrial parks in Guadalajara, Mexico, and Zhuhai, China.

Despite the longest economic boom in history, the rust belt continued to rust. Many manufacturing industries suffered from the same ills that plagued them ten and twenty years before. Detroit's auto producers continued losing market share. Japan may have been suffering from economic stagnation, but Toyota wasn't, and it steadily ate away at Detroit's position. Nissan, once thought to be at death's door, was revived by none other than the longtime French government auto champion Renault. Korea's Hyundai Motor Company also made its debut in the U.S. by nibbling more of Detroit's lunch. Actually, Detroit tried hard and made a lot of improvements. Its quality and productivity improved dramatically over 1980s levels. But whatever Detroit did, it wasn't enough, and its market share kept slipping, from 77 percent in 1985 to 62 percent in 2004.[12]

The steel industry was an even sorrier story. All the integrated steel makers except U.S. Steel went belly up. For a while it seemed the new nonunion minimills were the answer, but by the end of the century even they couldn't compete. In earlier years they had disdained the protectionism of the old-line steel companies, but now they joined the call for import restraints.

Other industries simply disappeared. No one thinks much about machine tools and they don't make hot Christmas gifts. But they are the foundation of all other industries; you can't make anything without them. Yet the U.S. machine tool industry has become a shadow of its former self. At the same time, things like ball bearings and forgings, which are in nearly anything that moves, have almost ceased being made in the United States. Although these industries all involve important technologies and support significant R&D activity, they are typically not thought of as high-tech, and many economists argue they are precisely the activities developed countries should abandon in favor of more advanced technology areas.

From this point of view, the problems of industries in which the Americans were supposed to be winners loom even larger. The name Boeing has become almost synonymous with airplane, and American manufacturers have owned the global aircraft market since the end of World War II. Year in and year out, through all the trade deficits, there was always one bright spot in the U.S. export statistics—aircraft. Boeing was almost always America's biggest exporter. But in 2003, Boeing orders dipped below those of the European Airbus and have stayed there. Airbus has long been the recipient of development subsidies provided by the EU authorities. These are very unlike the benefits Boeing derives from U.S. defense contracts. In the first place, Airbus gets defense work too. Secondly, while Boeing may make a profit on its defense contracts, no one guarantees to make up its losses on military or commercial aircraft. That's what the EU does for the Airbus. Not only does the United States not do that, but, until very recently, it didn't even challenge EU subsidies as illegal under WTO rules.

Recently Boeing announced plans to develop a new generation 787 Dreamliner. In an effort to match the EU subsidy of Airbus development costs, Boeing turned to Japan, where it partnered with Japanese aircraft parts makers like Mitsubishi Heavy Industries and Fuji Heavy Industries. Japan has long nurtured an aircraft industry and provides development subsidies to these companies. Over 50 percent of the 777, for example, was developed and produced in Japan. In the case of the 787, that portion will rise to well over 60 percent and will include the wings, which are one of the two crucial parts of an airplane (the cockpit being the other). Although Boeing CEOs once told me they would never outsource the wings, 787 wings will, in fact, be made in Japan. Development of the cockpit and overall integration of the project will remain in the United States for now. So in addition to losing market share, Boeing is also losing work. This does not augur well for future aerospace leadership. Nor does the abandonment of the U.S. commercial satellite launch capability. Today the nation that once sent men to the moon on the mighty Apollo rockets launches its satellites on Russian, Chinese, and European rockets and from their spacedromes because U.S. commercial rocket makers have fallen behind in technology.

The American semiconductor industry received a new lease on life following the semiconductor agreement with Japan and the rise of the PC. Its global market share, which had fallen from 70 percent to about 20 percent in the 1980s, rose to over 50 percent in the mid-1990s.[13] By mid-2003, however, its share was falling again, and it was warning of loss of technological leadership.[14] The industry's condition resembled that of the early 1980s, with a few new twists. The equipment industry that Washington and the semiconductor producers tried to revitalize with the SEMATECH consortium continued to slip away. Steppers that do the lithography are the most important single piece of semiconductor production equipment, and both U.S. stepper makers went out of business. Because the new semiconductor production facilities were being built in Asia, the United States, which as recently as 2000 accounted for 30 percent of global production capacity, held only 21 percent in 2003, and that share would probably keep falling. Even at the leading edge, the U.S. capacity was only 25 percent of the total.

Consider the development of the "fabless" semiconductor firms: companies of high-powered engineers designed chips and then had them manufactured by semiconductor foundries in Taiwan and China. Even counting this production as American, the U.S. chip makers' share of the global market was down to 48 percent and falling. Appearing before Congress on July 8, 2004, a panel from the National Academy of Sciences testified that the United States risks losing a substantial portion of its most important manufacturing industry.[15]

As more and more U.S. manufacturers struggled to stay in business, there were more and more things no longer made in America. Elkus and Morita were right about the importance of linkages. Flat-panel displays, though invented in the United States, had followed the television, VCR, and laptop computer to Asia—or perhaps it is more accurate to say the laptop went because the flat panels were there. The VCR had morphed into the digital camera, made in Asia along with the tiny motors that drive them and the displays that make them so user-friendly.

Then there is high-definition television (HDTV). In 1987 the Federal Communications Commission sponsored a contest for development of a digital HDTV standard. The Digital HDTV Grand Alliance, composed of Zenith, North American Philips, AT&T, General Instruments, MIT, Thomson, and the David Sarnoff Research Center, succeeded and prompted boasting among the U.S. commentariat about how the ever innovative Americans had leapfrogged the Japanese. Actually they had done the Japanese a favor. With a clear standard established, the Japanese manufacturers concentrated on making the sets. Ironically, the FCC has mandated that all TVs sold in the United States from 2007 be HDTVs. Naturally they will all be produced in Asia, adding to the already gigantic U.S. trade deficit of over $600 billion.

For many years as the deficit in manufactured goods rose, economists told us not to worry: America still had a surplus in high-tech products. In the late 1980s a special advanced technology products (ATP) category was created for U.S. statistical reports so that this point could be easily understood. In 2001, however, that index went negative. Today the U.S. high-tech trade deficit is over $30 billion and climbing, powered by a high-tech deficit with China that has gone from nothing in 1998 to $21 billion in 2003. This deterioration of trade occurred as overall manufacturing declined as a percentage of GDP to the point that the United States now barely leads Japan in total manufacturing output, despite being more than twice as large in both population and GDP.

The Dying Tech Ecosystem

These developments have elicited warnings about U.S. technology similar to those of the late 1980s. The euphoric new economy of the 1990s masked issues that were never resolved. Today's warnings always begin by noting that the United States "enjoys global technological preeminence" with the world's biggest concentration of technologists, the best universities, leadership in nearly all areas of basic research, and an annual R&D budget that dwarfs that of any other nation or economic entity.[16] This is all true, but then come the caveats. Thomas Hartwick, chairman of the Defense Advisory Group on Electronic Devices, told Congress that "the structure of the U.S. high-tech industry is coming unglued with innovation and design losing their tie to prototype fabrication and manufacturing."[17] This broken link leaves inventions "on the cutting room floor because they cannot be manufactured." In a few years, the U.S. manufacturing base may not exist to create "mega-billion dollar industries like microelectromechanical systems or nanotechnologies." Microsoft chief technologist Craig Mundie echoed that concern in a March 16, 2004, interview with *Business Week*, saying that U.S. research investment has declined and "I think that's producing long-term weaknesses in the U.S. technology effort."[18]

An example of weakness was explained to a House Small Business Committee hearing in October 2003. While the U.S. military proudly claims to "own the night," Siva Sivananthan, the inventor of the cadmium mercury telluride semiconductor materials that make night vision possible, told the committee that U.S. forces won't own it for long because the critical materials suppliers are all in Japan. Since the U.S. suppliers who developed the most advanced systems have licensed or transferred their production to overseas firms, he noted, no U.S. company is capable of producing the necessary equipment. He had to license his own technology to a French company that is now selling the equipment to China. Sivananthan further explained that research and university study in the area has ceased in the United States due to the absence of manufacturers. China, India, Israel, France, Germany, and Britain, however, are all investing heavily in new systems.[19] Surely one or all of them will appropriate the night fairly soon. Similarly, the twelve-member Commission on the Future of the United States Aerospace Industry told a Washington press conference that "the industry is in a nosedive and if it doesn't pull up soon it's going to hit the ground."

The President's Council of Advisers on Science and Technology (PCAST) made perhaps the most balanced and comprehensive assessment of the U.S. technology situation in January 2004. It emphasized that "the big winners will not be those who simply make commodities faster and cheaper than the competition. They will be those who develop talent, tools, and techniques so advanced that *there is no competition*" [my italics]. The report then noted that while the United States retains global technological preeminence, its continued leadership is not assured. While the United States may still have the best and most flexible R&D, workforce, universities, rule of law, infrastructure, and entrepreneurial business climate, along with the world's largest market, key elements of this "innovation ecosystem" are eroding rapidly. One reason for this is that "we are not just competing against foreign companies, but against foreign countries."[20] Overseas governments provide attractive packages of capital grants, tax holidays, free land, worker training, and other incentives to induce investment by foreign technology companies. Many technology CEOs told PCAST they had to move their manufacturing operations overseas to stay competitive. Moreover, having learned to manage complex global manufacturing, technology companies increasingly find that the incentives make offshore manufacturing almost irresistible even if there is no competitive necessity.

The PCAST drew particular attention to the absence of U.S. companies from the ranks of many industries that are heavy users of hightech devices. It described loss of manufacturing employment as not a problem per se (workers might disagree), but emphasized that the decline of manufacturing as part of the U.S. economy is perhaps the single most important problem. The reason is that the "research to manufacturing process is not sequential in a single direction, but results from an R&D-manufacturing ecosystem consisting of basic R&D, precompetitive development, prototyping, product development and manufacturing" all operating in such a way that "new ideas can be tested and discussed with those working on the ground."[21] The PCAST concluded that "locations that possess both strong R&D and manufacturing capabilities have a competitive edge."[22]

In other words, there is a link between the factory floor and the research lab. Neither can survive without the other. In this, the PCAST echoed the Senate Manufacturing Task Force, which had earlier concluded that the United States cannot lose its manufacturing base and still maintain its leading edge in design and R&D. "It all goes together," said IBM Technology Group vice president Randy Isaac. "You can't do effective R&D if you don't have the manufacturing to ensure that the R&D is actually relevant. If the United States loses its manufacturing lead it will lose everything else with it."

The PCAST, National Academy of Sciences, and Senate Manufacturing Task Force all noted the long-term implications of escalating capital costs combined with market absence or exclusion—or what Elkus and Morita refer to as the strategy of leverage and linkage. If a country or a company or some combination of the two can keep competitors out of an industry whose capital investment requirements are steadily rising, at some point market entry will simply be prohibitively expensive for competitors unless they can get help from their governments or deep-pocketed cartels. Leaving a fundamental technology area means that participating in technologies that evolve from it becomes virtually impossible. This strategy was identified as a very real threat to long-term U.S. technological competitiveness because of the willingness of governments and industries in the rest of the world to use it.

Two other elements of the ecosystem, scientific education and overall R&D effort, were seen as weak. With regard to education, the number of Americans obtaining science and engineering degrees is small and declining. In 1999, for example, the United States graduated 220,000 students with B.S. degrees, about the same as in 1985 and down 5 percent from ten years ago. China graduated 322,000 and India 251,000. Both countries have much larger populations, but their economies are only a fraction the size of the U.S. economy. And the Indian and Chinese numbers are set to double in the near future. Japan, with half the U.S. population, graduated 235,000 with B.S. degrees, and the EU-15, with a population about one-third larger than the United States, graduated 555,000 with B.S. degrees. Except in the life sciences, the U.S. number is lower now than it was in 1985.[23]

The picture in graduate education is worse. The proportion of university doctorates awarded to foreign students has grown from 35 percent in 1987 to over 40 percent in 2004. And whereas 80 percent of foreign-born graduates stayed in the United States in 1987, now the majority go home after receiving their degrees.[24]

Even more disturbing is the declining performance of U.S. grade school students. It appears that the longer they stay in school, the worse they do. International tests show U.S. fourth graders in the eighty-fifth percentile in science and the fifty-fifth percentile in math. By the twelfth grade, however, they have slipped to zero in science and the tenth percentile in math.[25] But never mind, the same tests show that they rank first in the students' assessment of their own performance—making the Americans number one on the feel-good scale.

As for R&D, while the United States is the biggest spender, its rate of investment has been lagging and is skewed toward the life sciences. At $295 billion, the U.S. R&D budget is about double that of Japan and about a third more than that of the EU as a whole. In terms of purchasing power parity (ppp), it is just about equal to China's $60 billion. (China's prices are much lower, so that $60 billion there buys as much as $300 billion in the United States.) But the U.S. budget is only 2.7 percent of GDP, as opposed to the 3 percent level at which it stood in 1960. This compares with Japan's 3 percent level, Singapore's 3.2 percent, and Korea's 3 percent. Europe as a whole is at 1.9 percent, but Sweden and Finland are in the 3–4 percent range while Germany is at 2.6 percent.[26]

There are two important points. First, of the U.S. spending, industry R&D in 2004 accounts for about 66 percent and government the rest. These ratios are the reverse of the 1960s. Because industry does mostly D and not R, the shift in ratios means less R is being done in the United States, relative to GDP, than in the past. Second, although government spending has been rising for several years, the increase is almost entirely in biotech. The physical sciences have actually been cut by 37 percent since 1970. Today, total U.S. government spending on physical science is less than the $5 billion Intel spends annually. The result is declining U.S. performance. Last year the only American company among the top ten U.S. patent recipients was IBM. All the rest were foreign firms.[27] Similarly, EU scientists have topped Americans in the numbers of articles published and cited over the past several years.[28] Until the late 1990s, U.S. publications outnumbered the rest of the world combined. Finally, the grand old industrial labs like Bell Labs have been turned into mere husks. It has been twenty years since anyone at Bell Labs received a Nobel Prize. In times past, this was an annual event, but as its budget and staff have been slashed, some of its scientists have been doing consumer expectations research instead of studying basic physical problems.[29] If you want to see the future, you won't find it at Bell Labs anymore. You'll have to take a long plane ride to Asia or cross the Atlantic to the European Union.

CHAPTER 7

High Tech II:
The World's Baby

We're falling behind. We're not keeping up with
other countries in our investment in science and
engineering. The science and math scores for our high
school graduates are disastrous. We're underfunding
research in the physical sciences and lagging
seriously on publications in these sciences. This is a
problem for our economy, and we have to think about
what we want to be in twenty to forty years.
—SUSAN HOCKFIELD, MIT PRESIDENT

Today technology centers of excellence are proliferating around the
globe. Progress no longer depends on a few talent pools in developed countries. Researchers are being linked to one another in ways
that should produce new technologies and products never before
dreamed of as companies manage R&D on a global scale. The Internet
and the globalization of corporations have enabled twenty-four-hour
development operations that shift work back and forth across time
zones. Asia is becoming a powerhouse of technology, tightly linked to
the United States but also driving to achieve technological independence. While many Americans think the European Union is technically
inept, it is not. Actually Europeans, more than Americans, seem to understand the importance of the technology "ecosystem" and are aggressively trying to foster it. Consequently, the question of America's future
in technology is up in the air. To see why, it's important to understand
what's happening in all those new centers of excellence.

Asia

Though Japan has long been a technology leader and remains so, the real surprise in Asia is Korea's drive to the top of the tech world. India, as we have seen, is powering its growth with technology and trying to move from there to a broader manufacturing base while China is going the other way and rapidly turning manufacturing leadership into technological strength. Despite their varying situations and capabilities, you will see that they share a firm national commitment to achieving technological leadership.

South Korean Firehose

You may think of South Korea as a developing country, an "Asian tiger" defended by 30,000 U.S. troops. But as we arrive at the new Inchon International Airport, you see that you've been living in the past. The airport itself is at least two generations ahead of anything in the United States. Your cell phone works better than you ever imagined. The drive into Seoul takes about an hour if you're lucky, but you needn't fret. Just switch on your cell phone to pick up one of the eight channels of streamed television. Or maybe you forgot to change money at the airport. No problem. Just dial up any local bank, submit your credit card number, and give the address of your hotel for delivery. Or better yet, just open a telephone account and don't bother with cash. It's so old-fashioned. You can learn a lot by watching your cab driver. If he turns off the freeway onto a bumpy local road, it's because his phone has a tracking device that allows road watchers to monitor him and tell him when and where to bypass an upcoming traffic jam. On the other hand, he might just be making a detour to check on his kids, who carry their own location-based phones.

Once you get to your hotel room, turn on your TV or connect your computer and download your favorite movie. I don't mean one from the hotel's menu, but whatever movie you want. This is a real broadband connection at 20 megabits per second. About 75 percent of Koreans have this kind of connection and, in less than ten years, they will have 100 megabits per second. Think of this as a fire hose compared to the little garden hose of U.S. broadband that, even now, only 20 percent of Americans have. Don't even mention dial-up. No one in Korea knows what it is.

You notice that the television is a flat panel hanging on the wall. (No need for a huge armoire with swinging doors to house a bulky cathode ray tube TV set.) Naturally it is high definition. Although the panel could not have come from the United States, it might have been produced by several Korean electronics companies. Chances are good, however, that it was made by Samsung, the $53 billion colossus leading the global high-end television market; it is also the world's largest producer of LCD flat-panel computer monitors. But Samsung doesn't stop there. It is the world's second largest and fastest growing semiconductor producer, with a 53 percent increase in sales last year. Although all American producers but one got out of the DRAM business years ago, Samsung makes a nice profit out of being their biggest producer. In the fall of 2004, it joined with Sony and IBM to develop a microprocessor that could one day challenge Intel's dominance in that field. Indeed if you ask Intel's chairman, Craig Barrett, to name his most dangerous competitor, he'll tell you it is Samsung. Samsung is also coming on like gangbusters in mobile phones, having shot past Motorola to gain second place in the global market[1] while growing at 49 percent between 2003 and 2004.[2] It would be a little awkward to try to take home a dishwasher, refrigerator, microwave oven, or rice cooker, of which Samsung is also a leading producer. But you should get yourself a hidden antenna, flip screen, digital phone camera. You can use the 5 megapixel pictures it takes to prove to your friends back home that you are not lying about all the high-tech stuff in Korea that you can't find in America.

For Samsung and other Korean companies, the rise of China has been nothing but good. They are selling more to China than they ever did to the United States. Korea has a trade surplus of $29 billion with China and is gaining most of its growth from the Chinese market.[3] But Korea Institute of Industrial Technology president Doug-young Joo says China's rapid progress is forcing Korea to adopt more aggressive industrial strategies aimed at retaining and promoting high-value-added manufacturing. This means stepping up its investment in manufacturing research and development. "Our success didn't happen by chance," says Joo. "It happened through R&D and significant technological breakthroughs in manufacturing."[4]

The Korean government played a major role in two ways. On the one hand, it deregulated key industries like telecommunications and opened up a number of markets to competition by cracking down on insider dealing by the giant Chaebol conglomerates. On the other hand, it has never been loath to imitate President Wilson's RCA initiative or the DARPA Internet project. The broadband capacity is in place because the Korean government mandated development of high-speed Internet capacity as a top national mission and put $60 billion in the budget to make sure it worked.[5]

To keep ahead of China, Korea is dramatically increasing spending on R&D and education. With one-sixth of the U.S. population, Korea already turns out about half as many engineers, and in a recent international assessment of math literacy for fifteen-year-olds, Korea scored second behind Finland, and far ahead of twenty-fourth-ranked United States.[6] Nor is Korea anxious to share its hard-won technological gains. When rumors circulated that the flat-screen TV maker Orion Electric might be acquired by a Chinese competitor, a senior company executive said he received an unusual phone call from the National Intelligence Service: "Why do you want to sell overseas? Can't you raise capital at home?" Although the NIS denies making the call, the Korean government is introducing legislation that would require government permission for certain companies to engage in sales or investment that might transfer key technology abroad.[7] Seoul is particularly worried about Chinese companies that are acquiring or merging with advanced technology firms. But the horse may be out of the barn already. Last year, China's BOE Technology Group acquired Korean flat-screen maker Hydis and is now building a factory near Beijing that will produce 60,000 glass sheets for LCDs per month.[8] Other Korean companies in the hands of creditors as a result of the 1997 financial crisis are also anxious to be bought.

Japan: The Best Competitor Is No Competitor

Across the Korea Straits, Japan is proving that reports of its death are exaggerated. Powered by exports to China, the Japanese economy has begun to show some signs of life for the first time since 1994. The trade situation with China represents a big turnaround. Only a few years ago, Tokyo dreaded the same kind of *kudoka* (hollowing out) that the Japanese see themselves as having inflicted on the United States. Low-cost Chinese goods were flooding the Japanese market, and Japan began to run a trade deficit with China. Japanese manufacturers who had long resisted the temptation to move production abroad found they could resist no longer. The share of Japanese owned-production capacity located abroad had long remained at about 8 percent, compared with 50 percent of the United States. But in the late 1990s, it grew quickly to today's 45 percent.[9] Just when the old Japanese export model seemed finally doomed, however, it came roaring back. Today Japan enjoys a $45 billion trade surplus with China to go along with its traditional surpluses with the United States, Korea, and most other countries.[10]

How can that be? After all, Japan is no low-wage sweatshop. If its manufacturers are moving to China, what does it sell there? The answer is a concrete demonstration of the point made in the PCAST report that the big winners are those with no competition. Japan has embraced that view with a passion. It mostly sells things no one else can make or make as well. The stagnant 1990s led some Japanese producers to try reducing costs by making strategic alliances with Asian competitors that involved transfer of key technologies such as the manufacture of flat-panel displays and semiconductors. But this strategy backfired when the Koreans and Taiwanese took the technology and undercut the Japanese in markets they had long dominated. Says Toshiba's Tadashi Okamura, "We did not expect the Koreans to catch up so quickly."[11] Fortunately, he continues, the digital revolution is "a major transformation similar to the shift from radio to television. We have passed the age of language-based information technology and entered a period of video networks. It is a technology innovation and cultural transformation that happens only once in several decades." This shift plays to Japan's strength and promises to make it preeminent, without any competitors.

Japan's producers dominate the global markets for video camcorders (the grandchildren of AMPEX and the old VTR), digital still cameras, DVD recorders, and 2.5-inch hard drives like those used in the Apple iPod. They have a monopoly on charge-coupled devices (and here is linkage again), the chips at the heart of digital cameras. While facing stiff Korean competition in LCDs, Sharp still has the largest market share, and Japanese companies, led by Fujitsu, have a stranglehold on plasma flat-panel displays used for large TVs. On top of that, Japan's mobile network infrastructure is the world's best, and Japanese cars and appliances all have communication capability. On a recent visit to old friends in Japan, I was startled when a voice from the *ofuro* (bathtub) told me the water was too hot. My host regularly turned on her rice cooker from the car while driving home from work. Products and services stemming from this environment will no doubt spread around the world without much competition.

Groups like Sony and Toshiba are marketing PCs with TV tuners to satisfy a growing demand for multimedia terminals. Indeed, 60 percent of PCs for home use in Japan have a TV tuner, and Sony has changed the color of its Vaio PC from mauve to black and silver to make it look more like a TV. This move is in interesting contrast to IBM's announcement late in 2004 that it is selling off its PC division to China's Lenovo. Sony has a smaller share of the PC market than IBM, but like Samsung, it does not believe in dogs, stars, and cash cows. While IBM is divesting itself of the PC it fathered, Sony is linking its PC with its TVs, camcorders, and other technologies to turn it into a multimedia terminal that may create a major challenge for the likes of Dell, HP, and even Intel and Microsoft. By tying together more and more parts and products no one else makes, and doing so in capital-intensive industries where the cost of entry rises exponentially (Sharp and Samsung have just announced a $21 billion joint investment in flat-panel production. How many can match that?), the Japanese are bent on ensuring the absence of competition.

And they intend to keep the production at home. Sharp recently opened a sixth-generation flat-panel production plant in Kameyama, Japan, in order to protect its technology, and Canon CEO Fujio Mitarai has vowed that the bulk of Canon production will continue to be done in Japan. Says one leading Japanese CEO, "We keep the brain work in Japan and just ship black boxes abroad for assembly in China or Southeast Asia."

Even more powerful, however, may be the Toyota approach. Its executives tell me they don't worry about being copied because they don't think their product *can* be copied. To produce a Toyota, you have to imitate the company's integration of technology, manufacturing, and human behavior. And that would require an organization almost identical to Toyota's, and that, they believe, is nearly impossible.

The formidable Japanese industrial technology base is supported by an equally formidable government program to remain competitive. Japan devotes 3 percent of its GDP to R&D and has been spending at a higher rate than the United States since 1990. Moreover, in the absence of a military component, Japan's R&D is aimed solely at commercial markets. With half the population of the United States, Japan annually graduates two-thirds as many scientists and engineers, and its students rank near the top in international math and science assessments.[12] Japan's sixty-nine patents per million of population put it just behind number one Singapore's seventy-three and far ahead of America's forty-two. Perhaps most significant, no one in Japan seems concerned about their ability to compete in leading-edge technology. Ministry of Economics and International Trade officials recently told me they have full confidence in Japan's ability to stay on top.

China and India "Get It"

As we have seen, the main driver of India's recent rapid growth is technology. America's $30 billion advanced technology trade deficit with China is proof of China's technology skills, and more proof is appearing as I write. The lead business story in this morning's (December 7, 2004) newspapers is about the IBM-Lenovo deal. Once the world's dominant technology company, with the product line that made Microsoft and Intel the cornerstones of America's technological leadership, IBM is selling out to a Chinese company with aspirations for global technological leadership. Of course, the PC is no longer at the cutting edge and the real technology is in the Intel chips and the Microsoft software; still, I couldn't have made up anything that would have better made the point. So let's go back to China and India for just a moment and take a look at what's happening in technology.

For companies like Intel, Microsoft, Siemens, and others that search for the world's best talent, the Chinese and Indian brain pool is a powerful magnet. This would be true even if pay levels in China were equal to those in Japan, Europe, and the United States. But, of course, they are far lower. Adding to China's attraction is the fact that virtually all top Chinese officials are trained as engineers. In the words of Intel CEO Barrett, "they get it," they understand the linkages of technology development to manufacturing, university, and infrastructure "ecosystems."

Although India's leaders are not all engineers, they too are beginning to "get it." Both India and China are developing the right kind of "ecosystems," frequently by offering investment incentives to foreign companies. While I was in Delhi in the fall of 2004, both Barrett and Microsoft CEO Steve Ballmer had just arrived in town from China. Executives like them are routinely offered powerful incentives on these trips. A company that invests in a major manufacturing facility in selected parts of China pays no taxes for twenty years; land is provided free; the company is exempted from all import duties and value-added taxes and can expect grants to help train the workforce. On top of that, grants of up to half the amount of the capital investment are also available. Compare that to a similar U.S.-based investment, where federal authorities would offer nothing. States might offer some tax breaks and utility cost abatements. You can see why China looks so good. India is not yet as generous as China, but it is learning, and the offers it makes with its biotech and software industrial parks are very interesting. That's why Ballmer announced a big new Microsoft R&D campus while he was in India, and Barrett, who already has lots of Ph.D. engineers and computer scientists in Bangalore, talked about adding more.

Another factor in their thinking goes beyond money and talent to desire. Barrett and Ballmer are better known in China and India than Britney Spears. Barrett is feted by millions of Chinese at personal computer festivals. "These people are crazy in love with technology," he says. The flip side of Barrett's status is that the Chinese government wants its own rock stars and is moving aggressively to create China-based standards. In 2004 China nearly established a wireless computing standard that would have forced Intel and others to abandon existing standards and equipment in order to sell in China. The global technology community eventually persuaded the Chinese to back down, but in the future more and more standards will be set by the Chinese.

The five hundred engineers and scientists at Microsoft's Advanced Technology Center outside Beijing have already put seventy-two innovations into Microsoft products, including the "digital ink" used in software for tablet PCs. They are also developing graphics, handwriting recognition, and voice-synthesization technologies.[13] In September 2004 Motorola announced a new R&D center in Beijing, and a few days later Lucent Technologies stated its plan to invest $70 million in an R&D center in Nanjing for its 3G cellular unit. About a month later, Steve Chen, who is to supercomputing what Michael Jordan is to basketball, announced he was leaving the United States for China. When he worked at Cray Computer in the 1980s, he was almost singlehandedly responsible for keeping the United States in the lead in supercomputing. A native of Taiwan, he came to the United States in 1975 to pursue his love of fast computing. Now, however, he has decided to join Galactic Computing in Shenzhen, where a group of Hong Kong investors is financing a major new supercomputing effort. Chen's move tells you all you need to know about China's technology development.

Not to be outdone, the Indians, too, are moving into the global technology big leagues. GE's research center in Bangalore is its largest outside the United States. Here 1,800 scientists and engineers are working at the cutting edge of plastics, jet engine, medical, and other technologies. Last year this group was awarded ninety-five U.S. patents. Just down the street, Intel's IT Ph.D.s copped sixty-three patents, and total Indian filings for U.S. patents last year topped 1,000.[14] Rick Wallace, executive vice president of leading semiconductor equipment maker KLA Tencor, says, "You begin by giving the Indians some routine stuff to do because you think you will save a lot of money. And you do save money. But pretty soon, you realize the work is getting done faster and better, and you start sending more and more of it. You also start sending more advanced work and then have to figure out what, if anything, you really don't want to send."

The European Union: From Airbus to Linux

No one would confuse Europe with Silicon Valley. A recent article in *Time* Europe entitled "How to Plug Europe's Brain Drain" explains how America's labs are teeming with bright young Europeans fleeing the dead hand of convention and bureaucracy in favor of entrepreneurial freedom and more money.[15] There are now 400,000 European science and technology graduates working in the United States, with thousands more on the way.[16] One reason for this is that Europe is spending only 2 percent of GDP, about $166 billion, on R&D annually, with a resulting twenty-eight patents per million inhabitants.[17] Europe faces many of the same offshoring pressures as the United States. For example, Siemens CEO Heinrich von Pierer was recently asked by *Der Spiegel* why the CF-62 mobile phone he carries everywhere was developed in China rather than in Germany. He replied that Siemens will sell 14 million phones in China this year and 18 million next year, in what is by far the biggest mobile phone market in the world. In order to understand the customers' needs, he said, the developer must be nearby. Likewise, because production cannot be separated from development, the production must be nearby as well. Von Pierer recognized that this was a problem for German workers but emphasized that Siemens had to go where production costs are low in order to survive.[18]

On the other hand, Europe also has some strong cards to play. With 555,000 science and engineering graduates every year, the EU has more technologically trained people than either the United States or Japan. Germany, like Japan, enjoys strong exports to China. Again, you may ask how a high-cost, stagnant, union-bound, over vacationed welfare state like Germany can sell anything in China against competition from the likes of Japan, Korea, and the United States. But if you take that 267 mile per hour maglev train ride from the airport into Shanghai, you know the answer. It is the same as Japan's: sell things no one else makes. The maglev is Germany's answer to Japan's bullet trains, except it is newer and better.

The Germans also sell steel and machine tools and printing presses to China made with a quality of steel neither the Chinese nor the Americans can make. I have already noted that the European Airbus has taken the lead from Boeing in commercial aircraft, taking 315 orders in 2004 to Boeing's 285. Its planes are more technologically advanced, and the new 800 passenger Airbus A380 will soon be replacing the venerable Boeing 747 as the international long-haul aircraft of choice. Although the mobile phone is a U.S. invention, its rapid development and deployment were led by European companies, which continue to hold the largest share of the global market.

Finally I should mention two important European names in software, Linus Torvalds, the developer of the Linux computer operating system, and Tim Berners-Lee, the Geneva-based developer of the World Wide Web. Neither will ever challenge Bill Gates for richest man status. But both invented software systems that are essential to our modern information society. Linux was offered by Torvalds as an open operating system available at no charge and has become the system of choice for big league industrial computing. As for the World Wide Web, who could live without it? If it had been patented or copyrighted, Berners-Lee might be the world's first trillionaire. Maybe Europeans don't have more patents because they give the technology away.

European secondary school students score near the top of the international assessment table, and the EU has launched an official effort to become the "most competitive economy in the world" by 2010.[19] Although the project is currently lagging, it at least exists. That fact, coupled with its many strengths, means it would be a mistake to count Europe out of the global technology sweepstakes.

The Future of the United States in Global Technology

As a result of all this R&D diffusion, new products are emerging from a veritable United Nations of suppliers. Take a look at your new PDA or digital camera phone. Its central processor is probably from Intel or Texas Instruments while the operating system is likely from Blackberry, Symbian, or Microsoft. The circuit board and specialty chips could have been designed in China, Taiwan, Ireland, or India. The color display probably came from Korea and the high-grade lens from Japan or Germany while the cellular links could be from Finland or

France. If you have Bluetooth technology that lets digital devices talk
to each other, it was probably licensed from Israel's IXI Mobile. Says
Doug Raser, head of global strategic marketing at Texas Instruments,
"The more we can leverage outside talent and companies with great
ideas, the more product we can get out." By the same token, the new
global innovation supermarket lowers entry barriers and speeds the
ideas of new players to market. Austin-based Motion Computing, for
example, is a 110-person company that has suddenly become the number three supplier in the tablet PC business, which is forecast to hit $7
billion in three years. Says CEO Scott Eckert, "This business model
lets us bring core technologies from around the world to market faster
than our competitors."[20]

The spread of technology development promises enormous benefits, with complex implications for America. The United States cannot
and should not hope to dominate all technologies for all time. But the
PCAST prediction that the big winners in the future will be those with
technology for which there is no competition is significant. To maintain its standard of living and ability to defend its interests and values,
the United States needs to remain strong in many and stay on top in
some. There is no cause for immediate despair. Diana Hicks of the
Georgia Institute of Technology says, "America is not yet in large
[technological] peril."[21] As *Business Week* says, others are "gunning
for U.S. technology because it is the best." No one disputes that the
elite U.S. technology universities are the world's finest, and despite
many foreign efforts to clone it, the American entrepreneurial system
epitomized by Silicon Valley remains unique. The scope of the U.S.
technology effort is far broader than that of any other country. Says
Bell Labs senior vice president Cherry Murray, "The United States is
pretty much in the lead in all science. While it is painful to lose some
ground in the physical sciences we are doing very well with biology
and medicine." A look at researchers weaving transistors atom by
atom out of carbon fibers at IBM's Watson Research Center or at Stanford Research Institute's work on artificial muscle confirms that American science is far from dead.[22] Optimists argue that America answered the last threat; the Japanese technological challenge of the
1980s, with the world's fastest microprocessors, best software, and

leading edge equipment to fabricate semiconductors.[23] Concludes *Business Week*, "It's a safe bet that somewhere in America's vast research enterprise, excited researchers are on the cusp of the Next Big Thing."[24]

While there is reason for optimism, the concerns of the PCAST and other technology leaders and economists cannot be dismissed. MIT president Susan Hockfield agrees that "U.S. biotech and life sciences are fabulous right now" but insists nevertheless that "we're falling behind in science and engineering.[25] Intel chairman Andy Grove adds that the U.S. software industry could become an endangered species.[26] Like Hockfield, he is alarmed at the state of American education and the decline of U.S. funding for engineering and the physical sciences. Grove is also frustrated that even as the number of U.S. science and technology graduates declines, the U.S. government is making it harder for foreign students to get visas for study at U.S. universities. In sum, while the United States still has the best technology assets, the trends in America seem to be mostly down while those elsewhere are mostly up.

Conventional Remedies Won't Work

The remedy normally prescribed is a combination of increased spending on education, engineering, and the physical sciences, reform of K–12 education, granting more visas to talented foreign students, more incentives for U.S. entrepreneurs, and better protection of intellectual property. But these measures are probably insufficient to reverse the trends. During a week of interviews with leaders of venture capital and technology firms in Silicon Valley, I found that the tech company executives are moving R&D out of the U.S. base as fast as they can, not only for reasons of cost and quality but also because of the link with manufacturing, which is increasingly being done abroad. The head of one major semiconductor manufacturer quipped that the only reason for staying here is because some of the top execs like the neighborhood. Extra funding and more science graduates will not change this trend. One Santa Clara University professor told me enrollment in engineering is falling by 30 percent a year because the kids have figured out that there won't be any jobs in those disciplines. They'll all be in Asia.

While they lament these trends, the CEOs and venture capitalists find themselves in the peculiar position of being pushed to move jobs and transfer technology. American thinking eschews economic strategy and offers no countervailing pressures. On the contrary, it embraces whatever the companies do as by definition the best outcome. Thus Cisco CEO John Chambers says China will become the information technology center of the world sometime between 2020 and 2040, and Cisco is trying to develop a strategy for becoming a Chinese company. Another top CEO says although he is concerned about the drift of things as an American citizen, he has a fiduciary responsibility to do what is necessary to keep Agilent healthy and has to depend on the guys in Washington to take care of America.

One venture capital manager urges all the biotech start-ups he funds to move as much research and development as possible to China and India. When I asked how he felt about the long-term implications of that to the U.S. economy, he acknowledged some concern, but then said, "Look, I'm a loyal citizen but what happens to the United States is not my job. I have a fiduciary responsibility to my investors. The guys in Washington are supposed to be worrying about the United States." This is a logical assumption. Americans hold elections and send people to Washington to worry about the nation. But no one in Washington is minding the store because American economic doctrine holds that worrying about this sort of thing is not Washington's job either. If you asked leaders in Washington about these issues, they would respond by asking what the business community thinks. Nobody is taking an interest in the health of the long-term economic structure of the country because America's economic ideology says it is wrong to do so.

Sometimes those worried about what they see as negative trends suggest that business leaders are "Benedict Arnold CEOs." This puts the CEOs in a difficult and unfair position. They are being pushed offshore by an alignment of forces. American business doctrine and law holds that their primary responsibility is to their shareholders. No one in Washington is concerned. It might be heroic for the business leaders to resist these forces, but it could also be suicidal.

Thus the logic that is moving manufacturing to China and services to India is moving R&D to those countries as well. I have spoken with hundreds of American business, government, media, and academic leaders on the topic of long-term competitiveness over the past twenty years. Their advice is always the same as Marc Andreesen's: America has to invent the next new things. This response assumes that the next new thing invented by Americans will also be commercialized in the United States and thereby create high-wage employment for ordinary Americans. This is what Andreesen assumes with his "always, always, always" comment. The problem for Americans is that the assumption is only half right. Surely there will always be the next new thing waiting somewhere in the wings. But it won't necessarily be waiting in America, and even if it is, it almost certainly won't be commercialized in America and won't provide jobs for ordinary Americans. Intel's Barrett captured the situation perfectly when he commented that "Intel will be okay no matter what. We can adjust to do our R&D and manufacturing wherever it is most economically advantageous to do so. But in addition to being chairman of Intel, I am also a grandfather, and I wonder what my grandchildren are going to do."

CHAPTER 8

Cheap No More

In our lifetime, we will have to deal with
a peak in the supply of cheap oil.
—ROBERT K. KAUFMAN
OIL ECONOMIST, BOSTON UNIVERSITY

While the three billion new capitalists are making an important impact on technology, they may have an even greater impact on the
long-term cost of basic economic factors. The pricing of oil, a major issue since the crises of the 1970s, is likely to become even more fraught
as a result of rapid global growth and falling production. Less discussed
are the limited global supplies of critical minerals and materials. And
while no one expects a return of famine, the growth of global food production has slowed, and the United States, long a major food exporter,
has become a net importer. For all of these staples of modern life, the
laws of supply and demand are tending in the same direction.

Hooked

I have always thought of myself as a moderate guy. I don't smoke,
drink only an occasional glass of wine, have never done drugs (not
only didn't inhale, never even touched a joint); I exercise regularly and
control my weight. Yet I'm hooked and so are you.

We're hooked on oil and its close cousin, natural gas, in ways we
seldom recognize. For instance, I wake up in the morning and put on

my underwear. If it's cotton, the oil content is relatively low, maybe a half gallon or so for the fertilizer to grow the cotton, the fuel for the air-conditioned tractor used to plow and seed the field, and the fuel used to process and transport the shorts and shirt to the store and eventually to my door. But sometimes I wear Cool Max. It's 100 percent polyester, and that's all oil and gas. I brush my teeth. The toothbrush and toothpaste container are all oil. I shave, and the razor, shaving lotion container, and aftershave container are made of nothing but oil. Man, I've got oil all over my face. The plastic comb I use to part my locks is all oil. So now I've got the stuff in my hair too.

What am I wearing today? A pair of polyester slacks? Or maybe that neat new microfiber that doesn't wrinkle. It's all oil. Okay, I'm conserving by wearing a cotton shirt, but the tennis shoes with the synthetic rubber soles are oil intensive. When I go downstairs, my wife says we're out of milk. So I jump in the car for a hop to the supermarket. I get the milk along with some ground beef she also asked me to pick up for tonight's hamburgers. It takes nearly a gallon of oil to produce the pound of beef I just bought. I live in the suburbs, and when I get home the odometer shows I've made a round trip of sixteen miles. For my car, that means about a gallon of gas. I feel a twinge of guilt when I spy my neighbor's hybrid Prius, but hey, gas is cheap. It costs about half what I just paid for the milk.

It's been like that for most of my life. I got my first car in 1957, a 1950 Chevrolet, when I was sixteen years old and gas cost sixteen cents a gallon. Even as a kid, I could easily afford the cost of driving it just with my part-time jobs. However, I also remember a different time. In 1973 and again in 1978 Middle Eastern oil producers, who then provided over half the world's oil supplies, suddenly cut back production to force prices higher. Overnight, we went from cheap gas to no gas. Lines formed at every pump and stretched for miles; people literally came to blows over who got to the pump first. At this time the average car in the United States was getting about thirteen miles to a gallon. Prices soared, the economy went into a nosedive, and unemployment nearly doubled.

The response was twofold. The high prices spurred a burst of exploration. The North Sea oil fields were brought on stream along with

Alaska's North Slope. More oil was found in the Gulf of Mexico at depths that had previously been beyond reach. Other fields were developed in Africa, Latin America, and central Asia. As a result, the Middle East suppliers' share of the market dropped from over 50 percent to about 30 percent.[1]

The big oil-consuming countries enacted real conservation measures. In the United States, for example, Congress passed legislation requiring that by 1988, the average gas mileage of the entire U.S. auto fleet be double the thirteen miles per gallon of 1978. Cars were redesigned for front wheel drive and their weight reduced as newer, lighter materials were adopted. Tax incentives lured many people to install rooftop solar hot water heaters. Factories appointed energy conservation managers. Office building managers began to turn off the lights at night. Within eight years, the United States cut oil consumption by 17 percent even as the economy grew by 27 percent.[2] Oil imports fell by 50 percent and imports from the Persian Gulf by 87 percent. Imports as a percentage of U.S. consumption dropped from nearly 50 percent to around 30 percent. The ability of the Middle Eastern suppliers to dictate prices was broken, and oil again became cheaper than milk.

Old Habits and New Addicts

Since then, old habits have reasserted themselves. Cars, for example, have become more muscular with 93 percent more horsepower, making them 29 percent faster in getting from 0 to 60 miles per hour today than in 1981. A loophole in the law that sets mileage standards made trucks exempt, and because SUVs are classified as trucks, they were until recently not required to meet gas mileage standards. Over the past fifteen years, the U.S. auto fleet has shifted massively to SUVs, and consequently the average vehicle today weighs 24 percent more than in 1981 and gets fewer miles per gallon.[3] This shift has been facilitated by the U.S. tax system, which now allows as much as a $100,000 deduction on the purchase of an SUV for business use. At the same time, the office building lights have tended to stay on (although the bulbs are often vastly more efficient than in 1980), the population has grown, Americans are driving more miles per person than they ever did, and U.S. oil consumption has climbed by 25 percent since the mid-1980s to a record high of about 20 million barrels a day.[4] That comes to about three gallons a person every day. With 5 percent of the world's population, America accounts for over a quarter of global oil consumption of about 80 million barrels a day. Forecasters do not see these trends changing. Consequently, the U.S. government's Energy Information Administration projects that by 2025, U.S. oil consumption will be up by a third to 30 million barrels a day.[5]

Nor is the United States alone in thirsting for oil. The EU now consumes about 15 million barrels a day while Japan uses 5.5, and eastern Europe and Russia add another 5.5. Both the EU and Japan are far more energy efficient than the United States, getting a dollar's worth of GDP by using only 60 percent of the energy it takes to produce a dollar of American GDP.[6] These countries also have slower economic growth rates than the United States. As a result, their oil consumption is forecast to rise only modestly between now and 2025. Not so, however, in Asia outside of Japan. The entry of China and India into the global system and their rapid adoption of a developed-country lifestyle are creating a whole new reality.

China passed Japan as the second largest consumer and importer of oil in 2004, with daily consumption of about 6 million barrels. The first private vehicle went on sale in China in 1984. In 2004, 2 million were sold. Traffic jams in Beijing and Shanghai are worse than the worst of Los Angeles and Tokyo. And China is just beginning. As a result of its rapid growth and motorization, forecasters say that by 2025 China will be using 13 million barrels of oil a day, or close to half the amount now consumed in the United States. India is forecast to more than double its consumption from today's 2.2 million barrels a day to 5.3 million in 2025 while the rest of Asia goes from 5.6 to 10 million barrels a day. Thus total world consumption is forecast to climb from today's 80 million barrels a day to about 120 million over the next twenty years.[7]

Here's the catch. Oil is getting a lot harder to find. The lower forty-eight states of the United States are essentially tapped out, producing less than half the oil of their early 1970s peak. Production from the North Slope of Alaska and the North Sea is also declining. In 1973 im-

ports accounted for about a third of U.S. oil consumption, and that fell
to about a fourth in the early 1980s. Today it is 54 percent and is forecast to hit 70 percent by 2025.[8] Europe too will be importing more as
North Sea production falls. Japan has always been completely dependent on imports. Now China and India, along with much of the rest of
Asia, will also be huge and growing importers. The big question is
where all this oil is going to come from.

View from the Peak

Oil experts have recently engaged in a hot discussion of something
called Hubbert's peak. No, it's not a mountain filled with oil. In the
mid-1950s, Shell Oil geophysicist M. King Hubbert predicted that the
peak of U.S. oil production (in the lower 48 states) would occur in the
early 1970s. Although scorned by many experts at the time, Hubbert
turned out to be on target. But when the lower forty-eight peaked, the
North Slope, North Sea, and other major finds were still to be developed. Today many analysts are suggesting that a global Hubbert's peak
is in our future. They note that prospectors made their best finds in the
early 1960s and that succeeding discoveries have been fewer and
smaller despite intense search efforts.

Bear in mind that world demand grows by about 2 percent while
4–5 percent of global reserves are used up each year. To replace what
is depleted while providing for the rising demand, prospectors have to
find 6–7 percent more oil each year, and that number rises as global
consumption climbs. Today less than one-third that amount is being
found.[9] That's what leads Robert Kaufman of Boston University to insist that we'll see a peak of supply in our lifetime.[10] Forecasts for when
this will occur vary. David Greene of Oak Ridge National Laboratory,
using data compiled by British geologist Colin Campbell, has estimated a peak for 2006 in the world outside the Middle East and 2016 if
the Middle East is included. On the basis of data from the U.S. Geolog-
ical Survey, Greene has a more optimistic forecast of a peak for world
production around 2040.[11] Greene warns that his estimate doesn't factor in political or environmental considerations. Some experts think
the peak may be here already. They note that the performance of some

wells in Saudi Arabia casts doubt on estimates of total Saudi reserves. In any case, the main point is that being an optimist only means pushing the peak out by a few years.

Energy analyst Charles T. Maxwell says today's situation is entirely different from that of the 1970s. Then, he says, the issues were political. There was always enough capacity to produce the extra crude oil necessary to meet the world's needs. In the relatively near future that will no longer be the case, and there is likely to be a global energy crisis that will be painful and difficult to solve. Maxwell sees the crisis arriving in three waves. The first and smallest arrived with the spike in oil prices in 2004. He expects a second wave in 2009–2010, when non-OPEC oil output may peak, causing increasing reliance on OPEC and particularly on the Middle Eastern members of OPEC along with Russia.[12] Separately, the U.S. Energy Information Administration estimates that by 2025, the Persian Gulf will supply between one-half and two-thirds of global oil consumption. This is the same percentage as in 1973, meaning that in fifty years the world will have come full circle. Maxwell foresees the real crisis occurring around 2020, when OPEC and the Middle East peak. After that, oil production should decline inexorably, never to recover. Things could come to a head more quickly if there is a military or political crisis in a key Middle Eastern country. For example, half of Saudi production comes from one field. Two-thirds of Saudi oil goes through one processing plant and is shipped from two terminals, the larger of which was the target of a failed terrorist attack in mid-2002.[13] Simple attacks on key facilities could choke supplies for up to two years. An interruption of just a few months in the Saudi supply to the world market "would spell disaster" and "throw the global economy into chaos." Yet the chief economist of the International Energy Agency says, "reliance on the sole Saudi pillar will continue."[14]

None of this is to say the world is going to run out of oil quickly or even entirely in some ultimate long run. There are enormous reserves such as the Athabasca tar sands of Alberta, Canada, and the shale oil of the western United States. Experts believe they may contain as much as 3 trillion barrels of oil. Alberta is producing about a million barrels a day now and could double that in ten years. But producing it takes enormously more effort than drilling a hole in the sand in Saudi Arabia. The Athabasca sand has to be strip-mined, cooked to 900 degrees, and then churned with hydrogen gas and a catalyst. What comes out is clean, low-sulfur crude, but what is left is a huge hole in the ground along with enormous air pollution and deforestation. And the tar sands are easy compared to the U.S. shale oil. The point is that while the world may not run out of oil quickly, it could soon run out of oil that costs less than milk. Maxwell notes that from 1987 to 2003 the price of oil ranged between $10 and $40 a barrel, with the average being $20. Between 2005 and 2010, he thinks the price could shift to $40, and from 2011–2020 he thinks a range of $50–$100 with an average of $70 is very possible. The economic implications of Maxwell's forecast for the United States and global economies are enormous. Who could afford to wear Cool Max underwear or drive to the grocery store for a gallon of milk? The Japanese and Europeans who have long invested in energy conservation might at last get a decent return on their money, but they would not escape the pain of global recession or even depression.

The geopolitical implications could be even more significant. Former U.S. ambassador to China James Lilly notes that "the Chinese are on an aggressive quest to increase their oil supply all around the world; whether Iran, Sudan, or Venezuela, you name it, they are after it."[15] John Pike of the Global Security.Org policy research group observes that "it's a hard issue to ignore if one contemplates a billion Chinese driving gas-hogging SUVs."[16] Pike is obviously unaware that China has already adopted gas mileage standards for its cars and SUVs that no U.S. products can presently meet. He might better have said that it's hard to ignore if 300 million Americans insist on driving the gas guzzlers. But the larger point is that concern about oil supply and competition for access to oil could easily become major geopolitical flashpoints, not just between the United States and China but involving all major countries.

The situation is far from hopeless. China's adoption of tough mileage standards for its vehicles is encouraging. New technology offers many possibilities, ranging from a massive switch to telecommuting to adoption of lightweight, composite materials (e.g., those now used in advanced aircraft) to build autos and other vehicles. In the United States, conservation combined with simple things like coordinating traffic lights, fitting toll booths with electronic scanners, and using a mix of asphalt and ground-up tires for road surfaces could potentially save as much oil as we currently use. But for any of this to have an impact in time to avert trouble, new attitudes and policies must be adopted now.

Hard Things in Hard Places

While everyone has some awareness of the oil issue, few realize that a similar situation exists with regard to other important minerals and raw materials. There is a common misperception that the United States is well endowed with virtually unlimited mineral resources. At international meetings, countries like Japan frequently note their poverty of critical raw materials and point to the United States as blessed with an abundance of them. The truth, however, is that, like oil, other key materials often are found in only a few places, frequently the most inaccessible or the most politically hostile. And while the United States has more minerals than many countries, it is hardly self-sufficient.

Take tungsten, for example. For a long time you couldn't make light-bulbs without it. The United States imports about 70 percent of its needs, and its major suppliers are China, Russia, and Canada. Without Canada during the Cold War, we might all have spent a lot of time in the dark. Cobalt caused great anxiety in Washington in the late 1970s. Without cobalt you can forget about the metals essential in aircraft, missiles, and turbine engines. The United States imports about 80 percent of the cobalt it needs, and in the late 1970s the Republic of Congo was a major supplier. But when guerrilla activity in Congo's Shaba province disrupted supplies, prices shot through the roof and there was even speculation about possible U.S. military intervention. Tensions between the United States and the Soviet Union in the early 1980s fueled fears of a resource war. Indeed, some experts pointed to mineral resources as one of the reasons for the Soviet invasion of Afghanistan in 1979.

As in the case of oil, scarcity led to prospecting for new sources of supply, and the end of the Cold War put old supplies back on the market. As a result, most key materials have been plentiful over the past fifteen years and prices have been low. Indeed, these low commodity prices have helped control inflation over the past decade of unusual economic growth. But that is changing rapidly. On the one hand, the United States is increasingly importing materials it once exported such as superalloys and crystalline silicon. On the other hand, the rise of China and India has unleashed enormous new demand for many of these materials. We have already seen that China is the largest market for products like steel, aluminum, and cement and will eventually be the largest for many other products. This means China is beginning to inhale raw materials in the same manner as the United States. Currently China supplies the U.S. market with a large number of mineral commodities, including tungsten, yttrium, magnesium, antimony, indium, graphite, tin, tantalum, and fluorspar. But China's internal consumption is rising rapidly, as is that of India and much of the rest of the developing world. Consequently supplies are getting short and global prices are rising. Thus a new era of possible shortages and high commodity prices appears to be on the horizon, again with very significant economic and geopolitical implications.

Let Them Eat Golf Balls

John Blaska's family has a long history in Dane County, Wisconsin. In the 1880s the first Blaskas arrived in search of the opportunity that America's vast open spaces and fertile land seemed to offer. Like the majority of Americans at the time, they were farmers, and they answered the U.S. government's call to go west and fill the space with amber waves of grain. For more than a hundred years the policy paid off big-time. This was some of the best farmland in the world, and the government maintained a vast system of subsidies and price supports to keep farmers in business when the going got tough. It was the Blaskas and millions like them who peopled the Great Plains and the Far West and turned the land into the granary of the world. During the world wars, this area kept Europe from starving. It supplied the food for peace and other foreign aid programs. Shiploads of food exports for nearly half a century gave America agricultural trade surpluses that partially offset the rising deficits in oil and manufactured goods. Indeed, food supply became virtually synonymous with America in much of the world.

In the summer of 2003, however, John turned part of the farm into the Oaks Golf Course, saying, "We're raising grass rather than corn." That decision and thousands like it reflect another major impact of the new wave of globalization. In 2005, for the first time since 1959, the United States is projected to run a trade deficit in agricultural products. Nor is this deficit likely to be a one-time event. According to the U.S. Department of Agriculture's Economic Research Service, we can expect the United States to have a more or less permanent agricultural trade deficit from now on as a result of fundamental shifts in the patterns of world food consumption and production.[17]

On the one hand, the addition of 3 billion people with rapidly rising income to the global system has greatly increased demand for all kinds of agricultural products. Economic development in India and China has meant that people are eating more meat. Because raising livestock requires large amounts of grain, demand for animal feeds of all kinds has boomed. Just as its consumption of oil, minerals, and basic manufactured goods has soared, China has also developed a voracious appetite for food. For example, it has become the world's biggest customer for soybeans and is investing heavily in facilities and joint ventures around the world to ensure having a food supply along with its oil supply. India is developing similar kinds of demands and making similar investments and arrangements. On the other hand, global food supplies per capita have declined by 17 percent over the past twenty years as a result of population growth, loss of farmland to urbanization, erosion, and salinization in some irrigated areas. This has contributed to putting about 3 billion of the world's people in a condition of some degree of malnourishment. Such a combination of trends should create rising demand that spurs rising production. And it has.

This has been a boon for traditional food producers like Australia, Thailand, and Indonesia. And recently South America has arrived on the scene as a new food-producing heavyweight. Argentina has long been a top agricultural producer and a leading supplier of beef to world markets. But now Brazil, Chile, and other South American countries are getting into the game as world-class contenders. In fact, they are so competitive that they are driving others from some of the markets. That's why John Blaska is turning the family farm into a golf course. As Brazil has created a so-called "new Midwest" by turning much of its vast interior jungle into cropland, the future of farming in the "old Midwest" has become clouded. As Brazil overtakes U.S. exports of both soybeans and meat, Roger Borges, a University of Wisconsin soybean agronomist, says of his native Brazil, "they can bury the entire world in grain and meat if they use their full potential."

U.S. farmers are suffering from many of the same problems that plague U.S. manufacturers. For a long time U.S. farmers were the ones with the biggest economies of scale. They had the world's biggest farms, plowed them with the world's biggest tractors, and harvested the fields with the world's biggest reapers. They were supported by subsidies and protected by high tariffs and quotas on imports of many items. In the past fifteen years, however, the WTO and other free trade agreements have removed or lowered these barriers. Ironically, at the same time, government crop subsidies, which in 2003 amounted to $550 million in Wisconsin alone, have tended to be capitalized in the land values, keeping them high. As a result of these changes, low-cost dairy products from Australia and New Zealand have been making big inroads in U.S. markets, as have other products from which tariffs and quotas have recently been removed.

Meanwhile, Brazilian farmers have been bringing lots of cheap, virgin land into production. In the case of soybeans, for example, Brazil increased planting by nearly 50 percent from 1992 to 2001 and, aided by more open markets, raised its exports by 326 percent as it passed the United States to become the world's top producer. One result has been that, as Blaska says, "commodity prices for at least the last six to eight years probably, have not been the greatest."[18] The fact is that U.S. farmers are having trouble competing, and despite booming world demand, U.S. farm acreage is dropping steadily as thousands of farmers like John Blaska decide they'd rather play golf.

Of course, that's not the whole story. New foods have grown in popularity as immigration into the United States has risen. Hispanics and

Asians do not lose their taste for the spices, vegetables, and other spe-
cialities of their homeland when they move to the United States. At the
same time, increasingly well traveled Americans bring a taste for exotic flavors back from their trips. Each year they buy more imported
wine, beer, fruits, vegetables, and beef than the year before. Take wine
as an example. Between 1994 and 2003, U.S. wine imports rose from
about $1 billion to over $3 billion as Chilean, New Zealand, and South
African varieties became popular and gained entrance to the market.
In 2005 U.S. purchases of all these products are expected to rise to $56
billion, up $4 billion from last year and slightly more than U.S. farmers
and food producers are expected to export.[19] Particularly significant is
the fact that the weaker dollar of the past year seems to be having no
impact. Says Bruce Gardner, dean of the University of Maryland's
School of Agriculture, "the lesson of the weak dollar is how little difference it's making. Imports are more expensive, but we're buying
them anyway."[20]

The dollar has been a factor on the other side, however. The Asian
financial crisis of 1997 and the strong dollar of 1995–2002 stifled demand for U.S. agricultural exports just as big new acreage was coming
on stream to compete in Brazil and elsewhere. From 1996 to 1999, demand for U.S. products fell by $10 billion and has not recovered.[21] At
the same time, the globalization of business has also had an impact.
About 15 percent of U.S. food imports are supplied by U.S. food companies through their farms and plants in other countries. Dole supplies
banana-growing Hawaii with bananas from Latin America. Like other
multinational companies, food suppliers take advantage of lower costs
of land, labor, raw materials, and capital abroad to produce there and
export back to the U.S. market. Thus the United States imports more
soft drinks than it exports, even though Coca-Cola and PepsiCo are
the world's largest soft drink makers.

Water, Water Nowhere

In the future, however, the big factor is likely to be water—or the lack
of it. In Tucson, Arizona, Reese Woodling remembers when he could
walk his ranch in the morning and get his clothes soaked from the dew

on the grass that fed his five hundred cows. But twelve years ago the dew began to disappear as shrubs took over from the withering grass. By 1998 Woodling had sold off half the cows, and in 2004 he abandoned the ranch.[22] What drove him off were persistent drought conditions that, despite some recent rain and snow, are projected to combine with growing population to cause an eventual water crisis in the West.

Jonathan Overpeck directs the Institute for the Study of the Planet Earth at the University of Arizona. Says he, "Twenty-five years ago scientists produced computer models of the drought Arizona is now experiencing. It's going to get warmer, we're going to have more people, and we're going to have more droughts more frequently and in harsher terms."[23] Of course, not everyone agrees. Sherwood Idso of the Center for the Study of Carbon Dioxide and Global Change says there were more severe droughts between 1600 and 1800 and this one will go away as they did.[24]

But it's hard to get away from certain facts. The Colorado River, which supplies a large part of the water consumed in Arizona, California, Colorado, Nevada, New Mexico, Utah, and Wyoming, is lower than it was during the Dust Bowl years and is so taxed that it literally runs out before reaching the Sea of Cortez. The region's two biggest reservoirs, Lake Mead and Lake Powell, have shrunk to half their capacity. More rain and less snow is falling, and it is coming earlier in the year, meaning it runs off and is lost more rapidly. The Scripps Institution of Oceanography predicts that by the end of the century the Sierra Nevada snowpack, which provides half of California's water, will be reduced by 30 to 90 percent.[25]

What this means for the West and agriculture is conservation, rationing, and probably reduction of farm and ranch acreage. Nine of the fastest-growing U.S. states are in the West. California's population has doubled since 1960 and will triple to 50 million by 2025. Water supplies are not keeping up with demand, and metropolitan populations are beginning to compete with agricultural users. For example, in California, agriculture accounts for 3 percent of state output and 85 percent of state water usage.[26] The enormous potential for conflict is obvious, as is the likely direction of resolution. Rain-short areas all over the country, but particularly in the West, depend on underground aquifers. But these are being drawn down much faster than they are being replenished. They supply more than 40 percent of U.S. irrigation, and the tripling of irrigation since 1950 is rapidly depleting them.

Public utilities get 40 percent of the water from the aquifers and their withdrawal has tripled over the past fifty years.[27] As a result, cities like Denver, Las Vegas, and several in southern California are scrambling to reserve secure backup sources. Some cities are buying farms in order to stockpile their water rights. In Nebraska, Lake McConaughy has dropped to its lowest level in years and irrigators on it and the aquifers of the Republican River are facing restrictions on withdrawals. Parts of the Platte River system are virtually bone dry. In another move, the Nebraska Department of Natural Resources ordered no new irrigation wells to be sunk in three key areas.[28] This means farmers cannot increase irrigated acreage for the time being.

The heart of the problem appears to be that the American West built itself on unrealistic assumptions during a period of historically unusual wetness that has now ended. This means major adjustments in the future of individuals, groups, businesses, and communities. The impending energy crisis will only add to the seriousness of the problem. Already, for example, 375,000 acres of U.S. agricultural land have been abandoned because of the high cost of pumping water for irrigation. All of these trends mean less agricultural land and less agricultural production in the United States unless there are dramatic technological advances. It is unlikely, therefore, that the United States will be supplying the booming world demand for food.

All of which poses an interesting question. If China is going to be the world's major manufacturer while India provides a lot of the services, and Asia and Europe lead the way in many areas of high technology, with Latin America supplying the world's food as U.S. production declines, what will happen to the U.S. trade deficit and the dollar?

CHAPTER 9

The End of the Dollar

Sorry, son, all my money's tied up in currency.

—W.C. FIELDS

At a recent conference in New Delhi concerning the future development of India and China, I was the only American on the program—or in the audience. Nevertheless, the economic discussion was couched in terms of dollars. Charts and tables relating to Indian or Chinese GDP growth rates, export and import volumes, foreign reserve holdings, and other variables were all denominated in dollars. Even when I had the bad luck to run short of Indian rupees in the middle of the conference, the coffee service gladly took my dollars. Nor was this surprising. Wherever I have traveled for the past forty years, people always and everywhere have readily accepted dollars. Few of the conference participants considered that the Indian and Chinese economic developments they were discussing could serve as catalysts for the end of the dollar era.

Yet that possibility was made clear to me on the return trip, when I stopped in Frankfurt for lunch with some German friends. The conversation turned to how inexpensive things are in the United States these days. When I mentioned the price of a new house in Washington, one of my friends became a bit confused and asked what that would be "in real money," by which he meant euros. It was a perfect reversal of the classic American tourist's question to anyone spouting prices in currency other than dollars. It was also a brutally insightful commentary on a developing financial shift of truly global proportions. Over the past four years, the chronic U.S. trade deficit has reached unprecedented levels, and the dollar has begun to weaken as a consequence. Of course, this has happened before and the dollar has not lost its global primacy despite a cumulative decline of 70 percent over the past fifty years. But this time it is different. If you don't believe me, listen to George Soros and Warren Buffett.

A Bet Against the Dollar

On matters of money, these two have established their bona fides beyond any doubt. Soros is one of the great currency speculators of all time, and Buffett is perhaps the all-time greatest long-term investor. Soros gained fame in the early 1990s as the man who broke the British pound by betting $10 billion that it would fall and making a quick billion when it did. Subsequently, when he warned in June 2002 that the greenback was in danger of losing a third of its value, it was worth taking notice. Of course, you could argue that, since Soros is a professional hedge fund manager whose job is to play the ups and downs of currencies, this remark may have been more manipulation than prophecy. Here's where Buffett comes in. No currency speculator he: in a November 2003 article in *Fortune*, he noted that he had begun worrying about mounting trade deficits way back in 1987, but he had never bought a dime of foreign currency—until the middle of 2002, when the deficit went from big to enormous. Since then, he says, he has felt it only prudent to begin moving some of his money into non-dollar assets. Buffett's commentary is fascinating for both its modesty and its conviction.[1]

Nevertheless, he says he's crying wolf again and backing it with Berkshire Hathaway's money this time by investing in several currencies. He insists he is doing this reluctantly and actually hopes, as an American and as an investor in many U.S. companies, that it doesn't pay off. But he emphasizes that he has to invest prudently, and the U.S. trade deficit has now grown so large that the country's "net worth" is being transferred abroad at such a rapid rate that the value of dollar-based assets may be at risk. To demonstrate why he is concerned, Buffett describes economic developments on two side-by-side islands, equal in every way except in the lifestyles of their inhabitants, which are captured in the names of the islands—Squanderville and Thriftville.

Land is the only asset in these islands, and the inhabitants need only food, of which enough for the needs of all can be produced by each inhabitant working eight hours a day. For a long time, things go along smoothly and pleasantly as everyone works his or her eight hours and each society is contentedly self-sufficient. But then Thriftville is seized by an extraordinary work ethic and everyone starts working 16 hours a day, exporting their excess food to Squanderville where the citizens are more than willing to quit working altogether and enjoy life while living off the food provided by their Thrifty friends. Even better, the Thrifties are willing to supply all this food in return for pieces of paper, Squanderbonds denominated in Squanderbucks. After a while the Thrifties have a lot of these Squanderbonds, which are essentially claim checks on Squanderville's future output. A few Squander pundits are nervous because they foresee that to pay off their growing debt the Squandervillians will, at some point, not only have to go back to work, but will have to work more than eight hours a day. But the pundits are dismissed and accused of being unpatriotic and having insufficient faith that Squanderville's best days are yet to come.

But a lot of Thrifties are getting worried too because they begin to doubt that the Squanders will ever be able to pay off any of those IOUs. In fact, there is some talk in Squanderville about printing more Squanderbucks to create inflation and dilute the value of both the bucks and the bonds so that they are easy to pay off. This talk leads the Thrifties to sell off the bonds quickly for Squanderbucks with which they start buying Squander land. After a while the Squanders are forced to wake up to a grim reality. The party was great while it lasted, but now they have to work eight hours a day to provide their own food plus extra hours to cover the rent on the land they so blithely sold. It is to hedge against the Squanderville syndrome that Buffett is moving some money into non-dollar assets.

The Ponzi Scheme Economy

What has Buffett and Soros worried is the enormous imbalances in the global economy. Indeed, in some ways it resembles the scheme made famous in 1920 by Boston's Charles Ponzi. He operated a fund in which early investors were guaranteed huge returns to be paid from the money contributed by new investors. The problem was that since the fund had no other source of income, it needed to add investors at a geometrically accelerating rate in order to keep paying the promised returns to the ever growing pool of previous investors. Eventually the entire population of the world would not have been sufficient to keep the fund afloat. When the scheme collapsed, Ponzi was sentenced to five years in federal prison and investors lost most of their money. (Ponzi somehow managed to disappear before serving an additional sentence on state charges in Massachusetts and started a land scam in Florida.)

In today's global economy, one net consumer—the United States—is accumulating a huge trade deficit by buying more than it produces at an ever accelerating rate. While it imported $600 billion more than it produced in 2004, it will import an excess of nearly $700 billion in 2005. The money to pay for this excess has to be borrowed from the rest of the world. So far that has been no problem because the rest of the world saves by consuming less than it produces, and then lends the savings to the United States so that we Americans can import the excess production of the other members of the global community. These U.S. imports create export-led growth for the rest of the world while adding to the growing U.S. trade deficit. Thus Americans borrow and buy more and more while the rest of the world saves and produces more and more. It then lends more and more to the Americans so they can spend more and more on imports from abroad.

As Buffett noted, this has been going on for a long time, and for a good reason. It suits all the players fine. The Americans (Squanders) get to live beyond their means, and they love it. The best part is that because individual Americans are not borrowing the money, they get to believe they are actually earning their high standard of living. The non-Americans (Thriftvillians) also like it. The extra American demand enables them to invest more and grow faster than they otherwise could, particularly in what they consider key industries. It also allows them to earn a reserve of dollars that can cushion shocks and provide leverage in global financial negotiations. So everyone is happy. If the Americans could guarantee to buy more than they produce at an ever accelerating pace indefinitely, while the rest of the world guaranteed to keep lending to America at the same pace, everyone would remain happy. Unfortunately, as Buffett points out, neither side can make those guarantees.

Here's why. American consumers have been buying so much on their credit cards and home equity lines that U.S. household debt is now at an all-time high of 120 percent of household income.[2] Once the credit cards and home equity lines are maxed out, the kids all have part-time jobs, and mom and dad both work full-time, it is just not possible to consume more unless earnings start rising more rapidly. But earnings can't rise. The lack of domestic savings is holding investment down, and the rapid move toward outsourcing and offshoring, along with technology-driven productivity gains, is restraining all but executive wages and salaries. And an aging population with lots of retirees means less consumption and less growth over time. Finally, the United States is already absorbing a large portion of the world's internationally available savings. At current rising debt rates, there simply may not be enough global savings to fund the American need.

There are also pressures on the other side of the equation. The great pools of world savings are in Asia, particularly China and Japan. But the aging of Japan's population has already cut savings rates from 15 percent to 6.4 percent.[3] In China, which is also aging, popular pressure to realize the fruits of economic growth through more consumption is also likely to cut savings rates. This is broadly true for the rest of East and Southeast Asia as well. More immediately, however, many foreigners are growing uneasy about the long-term value of the American IOUs they have been piling up. Foreigners effectively lend money to the United States in several ways. Private investors, for instance, might buy U.S. stocks and bonds or real estate or locate new factories and offices on U.S. territory. All of which brings foreign money flowing into the U.S. coffers. Foreign central banks also invest in the United States by acquiring Treasury bonds or buying the dollar in an effort to prop its value up when foreign exchange forces are tending to push it down.

During the dot.com bubble of the late 1990s, the vast bulk of foreign money flowing into the United States belonged to private actors rushing to invest in the new El Dorado. In those years, however, the United States needed only $100 billion–$200 billion to balance its deficits.

Recently that amount has grown to nearly $700 billion annually, even as the crash of the U.S. stock markets and a recession have driven many private foreign investors out of the market. They were replaced by their countries' central banks, which are now sitting on enormous piles of U.S. Treasuries, dollars, and other assets. Twenty years ago, America was the world's biggest creditor. Now the Thrift-villians of the world's central banks are choking on close to a net $1.5 trillion of American IOUs and increasingly wondering if Americans are really going to make good on them. They especially wonder this when they consider two developments. One is the rapid offshoring of U.S. manufacturing, software, and services, and the other is the likely continued decline of U.S. savings, as the federal budget deficit widens under the impact of rising social security and health insurance obligations. Both will make the current account deficit get much bigger before it gets smaller.

The Making of a Pickle

How did we get into this pickle? Of the many factors, primary have been America's misuse of the dollar, our falling savings rate, our soaring trade deficit, and the myth of free trade, along with the excessively high savings rates, production, and exports of other countries. Let's start with the abuse of America's privileged role as the issuer of the world's money—the dollar.

Abusing the Dollar

When President Nixon announced the end of the dollar's link to gold and created today's dollar standard, he effectively made the global financial system dependent on America's good behavior.

With no necessity to make good on its obligations in a world with no alternative reserve currency, America was literally licensed to print international money. It could exchange green pieces of paper bearing pictures of presidents for whatever it wished to buy. Do America's gas guzzlers need more oil? Print greenbacks and send 'em to the Saudis. Are American kids in love with everything made in Japan or China? Just run off some of those presidential pictures and send them along. America could have anything it wanted without having to consider the value of what it was getting against the value of what it was giving because—except in a very abstract way and over a very long term (about which more later)—it wasn't giving anything of value.

With no potential discipline or real obligations involved, America's international trade accounts became accounting artifacts. When I was a student in the 1960s, the monthly trade and balance of payments statistics were prominently reported, and France's periodic demands for more gold from Fort Knox were hotly debated. After the Nixon shock, however, this all got relegated to page 42, and America stopped worrying about international trade. Other countries had to count their reserves and find ways to earn dollars in order to procure necessities from international suppliers. But not the Americans. They just ran their printing presses and bought whatever they wanted. If they happened to buy more than they produced, what difference did it make? In fact, it was actually good to buy more than you produced because the world needed an engine of growth, in view of the fact that the Asians saved too much and consumed too little.

No More Piggy Bank:
The Decline of Savings

America's emphasis—with the memory of the Great Depression still fresh—on consumption as the driver of economic growth after World War II has a twin—a declining national savings rate. From 1947 to 1973, America's national savings—the combination of household, corporate, and government budget surpluses and deficits—fluctuated between about 8 to 15 percent of GDP. Since 1980, however, everything has gone south. What lies behind this trend is both difficult and easy to explain.

The difficult part is personal savings. Over the past twenty-five years it has steadily declined, from nearly 10 percent of GDP in 1979 to almost nothing today. One factor, clearly, has been the heavy promotion of consumption. As a teenager in the late 1950s, I never received an unsolicited credit card in the mail. When my children were teenagers in the late 1980s, they were each getting two or three a month. In 1968 outstanding consumer credit (calculated in year 2000 dollars) was $119 billion. By June 2000 it had soared to nearly $1.5 trillion. In 1970 only 16 percent of households had a bank type of credit card. By 1998 that figure had climbed to nearly 70 percent.[4] So aggressive are the credit card companies that they use data-mining techniques to identify people with high debt balances on their present cards in order to ply them with additional card offers. I can remember when most retail stores were closed on Sundays. For my children, that is unimaginable.

This shop-till-you-drop mentality did not evolve unaided. For a long time, the interest on credit card debt was tax deductible because the government thought shop-till-you-drop was good for the economy. Even when the feds eliminated the deduction, they provided for tax deductibility on home equity loans, meaning you could keep shopping as long as you owned a house. And don't forget President Bush's stirring injunction to the nation following 9/11. After declaring "war on terrorism," he urged Americans to support the effort by shopping to keep the economy going. The same year, Alan Greenspan, director of the Federal Reserve system and the nation's top economist, slashed interest rates virtually to zero after the collapse of the dot.com bubble in an effort to hold up consumer spending by encouraging home equity loan–based buying. Over the past fifty years, "saving" has almost become a bad word. Hardly anyone wants you to do it.

But the rise of consumerism only partly explains the decline of saving. There has also been a tightening squeeze on the average family's finances. After more than doubling from $21,201 to $43,219 (2003 dollars) between 1947 and 1973, median family income went nowhere for the next twenty-two years, rising only to $48,679 in 1995.[5] It jumped to $54,191 in 2000 but then dropped back to $52,864 in 2002.[6] Had the

1947–1973 trajectory held, median family income would now be approaching $100,000. Even more revealing, over 80 percent of households in my youth in the early 1950s only had one earner. Today over 70 percent have two.[7] One could argue that the real per capita standard of living has declined. Of course, I must quickly acknowledge that today's houses are bigger than yesterday's, and families now drive two or three cars in place of one and shop online instead of driving to the mall on Saturday. Moreover, the imported clothing, toys, and PCs they buy are very inexpensive and have given families a kind of income boost through lower prices. Michael Cox, of the Dallas Federal Reserve Bank, has written that if you calculate retail costs not in the familiar constant dollars but in the amount of average-wage work time needed to earn something, most consumer goods have grown significantly cheaper over the past generation. Cox argues that the material possessions of Americans at the poverty line in 2000 roughly equaled those of middle-income Americans in 1971.[8] So perhaps "decline" is too strong a word. Still, the average American family has been under increasing pressure to find ways to pay for the average lifestyle. One way to do that has been to save less.

The part of the falling national savings rate that is easy to explain is the government portion. The Reagan tax cuts of the early 1980s did not generate enough economic growth to offset the revenue loss arising from lower tax rates. As a consequence, the federal budget deficit soared to an unprecedented 6 percent of GDP and further accelerated the decline in the national savings rate arising from the fall in private saving.[9] America was spending far more than it was earning, and conventional analysts began to warn that government borrowing might soak up all the savings necessary to fund private investment, causing a spike in interest rates.

It never happened, because all that American buying included lots of imports that put billions of dollars in the hands of foreigners, especially of Japanese, who seemed to be making everything at the time. With global trade now denominated mainly in dollars decoupled from gold, the foreigners had no alternative but to accept and hold those green presidential pictures in return for all the Hondas, Walkmans, and Airbuses they were selling us. But rather than just look at the handsome pictures, they used them to buy U.S. Treasury bonds. This funded the burgeoning budget deficit and kept interest rates under control. Americans could have their cake and eat it too. Deficits, whether fiscal or trade, didn't seem to matter for the United States. By implication, neither did savings because, in lieu of its own, America could soak up the savings of the rest of the world. How good could life get?

Actually there were a few clouds in this picture. Social security was looking as if it would run out of money, and the federal budget deficit projection was getting so big that all the savings in the world might not be enough to offset it. So Reagan eventually raised taxes, and Bush I and then Clinton raised them even more. That, along with the 1990s dot.com bubble that produced rising tax revenue, put the federal budget in surplus and offset the continuing fall in private savings to keep total national savings at least in positive territory. Mind you, this was not enough to fund America's investment needs. The country was still borrowing like crazy, accepting those green pictures back in return for Treasury bonds or shares in U.S. companies and golf courses.

Then came the election of Bush II in 2000, and new tax cuts at the moment when private savings were collapsing completely. The budget deficit set new records in each following year, and America's national savings evaporated. In 2004 the Congressional Budget Office and several other public and private groups calculated a U.S. financial shortfall of $2.3 trillion over the next ten years.[10] But official Washington was not worried. As Vice President Dick Cheney said, "Reagan proved deficits don't matter."

Americans in Squanderville

Cheney actually had a point. What's the big deal about national savings? So we consume more than we produce, run a trade deficit, and have no savings to fund further investment. But our economy grows and stimulates growth in the rest of the world. Saving is a virtue but not an end in itself. It simply provides investment capital for the real objective: growth and higher living standards. If you can get the capital without saving, that would seem pretty close to paradise. This is where

American conservatives like Cheney think they are. They firmly believe that American democracy holds the secret to superior economic performance. Conservatives know that America's investment needs have long outstripped its now nonexistent savings. But they fully expect that foreigners will cover the gap indefinitely, both because they have no alternative to keeping their reserves in dollars and because they believe the U.S. economy will always yield the best return.

Recent history has seemed to justify this view. After raising concerns about declining competitiveness in the 1980s and recession in the early 1990s, the U.S. economy turned around to produce the longest boom in its history. It seemed to far outstrip the Japanese and European economies in both growth and productivity. On top of that, the Silicon Valley phenomenon, with its stock options, and the boiling NASDAQ market, were making everyone rich. Of course, foreign investors were putting their money in the United States. And who said Americans had no savings? Look at their capital gains in the stock market and at the skyrocketing equity in their homes. If you counted savings properly, it was argued by conservative economists, Americans were the world champions.

Then the market crashed, destroying $8 trillion of value. This is one reason market gains on paper don't count as savings. There were other flaws in the argument as well. Much of the growth was phony. The United States had experienced one of history's great investment bubbles, comparable to the South Seas bubble in the early eighteenth century, the Tulip bubble in the 1630s, and the Japanese bubble of the 1980s. The growth of such bubbles and their collapse are not usually considered signs of robust economic health.

Another apparent justification has been productivity growth. Productivity is the single most important thing in economics. It's the difference between a rich economy and a poor one. If I can produce twice as much as you in the same amount of time, I am going to be a lot richer than you. During the golden age of 1947–1973, productivity grew faster than it ever had, at about 2.8 percent annually. That's why real income more than doubled. For the next twenty years, however, productivity growth languished at about 1.5 percent and real income hardly moved. Then there was a huge jump to 2.5 percent annual productivity growth in the late 1990s, and everyone became euphoric about the new economy and its magnetism for foreign capital.

Still, it's not entirely clear that this jump was real. By creating huge excess investment, bubbles generate high rates of production, and factories running at 100 percent of capacity are always more productive than those limping along at 70 percent. The argument has been made that the huge infusion of IT equipment and processes that accompanied the bubble was a major factor in the jump in U.S. productivity, and it contains some truth. Although productivity growth fell off somewhat in the recession of 2001–2002, it has remained good over the past several years. U.S. analysts, comparing this to the approximately 1.5 percent rates of Europe and Japan, have not hesitated to attribute foreign capital flows to America to its apparently superior productivity.

Yet the way productivity is calculated and the effect of offshoring make it very hard to get an accurate accounting. For example, U.S. productivity calculations are done by a method known as hedonic scoring. Here's the deal. Last year you bought a laptop with a one gigabit hard drive and a Pentium 3 microprocessor for $2,000. This year you got one for your wife, but it had a two gigabit hard drive and a Pentium 5 chip, and it cost $1,000. Did computer production fall in the United States or did it double? Measured by price, it fell in half; but measured by computer power, it doubled. The U.S. government, using hedonic scoring, says it doubled. (It's actually more complicated than that, but you get the idea.) For sure, it didn't fall by half, but is your wife really using all that extra power? Maybe it didn't double either. After all, when you buy your new Cadillac with 400 horsepower to replace an old one that only had 200, you don't consider that you got two cars in place of one. Anyway, the key is that other countries don't use hedonic scoring, so it's not entirely clear how our productivity compares to theirs.

Then there's the effect of offshoring. When companies close factories and move production offshore, they close the worst plants first. Remember that productivity is the amount produced per worker per hour. When the unproductive plant closes, output per worker rises. That's very good, but what of the workers from the plant that closed? Unless they get new jobs that pay as well as and with the same productivity as the old jobs, they become a drag on the economy.

Offshoring adds another complication as well. When my tax accountant moved his back office to Bangalore, it didn't mean he was doing more tax returns. Rather, as he explained to me, by laying off his back office staff and outsourcing the work to India, he would save a huge amount of money. How would this play out in U.S. productivity accounting? Here's how it seems to work. Say my accountant sells $1,000 of tax returns. He pays nine back office employees a total of $500 to crunch the numbers and pockets $500 in profit for himself. Thus, before the switch to Bangalore, the U.S. economy gets to add $1,000 to GDP, and productivity is $100 per person employed. After the switch, the nine American back office workers have become fifteen Indian workers. The cost of doing the work in India is $100, which has to be deducted from the $1,000 gain to U.S. GDP. Thus the number of people required to do the work has increased, but as far as U.S. accounting is concerned, there is only one, my accountant. He is now making a profit of $900; and because he is now the only worker in the firm, productivity has gone to $900 per worker. U.S. GDP has decreased, and the number of people required to do the job has increased. But because most of those people are not in the United States, American productivity has taken an enormous jump. You see how slippery all this can become.

In truth, superior U.S. performance presently explains little of the foreign capital flow. The money now coming into the United States is largely not funding private investment. Rather, it is going into treasury bonds that fund budget deficits and excess U.S. consumption. When you borrow to invest, you expect to eventually pay off your loan and make a return. But when you borrow to throw a big party, you can expect only bigger credit card payments down the road, along with less money available for investment. That's Buffett's Squanderville, that's where the United States is right now.

Overstuffed Piggy Banks

The fault, however, doesn't lie entirely with the Americans. In their efforts to achieve rapid economic growth, first Japan, then the Asian tigers like South Korea and Singapore, and now China have all contributed to the American problem. In *The Wealth of Nations*, Adam Smith argued that the objective of economic activity is consumption. While this may be true for the Asian economies in some long-term sense, their development models all involve the suppression of consumption, along with a heavy emphasis on saving, investment, and production. In Singapore, for example, the government mandates large contributions to a pension fund. In Japan, consumer credit is limited even today. Asian savings rates, at 30 percent to over 50 percent of GDP, are higher than Western rates have ever been except in wartime, which is perhaps not surprising given that industrial development is seen in Asia as a key element of national security and of avoidance of Western dominance. For similar reasons, savings have frequently been channeled not by the invisible hands of bureaucrats. They push investments in industries they think will grow faster and enjoy higher productivity gains than others or that will raise the general level of industrial technology and prevent undesirable strategic dependence. Whether the strategy is economic or geopolitical, it is not aimed at satisfying consumers today.

We have already seen a number of examples of this. The semiconductor industry has been a favorite, with Japan, Taiwan, South Korea, and now China all promoting its development through special financial incentives and regulatory policies. These countries are prepared, in effect, to buy semiconductor plants because those plants are seen as universities-cum-research centers that will bring quick technology transfer. Sometimes there is another factor. In capital-intensive industries with only a few competitors, dominant companies can become quasi-monopolies earning high profits and paying high wages. Sometimes policymakers aim to ensure that their country includes companies that dominate these industries.

Thus, while competition and market forces operate, they are subject to intervention. Nor are the Asians the only ones to use these techniques. Americans and Europeans invented them; RCA and Airbus are good examples. But in the past fifty years they have been used more extensively and consistently in Asia than elsewhere.

High productivity usually requires economies of scale that in turn require mass production. The high Asian savings rates and the drive for mass production mean these countries always produce more than they consume. Their high savings rates mean they cannot sustain their own production and would all go into recession or depression if they suddenly had to depend on their internal demand. In short, they save and produce too much.

The Elephant in the Room

There is a solution to this problem—exports. "Export-led growth model" is the phrase coined to describe the Asian approach to economic development. The model has a number of variations. For example, Singapore and China have welcomed foreign direct investment, while Japan, Taiwan, and South Korea have resisted it. But there is a common feature: if you are a country that produces more than it consumes and depends on exports for growth, you don't want a lot of imports. You might want to import raw materials or commodities you don't make, but imports of what you do make, or of products in industries you are trying to build, interfere with your growth. Thus there is a constant temptation to protect, particularly in "strategic" areas. In practice, this temptation has been yielded to in different ways. The Japanese market has long been notoriously difficult to penetrate, while Hong Kong and Singapore are pretty easy, and China is surprisingly open. However, one characteristic common to all the key Asian economies except Hong Kong (which is essentially dollarized) is managed currencies. They are either pegged to the dollar, like China's yuan, or the object of frequent central bank intervention in the currency markets to conduct a "dirty float." Either way, they usually keep their currencies undervalued versus the dollar.

International economics employs a simple accounting equation to explain the causes and dynamics of the U.S. trade (more accurately, current account) deficit:

Exports – Imports (the trade balance) = Private Savings + Government Budget Surplus (or deficit) – Domestic Investment

A trade surplus means the sum of private savings and government surpluses or deficits is greater than domestic investment. A trade deficit means the opposite. Over the past twenty-five years, nearly all the discussion of this equation has been based on the assumption that the action is from right to left. In other words, low private savings and government budget deficits have driven the American trade deficits.

Nonetheless, because the formula is an equation, the causality can run from left to right as well. An excess of imports over exports could be causing a reduction in private savings and/or an increase in the U.S. government budget deficit. This is the effect of protectionism, pegged currencies, and "dirty floats." Companies producing in the United States sell less than they otherwise would, workers earn less, the government collects less in taxes. The result is a shortage of savings relative to investment and an ever larger trade deficit. Just as foreign governments suppress their domestic consumption, so they also help suppress U.S. savings. This is the elephant in the corner that is rarely discussed in polite company.

It is not discussed because to do so would be to challenge free trade policies that have formed the bedrock of the international economy for over half a century. The mismanagement of the global economy that worsened the Great Depression and helped bring on World War II taught postwar leaders an important lesson. Protectionism not only doesn't work; it can be dangerous. That lesson was the foundation of the postwar economic institutions, of the spread of the liberal trading regime, and of the whole second wave of globalization. The new system, built on free trade principles, succeeded because those principles are essentially sound, and there is great truth in the free trade analysis when its major assumptions are operative. But like generals fighting the last war, economists have too frequently fought the last depression while ignoring important new realities.

The British banker and economist David Ricardo first elaborated the principles of free trade in the early nineteenth century by using the example of trade between England and Portugal. With its wet cool climate, England raised sheep and made woolens that were exported to Portugal. Conversely the warm, sunny climate of Portugal was ideal for growing grapes from which the Portuguese fermented wine that they exported to England. Of course, it was possible for the Portuguese to raise sheep and for the English to culture grapes in some locales, but neither of the climates was well suited to these tasks. Both countries would raise their standard of living by doing what they did best and trading for the rest. Ricardo further demonstrated that even if one country could both make woolens and ferment wine more efficiently than the other, each would still benefit by specializing in what it did best and importing to supply other needs. Or take the extreme case in which one country, say Portugal, insists on being self-sufficient even though this raises prices for its consumers. England is still better off by specializing in woolens and importing Portuguese wine. That the Portuguese irrationally penalize their consumers is no reason for the English to do likewise. The Portuguese are only hurting themselves. This theory of comparative advantage is mathematically unassailable and has been elaborated over the years to form the solid underpinning of international trade theory and of the myriad of free trade agreements that have dramatically lifted global living standards over the past half century.

It is important to note, however, that the theory rests on certain conditions. Ricardo was writing before the industrial revolution had really taken hold. By observation he could see that the direction of most of the trade of his day was determined by differences between countries in climate, resources, and topography. Gold was the international money and there was no "dirty float." Economies of scale hardly applied to sheep herding or winemaking, and both were mature industries without steep learning curves. Markets were mostly for competitive commodities in which producers had no power to influence the total quantity produced or the prices asked. No extra profits or "rents" were derived from dominant market positions. Finally, there was little intellectual property and technology, labor, and capital did not move easily from one country to another. Many of these conditions still apply to trade such as that in wheat or exotic flowers. But in the modern world, they frequently don't apply.

To see the limitations of some of the assumptions, let's take the example of hydro-generators, the machines that generate electricity from rushing water. In 1982, when I was counselor to the Secretary of Commerce, there were about ten manufacturers of such equipment in the world. Allis Chalmers was the last American corporation in the group. One day Allis representatives came to complain about unfair bidding. They had data showing a pattern of dramatic underbidding by several Japanese companies on a series of contracts let by various U.S. municipalities. On one contract, all the bids would be around, say, $10 million except Japanese company A, which would come in at $5 million. On the next contract, for the same kind of equipment from the same bidders, Japanese company B would be in at $5 million. Obviously illegal, collusive bid rigging was taking place.

The Commerce Department wanted to initiate an investigation, but to do so it needed the support of the Council of Economic Advisers. The brother of a close friend of mine happened to be on the council, so I approached him about the council's view. Amazingly, I was told the council saw no problem. The U.S. municipalities, he said, were getting cheap generators and making cheap electricity and selling it at low prices to consumers. Why complain? I answered that Allis Chalmers would probably have to go out of business and lay off several thousand employees. "So what?" was the response. "They can find other work in the service economy. Services are growing." When I noted that there were high costs involved in closing down a company and having whole communities look for a new livelihood, I was told that the gains to consumers outweighed these costs. Then I noted that in Japan these same companies monopolized the market and engaged in similar bid rigging, but at much higher prices because there was no outside competition. What would happen, I asked, when all the other companies had been driven out of the business and the Japanese began to raise their U.S. prices to Japanese levels? The response was that the American companies then could come back into the market. I was stunned. Here was a very intelligent person of great reputation who simply didn't understand the practical realities of the modern marketplace. Soon after this Allis did go out of business and prices did rise.

Not all economists are quite so ivory tower. Paul Krugman and Joseph Stiglitz, for instance, have done groundbreaking work on the issues of free trade, uncertainty, and modern market dynamics. Krugman is noted for his work demonstrating that free trade may not always be the best way for a country to raise living standards. He wrote in the 1980s that much of trade appears to require an explanation in terms of economies of scale, learning curves, and the dynamics of innovation—all phenomena incompatible with the kind of idealizations under which free trade is always the best policy. Economists refer to such phenomena as "market imperfections," a term conveying the presumption that they are marginal to a system which approaches ideal performance fairly closely. In reality, however, imperfections may be the rule rather than the exception.[11]

Krugman went on to explain two ways in which an activist trade policy might benefit a country more than free trade—by seeking rents and external economies. In economist-speak "rent" means profits or wages in one industry that are higher than those in a comparable industry (think of those Boeing 747 profits). The conventional view is that rents are not an issue because in a competitive economy there won't be many. If a particular industry looks very profitable, others will quickly enter and compete the rents away. In reality, however, there are often barriers—such as the need for very large scale production, huge upfront capital costs, or steep learning curves—that keep competitors out and profits high. Think of Microsoft, for example. Why aren't other companies rushing to write and market operating systems to compete with the hugely profitable Windows? Krugman demonstrated mathematically that in this type of situation, the use of government subsidies or protection of the market at a critical moment could well improve a country's welfare over the free trade scenario.

"Externalities" is economist-speak for benefits arising from an activity that can be diffused to others not engaged in the activity. Learning how to run laboratories, for example, is a kind of knowledge that can be diffused far beyond a specific lab. The acquisition of such "externalities" can also be stimulated by appropriate government intervention. This is why China offers free land and tax holidays to get semiconductor plants, and why so many central bankers seem to enjoy dirty floating.

Despite this new strategic trade analysis, the conventional wisdom has been hard to shake. In response to a statement by the chairman of the Council of Economic Advisers, Gregory Mankiw, that offshoring of jobs was good for the U.S. economy, a storm of protest arose in the Congress and on the shop floor. Then a roll call of big-name economists rose to Mankiw's defense with all the conventional free trade arguments. They were all true too—if you assumed full employment, no dirty float, no free land and tax holiday subsidies abroad, no learning from doing externalities, and no rents. But these economists should have known that every one of those assumptions is frequently at odds with the reality of today's markets.

Why did they make a defense that rested on an unreal view of the world? For two reasons. One was inertia: the strength of academic tradition, the old fear of protectionism, and the ingrained view that even if the other guy subsidizes and protects, you are still better off with free trade. The second was distrust of American democracy. Privately most economists accept the strategic trade analysis. But they fear how it could be mishandled by Congress. Better a suboptimal free trade regime, they believe, than a strategic trade policy dictated by K Street lobbyists. This is not an unreasonable position. The U.S. Congress and the government generally are capable of amazingly stupid things. The problem, however, is that if the other guy is doing it and you're not responding in some way, you become part of his policy—a policy aimed at beating you.

The Seen Hand at Work

This possibility has been brilliantly demonstrated by Ralph Gomory and William Baumol in a little noted but extremely important book entitled *Global Trade and Conflicting National Interests*. The essence of their argument is that while the Ricardian world of climate- and resource-based comparative advantage permits only one best economic outcome for both trading partners, that is not true for most of today's trade, where economies of scale and other factors are decisive. Rather, there are many possible outcomes that, once established, can be maintained indefinitely, depending on what countries actually choose to do, what capabilities, natural or manmade, they actually develop. These outcomes vary in their consequences with some being good for one, some for the other, and some for both. Often the best outcome for one country is a poor outcome for its trading partner. This means that in a modern free trade environment, a country's welfare is critically dependent on the success in international trade of the industries within its borders (that may or may not be its citizens).[12]

Gomory and Baumol show that because there is no universally best outcome, national trade interests often conflict. An industrialized country benefits from trade with a newly industrializing country up to a point. But after that point, acquisition of more industries by the developing country actually becomes harmful to its industrialized trading partner.[13] At that point, the developed country's interests are best served by competing vigorously to maintain its industrial and technological advantages. If it fails to do so, its prosperity will be diminished. For a long time, the United States and, to a lesser extent, Europe have not only failed to respond to the competitive challenge of developing countries but have actually embraced the disappearance of important industries.

The Gomory and Baumol work seems to have shifted the academic center of gravity. In several articles former Reagan administration assistant Treasury secretary Paul Craig Roberts has pointed to the current absence of most of the key conditions of classic free trade. He notes that

> for comparative advantage to work, a country's labor, capital, and technology must not move offshore. The internal cost ratios that determine comparative advantage reflect the quantity and quality of the country's technology and capital. If these factors move abroad to where cheap labor makes them more productive, absolute advantage takes over from comparative advantage.[14]

Lester Thurow has written in a similar vein. The conventional conclusion that everyone wins from trade, he notes, is subject to the assumption that full employment will be maintained. Otherwise, short-term economic losses could easily outweigh long-term gains. Moreover, the conventional analysis assumes that workers losing their jobs get new jobs at wages equal to what they had. In reality full employment is rarely maintained, and American workers who lose manufacturing jobs and manage to get new jobs in the service and retailing sectors can count on a 25 percent pay cut.[15]

Last but very far from least is the ninety-two-year-old dean of American economists, Paul A. Samuelson. Ricardian proof of the efficacy of free trade and comparative advantage, he says, "does not deny that the new technical Chinese progress in goods in which America previously had a competitive advantage can, all else being equal, permanently lower measurable per capita U.S. real income."[16] Thus do the winds of changing views blow through the academy. But whether they will have any effect on policy and business is very much open to question, because of another economic theory.

Equal Pay for Equal Work

Along with comparative advantage, "factor price equalization" is one of the foundations of international trade theory. It's simple. The idea is that in a world of open markets, the same factors of production ought to cost the same everywhere. The best example is the price of oil. There is a world price that is quoted on commodity exchanges around the globe every day. The same grade of oil costs the same whether it is sold in Tokyo, London, New York, Houston, or Singapore. Wheat and other commodities behave similarly. There is not an American price for hard red winter wheat and another price in India and yet another in South Africa. It's all about the same.

In principle, this should be true of labor too. Why should my wife's hairdresser cost more in Washington, D.C., than a hairdresser doing exactly the same job in the same amount of time in downtown Bangalore? Basically because my wife can't get to Bangalore conveniently. If she could, she would, and the cost of hair dressing would quickly equalize between the two cities. Right now, the Washington hairdresser is riding on the overall greater productivity and consequent higher living standard of the United States as compared to India. Even if she is not more productive, other parts of the economy are, and she gets a fee that reflects that generally higher standard. But if you could move people to Bangalore as fast as e-mail, a lot of prices would change quickly; hence the concerns I expressed in the prologue.

This is exactly what is happening as a result of the move to outsourcing offshore. When software is written in Bangalore instead of Silicon Valley, the price of the factor we call programmers is being equalized. There is the example of Jon Carson in Boston who, in a jam and needing programmers but uneasy about shipping the work to India, got U.S. programmers to accept Indian pay rates.[17]

While international trade and trade deficits are often blamed for "lost jobs," jobs are not the real issue. What really bites is what the jobs pay. Economists frequently ignore the factor price equalization discussion because they say wages in developing countries will rise along with productivity as the economies move up the scale of industrialization and as demand for labor bids up its price. There is no doubt that this happens. People used to talk of cheap Japanese labor, but now it costs more than American labor. The price of an English-speaking Chinese electrical engineer with an American MBA and ten years of experience is moving up very rapidly. But generally speaking, the addition of 3 billion new capitalists to the global labor pool almost overnight in the context of instant worldwide communications and networked production with express delivery is likely to have an equalizing effect on many wages. There is no doubt that Asian wages will rise, but the interval could be long.

I was therefore amused during the 2004 presidential election campaign to hear both candidates proclaim that "American workers can compete with anybody as long as the playing field is level." This is nonsense. They can't, and we shouldn't want them to. What is the point of all the public and private investment in education, R&D, and expensive equipment, if not to give our workers an advantage? As Paul Craig Roberts says,

> without different internal cost ratios, there is no basis for comparative advantage. Outsourcing is driven by absolute advantage.

Asia has an absolute advantage because of its vast excess supply of skilled and educated labor. With First World capital, technology, and business knowhow, this labor can be just as productive as First World labor, but workers can be hired for much less money.[18]

The stars are now aligned to drive more hiring of inexpensive workers. Countries may think in terms of comparative advantage, but businesses think in absolute terms. Consider my company and your company. I produce left-handed widgets, and you produce right-handed ones. You are the best in the world at making right-handed widgets. You can also make left-handed widgets more cheaply than I can, but for the moment you buy from me because that frees you up to concentrate on right-handed widgets, in which you are the world champ. This is comparative advantage at work, but it is not comfortable for me as a CEO. At any moment, you could decide to jump into my business and knock me out of the market or force my price down. So I look for any opportunity to get my costs under yours in absolute terms. If I can do that by moving my plant to China, that's what I'll do. Thus business is driving the global system toward trade based on absolute advantage rather than on classic comparative advantage. The comment by the President's Council of Advisers on Science and Technology that the only way to win is to do things no one else can do is an absolutist doctrine and comes from the heart of American business. But it could be coming from Japanese, European, or Chinese business as well.

Things That Can't Go On, Don't

In Washington you often hear the phrase "This can't go on." The late economist Herbert Stein used to answer, "Things that can't go on, don't." The $64,000 question before the world today concerns the U.S. current account deficit and the dollar. Will they go on? The recent prominence of the dollar in the world's leading periodicals reveals growing anxiety. Despite the nervous edge of headlines like "The Makings of a Meltdown," many analysts remain sanguine.[19] The U.S. economy is growing faster, they argue, and has more rapidly increasing productivity than any other economy and thus will continue to be the most attractive place for foreigners to invest their money. In early December 2004 the Federal Reserve Bank of New York released a report predicting strong productivity growth at 2.6 percent annually for the next ten years. This is far above the rate of 1973–1995 and represents a continuation of the strong productivity growth of the dot-com era. Combining this with population growth, the Fed predicted a trend growth rate for GDP of 3.3 percent, about double that of the European and Japanese economies.[20]

The growth argument is supplemented by the "no alternative to the dollar" view espoused by longtime Wall Street guru Henry Kaufman.[21] As the world's only superpower, he says, the United States has much better growth than other big economies with little risk of inflation, and it has deeper, broader, better organized markets that currently provide a better return than any other. Then comes Kaufman's final, intriguing point: realigning global economic and financial relationships in a smooth and orderly fashion is currently beyond the cooperative and organization capacity of the Chinese, Japanese, and Europeans. China would have to revalue the yuan by 50 percent to 70 percent, Japan would have to turn its aging citizens into bigger spenders than they have ever been, and Europe would have to turn inflationary. Since none of them are going to do any of this, Kaufman argues, they have no alternative but to continue buying U.S. Treasuries in support of the dollar. They may do it kicking and screaming, but they will do it.

Academic commentary has been less bullish on growth than the headlines, but also less nervous. One widely noted study by Catherine Mann looked at a number of countries and concluded that the United States could sustain a current account deficit of a little over 4 percent of GDP.[22] When the paper was written in early 2002, the deficit was 4.3 percent of GDP and thus presumably sustainable. Mann noted, however, that the deficit would become unsustainable at some point barring significant structural changes, and suggested that one such change could arise from global trade in services. Because the services share of GDP normally rises as economies develop, and because new technologies and trade liberalization have made it easier to trade services, there could be a dramatic shift in the U.S. trade account. U.S. exporters of services, said Mann, are "highly competitive" and could take advantage of the new technology to penetrate foreign markets and reverse the long-term trends of U.S. trade. Absent such a shift, however, Mann concluded with what seems to be the current academic conventional wisdom: things are sustainable for now, but Americans will gradually have to adjust to a falling dollar and pressure for less consumption and more saving.

These are all good arguments, but they accept American mythologies too readily and ignore the realities of the new capitalist road. It is comforting to Americans to keep telling themselves they have the best productivity and GDP growth and will therefore remain the location of choice for foreign investment. But is it true? While there is much evidence to indicate that U.S. productivity has indeed taken a jump, there is also cause for prudence about this conclusion. Beyond the weaknesses I have already outlined, other evidence suggests that the U.S. performance may not be as overwhelming as it looks. The *Financial Times* columnist Martin Wolf points out a paper by Credit Suisse First Boston showing that, from 1992 to 2002, real net domestic product per hour increased just 1.1 percent annually in the United States, while gaining 1.4 percent in the Eurozone.[23] If you remove the effects of the Internet bubble, in other words, the United States looks a lot like Europe. Another point is hours. While American productivity per worker per year is improving faster than that of Europe, on a per hour basis the Europeans are starting to come out ahead. This once again raises the issue of living standards. Americans are not only working more hours than Europeans or Japanese, they are working six more weeks a year today than they did twenty years ago.[24] Yet median family income has not risen much. What's going on? Wages are supposed to rise with productivity. Either the productivity gains are not really there or they are all going to shareholders. The latter would be consistent with the likely impact of 3 billion new capitalists on wages. In either case it is difficult to see how rapid GDP growth can be sustained

if workers don't get some of the benefits of rising productivity. Beyond this, the growth is also suspect. As chief IMF chief economist
Ken Rogoff says, the United States is getting the "best recovery money
can buy."[25]

The U.S. economy is a bit of a Potemkin village. GDP growth is high,
unemployment appears to be low, and household wealth appears to be
increasing. But a closer look reveals a more sobering reality. America's
growth is in part borrowed from the future. It's like a company striving
to make its annual sales projections by offering special incentives to
its accounts to stock up now, before the year closes, instead of waiting
to resupply at the normal time. We might call it "shipping in place."
U.S. consumers are consuming, but with borrowed money as they
have mortgaged their homes to maintain living standards. Yet because
investment and production have not kept pace with consumption,
more of this borrowed money is flowing overseas to pay for imports.
At a national level, Federal Reserve chairman Alan Greenspan says the
U.S. government budget deficit is a threat to long-term stability because it is not subject to correction by market forces.[26] At the same
time, the country's net international debt is high and rising rapidly.
This is not a healthy kind of growth, and analysts like Morgan Stanley's
chief economist, Stephen Roach, emphasize that it can't be sustained
in view of the "profound income leakage arising from global labor
arbitrage."[27]

As for unemployment, it's easy to keep it low if you put 2 percent of
all the men in the country in jail and don't count them as unemployed,
which the United States currently does. Further, we only count as unemployed those receiving unemployment benefits or who tell poll tak-
ers they are actively seeking a job. To see how this works, look at Kan-
napolis, North Carolina. When the town's only mill shut down,
reported unemployment soared. A year later, however, unemployment
magically disappeared—not because people got jobs, but because
their benefits ran out.[28] The real story of the U.S. economy is rising
hours worked, rising debt, and job creation largely restricted to low-
paying categories like retail sales and fast food restaurants. This is not
a formula for long-term prosperity.

The impact of 3 billion new capitalists on the United States, along with America's abuse of the dollar and its soaring public and private debt, has made foreign central bankers and finance ministers very nervous. They are all in a global game of financial chicken. If foreigners dumped a large portion of their dollar holdings, the dollar would fall dramatically and cause a recession or even a depression in the United States. Because the rest of the world lives by selling to the Americans, a U.S. recession could be devastating to the rest of the world's economies. Dumping dollars could precipitate global stock and bond market crashes that would bring huge losses to, among others, those doing the dumping. From this perspective, Americans are holding the world's financiers hostage. On the other hand, should things fall apart, the first player who gets out of dollars will take the smallest loss. Thus any hint of significant dollar dumping is likely to cause a chain reaction—fast.

If you are a finance minister or central bank director, this possibility creates two worries. First, if it looks like things are beginning to fall apart and you don't move, you could wind up losing billions for your country, along with your reputation. Second, Americans owe so much that they are sure to be tempted to inflate the debt away. If they do that while you are steadfastly holding on, you will again lose gobs of money, and your epitaph will not be heroic. So all the players, or nearly all (about which more later), are damned if they do and damned if they don't. So far they haven't, but tomorrow is another day.

Recently everyone's nervousness has been reflected in some interesting moves. As private money abandoned the dollar over the past two years, the European Central Bank followed free market principles and refrained from any intervention in the currency markets. American officials said they wanted a strong dollar, but their body language said weak dollar. Consequently the euro, which had languished during the dot-com boom, gained over 35 percent against the dollar in a two-year period, just as Soros had predicted. The Bank of Japan, on the other hand, engaged in massive intervention, buying over 623 billion dollars in 2003 in a largely successful effort to prevent the dollar from falling against the yen.[29] Because the Bank of China keeps the yuan pegged to the dollar by law, it doesn't intervene in the exchange markets as the Japanese do. But its trade surplus means that to hold the peg, the bank has to keep accumulating dollars. While doing so, however, the Chinese have quietly been buying lots of oil. They need the oil, and buying it now with strong dollars is a way to avoid investing in U.S. Treasuries, whose value could plummet in a crisis. The oil producers, in turn, have been taking the dollars from the Chinese and selling them for euros and euro bonds, putting more upward pressure on the euro. The Russians only added fuel to the euro fire when they announced the decision to reverse the dollar-euro ratio of their international reserve holdings. This activity has begun to price European goods out of international markets. As a result, the Europeans are now talking about "stabilizing" the dollar by organizing a joint buying operation with the Japanese. So far the system is still holding together, but it is increasingly shaky.

No one knows for certain what will happen, but clearly the global financial markets could implode very quickly. Former Federal Reserve chairman Paul Volcker says there is a 75 percent chance of a dollar crash within the next five years. This is Soros's great fear too. In public statements and in conversations with me, he has expressed concern about the market fundamentalist view that prevails in Washington and parts of Wall Street. This is the belief that markets are self-correcting and best left alone—a dangerous siren song, says Soros. Far from being self-correcting, he emphasizes, markets tend to excess. They overshoot. Anyone with any experience of markets knows this. When markets are going down, all the weaknesses get concentrated, and you need intervention at the right time to stop things from getting out of control. If the dollar started to melt down, the results could be really nasty. A 1930s-style global depression is not out of the question.[30]

The lack of an alternative to the dollar is the only reason it hasn't taken a big fall already. But now those alternatives are emerging. The euro, though not a perfect substitute, is becoming more attractive. Besides the Russians, others are also sneaking into euros, which is why it has recently strengthened so much.[31] In Asia there is serious discussion of creating an Asian currency unit, or Acu, in imitation of the European Ecu, which preceded the euro.[32]

In the end, it is very simple: the global economy is highly distorted. Americans consume too much and save nothing and the rest of the world, especially Asia, consumes too little and saves too much. There are three ways for this situation to work itself out. Americans could consume less and save and invest more. The fastest way to do this would be to cut the federal budget deficit. There are two problems. If Americans take all the adjustment, it would entail a big reduction of GDP. Since no political leader could survive that, it is not going to happen voluntarily. Nor is the federal deficit likely to be cut. If anything, it will increase as the baby boomers retire and cause a dramatic rise in social security and medicare payments. The second option would be for Asia and the rest of the world to cut saving and increase consumption. That will undoubtedly occur over the long run, but in the short run it would slow up the growth that is the raison d'être of these regimes, especially China's. Moreover, if it did occur, the reduction of the flow of Asian savings to U.S. financial markets would cause the dollar to fall.

That is, of course, the third and by far most likely event. When and how it might occur no one knows. Most analysts would like to see a smooth, gradual decline of 30–50 percent from present dollar values. How things develop will be significantly determined by China. To many Western economists China's policies seem foolishly mercantilist. But China's accumulation of dollar reserves has given it great negotiating leverage against the United States, and its policies induce rapid industrial development and technology transfer. So China might decide to prop the dollar up for a long time, as will, almost certainly, Japan. Europe might even join in to avoid the pain of the rising euro. But there is always the unexpected. Vladimir Putin is increasingly unhappy with the United States. Could he show his dissatisfaction by dumping dollars? What about OPEC? There are surely a number of members who have no love of the United States and might jump at an opportunity to dethrone the dollar. Remember also that before the Asian financial crisis of 1997, no one anticipated the damage hedge funds could cause. Recently a little bond market maneuver by Citibank caused a scary ripple in the European markets. There's no guarantee that something like that won't trigger a dramatic dollar crisis, and if it does, it won't just be another decline. It will be the end of the dollar's dominant role as the world's money.

It is on this—the end of the dollar's hegemony—that Soros and Buffett are betting. That, after all, is the logical outcome when some people squander their resources and others take thrift to the extreme.

CHAPTER 10

The Comfortable Road to Ruin

Nothing Is Safe

—JIM HEMMERLING

BOSTON CONSULTING GROUP

Leaders of both U.S. political parties frequently insist that American workers can compete with any in the world on a level playing field. I thought about that at a recent reunion of my high school class of 1959. We graduated at the peak of the post–World War II golden age, when the huge economies of scale of history's first mass market made American companies and American labor by far the most productive in the world. This was truly a time when American workers could compete with any on the planet—even as they earned the highest pay.

After graduation many of my classmates simply walked a few blocks down the road to the General Motors assembly plant near Wilmington, Delaware, and joined the production line. Outsourcing in those days was a matter of sending work around the corner to a local machine shop. Nobody had ever heard of offshoring. Meeting with all my friends forty-five years later, I was surprised that so many had been retired for so long. Most seemed to have condos at the shore. None seemed worried about medical care or adequate pensions. With no more than a high school education they had been able to get union jobs that paid up to $100,000 a year with overtime. These jobs also came with defined benefit pensions and lifetime medical care indexed to inflation. Most of them had sent their kids to college and many had put them through medical and law school as well. My class had truly lived the American Dream.

As we all chewed over old times, I wondered how our children and grandchildren would fare in the third wave of globalization with 3 billion new competitors. On the one hand, great benefits will accrue to those who know how. On the other hand, there will be immense challenges both at home and abroad. A lot will ride on how well they respond to these opportunities and challenges compared to their peers around the globe, who from now on will also be next door.

From Offshore to Inshore

In view of the investment, technology, and jobs moving to China, India, and elsewhere, the question uppermost in the minds of many of our children and grandchildren is, Will everything go offshore? To which the short answer is no. The United States, Europe, and Japan are not going to blow away overnight. Indeed, parallel to the "offshoring" trend is a significant "inshoring" movement in which foreign companies move factories and jobs into U.S., European, or Japanese markets. The United States has long been the leading recipient nation of direct foreign investment (i.e., investment in concrete facilities rather than portfolio investment in stocks and bonds). In 2003 China took over the top spot with an inflow of $55 billion. But the inflow into the United States was still $40 billion. The whole EU received about $125 billion, with France leading the way at close to $50 billion.[1] As a result of these inward flows, foreign firms employ about 6 million workers in their American operations.[2]

A good example of inshoring is the 2002 decision by the Swiss pharmaceutical giant Novartis to move its main research operations from Basel to Boston—a shift that brought four hundred top-level research jobs from Switzerland to Massachusetts. Another example, Glaxo-SmithKline, still maintains its legal headquarters in Britain, but its chief executive and head of research work out of Philadelphia. The Franco-German firm Aventis manages its research from New Jersey, and Pharmacia, formerly Swedish, is now completely U.S. run. Novartis chief Dan Vasella says he may move his Swiss operational base to the United States as well.[3] Behind these moves, three major factors make the U.S. market the most attractive one for pharmaceutical investment. First, the U.S. government and industry are spending more on medical and biotech research than anybody else. Second, the U.S. government is less restrictive than others regarding what pharmaceutical companies may tell the public about their products. Finally, the lack of medical price controls means that the U.S. market is by far the most profitable in the world.

The United States has also become a surprisingly popular location for investment by foreign automakers. In 1993, just as the Pentagon announced closure of the Charleston naval base and South Carolina's tobacco and textile industries suffered heavy losses, Mercedes Benz announced a new assembly plant that would bring the state 3,700 jobs. Things got even better when BMW broke ground for its first plant outside Germany and brought twenty-two of its suppliers with it. The combined $1.6 billion investment created 5,500 high-wage jobs just when they were most needed. A kind of bandwagon effect was created. Over the next several years, fifty-seven more German companies set up operations in the state along Interstate 85, which earned the nickname the "American autobahn."[4] This phenomenon has been repeated by Toyota, Honda, and Nissan in such states as West Virginia, Kentucky, and Tennessee.

Behind these investments is the fact that the U.S. auto market is the world's largest while skilled U.S.autoworkers now earn less than their Japanese and European counterparts. Further, labor costs for foreign makers in the U.S. market are lower than those of Detroit because the foreign-owned plants have younger workforces and no overhang of health and pension costs for retirees. Production based in China and elsewhere is not yet competitive in quality and overall cost. No doubt it will be sometime, but for now these "transplant" producers have found a sweet spot in the U.S. market. American plants are also a hedge against congressional protectionist backlash as well as a falling dollar. They also automatically obtain all the benefits of NAFTA.

Nor are investments limited to pharmaceuticals and autos. Despite the rush of semiconductor makers to invest in Asia, the giant Samsung Electronics of Korea recently decided on a $500 million addition to its $1.6 billion installation in Austin, Texas.[5] China's Haier invested $40 million in a refrigerator manufacturing plant in Camden, South Carolina—the Haier America Industrial Park.

What is true for America also holds in Europe. The Czech Republic has a manufacturing sector that is growing not only in absolute terms but as a percentage of GDP. Says Jan Mladek, the government's chief economic adviser, "We are the workshop of Europe."[6] Slovakia has attracted so much investment from foreign automakers that it produces more cars per capita of population than any other country in the world.[7] Even Mexico, despite the loss of many maquiladora plants, attracted nearly $15 billion of direct foreign investment in 2004.[8] In sum, while China and India are and increasingly will be the locations of choice for manufacturing, software, and services of all kinds, other locations will continue to have their own competitive or strategic advantages. How well they use those advantages will be the key to their future.

Moving to Equal

While the opportunities and benefits of the third wave will be enormous, no one should be under any illusions about the nature of competition in this new world of no time and no space with 3 billion new capitalists. My classmates lived comfortable middle class American lives on the basis of a high school education. That age is over. In the third wave of globalization, neither their children nor particularly their grandchildren will have the same kind of life, even with a much better education.

From Pekin to Peking

To see why, go to Pekin, Illinois. Said to be directly opposite Beijing (old Peking) on the globe, Pekin was named after the Chinese capital. Its high school teams were called the Chinks until 1981, when the more politically correct *Dragons* was adopted. Today Pekin has more serious concerns than the names of its teams. Excel Foundry and Machine Corporation, a local family-owned firm making parts for heavy construction equipment, has already moved 12 percent of its production to China in a last-ditch effort to hold onto business threatened by China's large, low-cost foundries. And Doug Parsons, CEO and family head, is thinking he will have to move much more, perhaps all of it, to survive over the next decade. Farther west, the blue jeans inventor Levi Strauss decided it had to move everything. On September 25, 2003, it closed its last U.S. factory with a loss of 2,000 jobs.[9] Toy maker Mattel, furniture producer Bassett, electronics giant Hewlett-Packard, and many more are moving to China. And companies aren't moving just from America. In Szekesfehervar, Hungary, the blue, green, and white facade of an IBM disk drive factory looks down from a hill onto a busy shopping plaza. Built just a few years ago, it still looks new. But the loading docks stand empty and the turnstiles are padlocked. IBM closed the plant over a year ago and sent the work to China, where wages are a quarter of those in Hungary.[10]

In Mexico the story is similar. Since 2003, as many as 500 maquiladora factories and 500,000 jobs have departed for China.[11] Half a world away, Japanese manufacturers are also rushing to China. NEC has moved its hard drive production from the Philippines to Shanghai; Toshiba has put its PC production in Hangzhou and thirty-three other locations scattered around China; Pioneer has 3,550 workers turning out DVDs around the clock in its plant south of Shanghai. Japanese companies have plowed $9 billion in new investment into Shanghai in the past five years.[12] Meanwhile Finland's Nokia, like its competitor Motorola, has moved much of its mobile phone production to China, and Siemens has moved half of its mobile phone R&D there as well. For Volkswagen, China is the most important market and production base outside of Germany. Ironically, the largest exporter from China in 2002 was the Taiwanese firm Honhai Electronics. With 40,000 companies and over $100 billion of investment on the mainland, Taiwan is by far the leader in outsourcing to mainland China. Its companies have over 50 percent of the world markets for keyboards, motherboards, monitors, and laptop computers, and production of this is all being moved to the mainland. The move by the Japanese is perhaps the most significant because they have long resisted transferring production offshore. But now the sentiment has changed. As Pioneer Shanghai chairman Hiroyuki Mineta explains, "We hesitated in the past, but we cannot say that anymore. We have to overcome our fear or we won't be able to survive."[13] Jim Hemmerling of the Boston Consulting Group (BCG) in Shanghai sums the situation up best when he says, "Nothing is safe."[14]

While most people only see the Chinese-made consumer products, BCG says the real battle now shaping up is in the $2 trillion market for industrial goods, everything from small motors to locomotives. Until now the first world's technological edge and established networks of high quality suppliers have kept production of these products at home. But no more. Now, says BCG, moving to China can save 20–35 percent, with no loss of quality even in production of the most sophisticated equipment. For this reason the Chinese will get most of the key manufacturing markets. How can China do this? Partly it is "pervasive industrial policies" that use both financial incentives along with hints of loss of favor in China to attract key investments. Very significant, however, is the fact that whereas Japan re-invented manufacturing during its rise to wealth, China is de-inventing manufacturing by removing capital and reintroducing skilled manual labor on the plant floor. Its low costs allow a rethink of every business process that, in addition to cost savings, enables less complexity in plant processes and a shorter time to market. Finally, there is the huge risk of opportunity loss by not being in China. To avoid that, business leaders will take risks to invest in China that they wouldn't consider in other markets like Mexico, for instance.

Thus manufacturing jobs in the advanced countries are either gone or going. Not all of them but a lot of them, and, more importantly, gone or going are their wage levels. In the United States in the past twenty-five years, manufacturing has declined from about 23 percent of GDP to about 12.7 percent while manufacturing employment has declined from 21 percent to 11 percent of the total workforce. Today, in 2005, 16 million people are employed in manufacturing in the United States, the same as in the early 1950s.[15] It is not that absolute levels of production have declined; actually they have doubled since 1980 and quadrupled since 1950. But they have not grown as fast as the economy. Most disturbing is the trend in wages and household income, which peaked in 1972 while manufacturing was 23 percent of U.S. GDP. Since then the relative stagnation of manufacturing has coincided with a steady decline in wage income levels.

Shedding Jobs

There is now a great debate over whether the main culprit is outsourcing and offshoring or the introduction of labor-saving technology. The answer, of course, is both. Most economists emphasize the introduction of technology and consider outsourcing and offshoring of minor significance. But the fact that the new factories in China are being dumbed down as a way to reduce capital costs in the context of a large supply of very inexpensive labor suggests that outsourcing and offshoring may be significant factors. Whatever the case, the entire debate misses the point. The real issue is whether there is going to be another source of good jobs. Over the years it has been argued that, with the United States in the lead, the advanced countries increasingly will shift to service-based economies. And certainly services have shown rapid growth. The 30 million service workers of 1950 have increased to 110 million in 2005.[16] This is why, as the U.S. trade deficit in manufactured goods soared in the 1980s and the early years of this century, many economists argued there was no need for alarm. It was assumed that software, sophisticated services like banking and product design, and high technology, where our native bent toward innovation is unparalled, would keep us comfortably in the style to which we had become accustomed.

As manufacturing jobs steadily disappeared over the past twenty years, workers made a major shift to software and service industries. But since the collapse of the technology bubble, good software and services jobs in the developed economies have also become harder to find. From 6.5 million in 2000, the U.S. IT workforce declined to 5.9 million in 2003 despite an upturn in the U.S. economy and a strong international economy.[17] The unemployment rate for computer programmers was 6.4 percent in 2003, and for electrical and electronic engineers, it was 6.2 percent. For the first time ever, this was higher than the 5.6 percent unemployment rate for all workers.[18] Not surprisingly, wage increases in these fields have fallen dramatically as well.

These figures reflect two developments. One is the aftermath of the collapse of the "irrational exuberance" of the 1990s. The other is the sheer number of companies moving or thinking of moving jobs offshore. Since 2002, the number of U.S. Fortune 500 companies moving work to India has tripled.[19] In January 2004, IBM announced it was moving 5,000 jobs from the United States and Europe to India, Brazil, and elsewhere. This caused a major stir because of IBM's history of paternalism and also because the affected employees fought back. But these kinds of decisions are being made daily. As Howard Rubin of Meta Consulting says, "U.S. companies are shedding 500–2,000 IT staffers at a time and these people won't get reabsorbed until they get reskilled."[20] At a company presentation not too long ago, a senior Microsoft vice president urged his staffers to "pick something to move offshore today."[21] Ann Livermore, head of services at HP, notes that "now we see some of the same trends in services that happened in manufacturing."[22] In the wake of the bad publicity IBM suffered, many companies have begun to suppress public announcements. But they aren't suppressing the move of key service work.

Estimates of the total number of service jobs at risk of being moved overseas in the next few years are all over the lot. A Deloitte research study based on a survey of the world's one hundred largest financial services firms in the spring of 2003 predicted that these firms would move $356 billion of their operations and 2 million jobs offshore over the period from 2005 to 2010.[23] In a report done for the Information Technology Association of America, Global Insight estimated that IT offshoring would actually result in net creation of 317,000 new jobs in the United States between 2004 and 2008.[24] The most widely cited study is one by Forrester Research that projects 3.3 million service jobs leaving the United States for offshore destinations by 2015. Another study by the University of California–Berkeley, however, says as many as 14 million U.S. jobs could be at risk.[25]

Since the United States now supports about 140 million jobs, 3.3 million or even 14 million are a relatively small share of the total. Jobs are frequently lost to technological change in the domestic economy. The Internet, for instance, has been a disaster for travel agents and has completely changed the lives of stock brokers. Yet no one would try to halt this evolution, as several state legislatures have tried to do with bills to prevent offshoring of state-related jobs. Nor does anyone complain about the 6 million U.S. jobs created as the result of inshoring or about jobs that would not exist were it not for the offshoring of others. Rosen Sharma, for example, is the CEO of Solidcore Corp., a start-up that makes backup security systems for computers. In 2004 he employed thirteen senior managers, engineers, and marketing people in Silicon Valley, but he says none of them would have a job without the eighteen engineers who work for him in India for one-fourth the salary of their U.S. counterparts. His venture capitalists wouldn't give him a nickel, says Sharma, if he didn't outsource to India.[26] But then he poses the key question, "As a father my reaction is different than my reaction as a CEO. Companies will always need senior people in the United States. But if you're graduating from college today, where are the entry-level jobs? How do you get to that secure, skilled job when the path that leads you there has disappeared?"

Production Line or Check-Out Line

What counts is not so much how many jobs go offshore. The answer is almost certainly a lot more than anyone thinks now. Who would have thought of medical tourism before it became a reality? Most of the projections I have cited are concerned mainly with software and IT jobs, but we have seen that tax returns, X ray reading, home design, and many more kinds of work are already being offshored, and the process has barely begun. But so what? If the United States and other developed countries continue to create new and better jobs, perhaps as a result of offshoring some of the lower-end jobs, everything should be fine. But what if the new and better jobs aren't there?

That question has also stirred a hot debate, with lots of industry association reports demonstrating that outsourcing and offshoring (done largely by their members) are good for the U.S. economy. The reports are essentially correct. But they make a key assumption—that most laid-off workers quickly find new jobs equal to the ones they lost. A much noted study by McKinsey & Co.'s Global Institute announced a $1.12–$1.14 benefit to the U.S. economy for every dollar of offshore spending. That's surprising because it implies that if we closed the U.S. economy and moved it to India, we could instantly increase GDP by 12–14 percent. The calculation begins with subtracting a dollar from U.S. GDP to be spent on services in India. That produces a saving of $0.58 as a result of low wages and costs in India. An additional benefit of $0.05 is gained from increased Indian imports of U.S. equipment and services resulting from growth in India. Another $0.04 comes from transfer of profits in India back to the U.S. parent company. So far a dollar has been deducted from U.S. GDP, and cumulative gains have been only $0.67. We are still losing. But then there is an additional benefit of $0.45–$0.47 from the reemployment of the worker whose job was offshored. This is calculated on the basis of a study indicating that 69 percent of such people are eventually reemployed at about 96.5 percent of their previous wage. Once the laid-off worker finds a new job, the total benefit comes to $1.12–$1.14. Subtract the dollar lost to offshoring and you have a net gain to the economy of $0.12–$0.14. Still, if the reemployment assumption is adjusted slightly to reflect lower rates of reemployment, lower wages, or both, the benefit can quickly turn negative. If employers took McKinsey's advice to increase their offshoring, it would almost have to. The more they sent abroad, the less likely workers would be to find new and equal jobs. That is what some key observers fear.

For the rosy scenario to work, as Steve Pearlstein has pointed out in his *Washington Post* column, several key assumptions have to hold. Full employment is assumed, as is free trade under a regime of floating currencies and perfectly competitive markets. In practice, as we now know, the currencies really don't float. Nor is there usually strong reemployment. The levels of the late 1990s, on which some of these studies were based, are more representative of the bubble than of normal reality. According to the U.S. Census Bureau, on average, 52 percent of job losers who are eventually reemployed take a substantial pay cut.[27] In another report, McKinsey itself says that over the past

twenty years only 36 percent of those displaced got new jobs at equal
pay, while 25 percent took pay cuts of as much as 30 percent.[28] With
this kind of reemployment experience, the McKinsey calculation
quickly turns into a disaster.

Morgan Stanley chief economist Steve Roach is one of the smartest
guys on Wall Street, and he's worried. He points to the phenomenon of
the equalization of wages and commodity prices in global markets that
was mentioned earlier. Roach notes that with their relatively small
populations, Japan and the Asian tigers gained manufacturing competitiveness that directly affected only 15–20 percent of the U.S. workforce. Yet they helped keep U.S. wages stagnant between 1973 and
1990. Now, with 3 billion new market entrants who may have an effect
on up to 80 percent of the U.S. labor force, the potential for equalization and first world wage stagnation is enormous.

As Roach sees it, there are two problems. First, the U.S. economy is
8 million jobs below where it should be in any kind of a normal recovery from recession.[29] Many of the missing jobs seem to him to be those
most subject to offshoring both in manufacturing and in services. Second, and more troubling, are the jobs being created. Although it is
good news that the economy is again creating jobs, both Roach and
Paul Craig Roberts, former Reagan administration assistant secretary
of the Treasury, urge a look behind the headlines. They note that low-
wage employers like Wal-Mart (now the nation's largest employer),
which account for 22 percent of the workforce, created 44 percent of
the new jobs. High-wage employers, who employ 24 percent of the
workforce, created only 29 percent of the new jobs. No jobs were created in any export industry. As Roberts says, "this is not even the pro-
file of a low tech developing economy."[30] Moreover, new part time employment was equivalent to 97 percent of the total of new jobs.[31]
Here's the crux of the matter: it's the kind of jobs that counts.

The advent of large-scale offshoring in service industries has surprised many sophisticated economists. For years as blue-collar manufacturing jobs disappeared under the impact of automation and offshoring, they urged people to have children study accounting or
computer science or radiology. Students who followed this advice
thought they would have a secure niche at least in the middle class and

perhaps higher. Now it's clear that this is not a safe bet. Snow removal is still safe: they really can't move the snow to India. Plumber, nurse, electrician—these are all jobs that will remain safe.

But many formerly safe jobs will now be subject to global competition and, as Roach notes, the narrowing of the knowledge gap between Asia and the West may actually inhibit knowledge job creation in the West. For example, whereas the United States today is producing the same number of new science and engineering graduates annually as in 1980—roughly 220,000, Asia is turning out 650,000, double the 1980 number.[32] If the tech jobs are going to Asia or if the salaries are going to be low, why go through the pain of becoming an electrical engineer when you could make more as car mechanic? The standard economist response is that growth in Asia will bid up wages and salaries there and thereby create more economic demand that in the long run will create more jobs globally. That is correct and, indeed, some bidding up of wages is already under way. But given the size of Asian populations, the long run could be really long. Furthermore, the semi-free market structure of both China and India means their markets remain somewhat protected, and it could take quite some time before they are soaking up imports from advanced countries. Japan, after all, is still not a big importer, even with higher than U.S. wages.

The Big Squeeze

So while the new globalization is bringing many wonderful things, its tendency will be to create a winner-take-all economy that will seriously squeeze the first world middle class and even retard income growth in some important developing countries. In fact, this squeeze has already begun, not only in the United States but in Europe, Japan, and Mexico as well, with the degree of the squeeze dependent on each society's buffers and safety nets. People often forget that the nineteenth- and early-twentieth-century versions of capitalism were both productive and brutal. The social impact of the industrial revolution had a lot to do with the rise of socialism, fascism, and communism. To compensate, most societies gradually introduced measures like labor unions, unemployment insurance, sick leave, antitrust regulations, environmental protection rules, and child labor laws to tame capitalism in accord with their values. My high school buddies escaped being equalized because they were members of a powerful union.

Now all this is being undermined. The economy is going global and the national taming mechanisms can't cope with the impact of new players who don't have similar taming devices.

In the United States the number of middle compensation jobs has been growing more slowly than those at the top and the bottom of the scale.[33] By the same token, income inequality is growing as the share of family income going to the top 20 percent of earners has steadily increased while that going to everyone else has stagnated or declined.[34] Top executive compensation has soared from thirty-five times the average worker's pay in 1978 to three hundred times in 2002.[35] In 1980 those with incomes in the top 10 percent accounted for 33 percent of total household income. By 2000 they accounted for 44 percent.[36]

In Europe and Japan, the differentials arc less but the trends are the same. The trend is also the same in China, where income inequality is growing more rapidly than in the United States. What is clear everywhere is the premium on skills. In China, it is the salaries of the educated and English-speaking that are being bid up. Grunt labor will remain very cheap for a long time. In the end, the 3 billion new capitalists are going to ensure that everyone is paid exactly what he or she is worth not on the old local scale, but on a new global one. To survive in this world, you'd better do something no one else can do or do what you do far better than anyone else.

This was made clear when the *Washington Post* recently ran a series of articles on people who make $17 per hour, the national average wage. The title of the series said it all: "Average Wage Earners Fall Behind." One is Teresa Geerling of St. Charles, Missouri, whom the *Post* described as living the life of a typical middle-income American. After years cleaning and polishing airplanes for American Airlines, Geerling, 50, was laid off. The job had been physically taxing, but the $32,000 salary with full health care benefits made for a good life in a small Midwestern town. Now Geerling works the night shift at a hospital as a nurse's aide while waiting to be certified as a medical assistant. The move to medical assistant is probably smart because it's a skill for which there is much demand. But the pay will be $2 per hour less than at the airline. There will be no pension beyond a 401K, and health care benefits will cost $200 per month. Geerling, said the *Post*, is at the leading edge of a new era that will require millions of Americans to shoulder more responsibility and take more risk. They will have to be nimble and ready to adjust to a constantly changing job market. Without some combination of special skills, higher education, and professional certification, they will be in danger of sliding down the ladder to low-paying service jobs with no benefits and no future.[37]

Who Will Be Safe?

All the world's major countries will be forced to respond to these forces and developing conditions. In the first world the challenge will be to maintain living standards. In the developing world it will be sustainable development. Each player brings different assets and attitudes to the table and who emerges in the best position may be a surprise.

United States

In the United States the situation for most people over the next five to ten years is likely to become more difficult, as indicated by Jim Hemmerling's epigraph comment that "Nothing is safe." ("America is on the comfortable path to ruin").[38] Behind the rising debt and deficits stand the fundamental philosophies, attitudes, and practices that have precipitated the present situation and are likely to make it worse.

Let's start with economics. If you want to make it big as an American economist, you had better be in macroeconomics. Macroeconomists study the big picture, things like interest rates, exchange rates, employment rates, and government budget policies. Industry structures and linkages are less exciting. Economists pay less attention to them, and the U.S. government collects little data on such things. In fact, if I need to know something about a particular U.S. industry, I often inquire at Japan's Ministry of Economics, Trade, and Industry. The Japanese usually know a lot more about American industries than the U.S. government does. In earlier times American economists and policymakers cared about these things too. State governors who work hard to attract factories and R&D centers to their states still do. But at some point the conventional wisdom concluded that these things are not important enough to rise above the purview of state governors. Consequently when China or Singapore offer big financial incentives to attract semiconductor plants and R&D centers, no one in Washington knows or cares.

Other countries look on these plants and centers not just as production units or even jobs but also as universities and critical pathways to a better future. For them, a semiconductor plant doesn't just make chips: it gives several thousand people skills that are transferable to many other things. The plant establishes ties with suppliers who may in turn locate facilities near it and educate more people in the skills necessary to produce their products and services. It can be used as an R&D center to develop new products or even whole industries. It provides jobs that justify and encourage the teaching and study of technical disciplines. These so-called externalities, which are not a direct part of the production process, are actually more valuable to these countries than the production itself. In the United States they are hardly discussed. American economists acknowledge externalities and even admit they can be important. But they are difficult to quantify and therefore suspect. If you want to be shunned as a retrograde mercantilist in a Washington economic policy discussion, one sure tactic is to suggest consideration of externalities.

By the same token, linkages and path dependence are hardly studied, and suggesting their possible importance is considered risqué in proper economic circles. The notion that by making one thing you open gateways to other opportunities or that, by not making it, you are locking yourself out of these opportunities, does not command attention. Think about the Ampex case, where the Japanese government had a whole program to help its industry clone the video recorder on the principle that if you made video recorders, you might someday make something like charge-coupled devices. Then you might use them to make something like digital cameras that you could export all over the world. No American economist or policymaker at the time gave any thought to the possible importance of this kind of pathway.

In 1985 I attended a White House meeting on what to do about European Airbus subsidies that were causing Boeing to lose market share and move some of its production to Japan, where the Japanese government would also provide subsidies. One of America's highest officials argued forcefully that there was no problem and nothing should be done. The Japanese continued to provide assistance over the years, and Boeing gradually moved more production there. Indeed, the new Boeing 787 will be mostly made in Japan. The Japanese wanted the skills and learning that go with the jobs. The American refusal to see any advantage in such an arrangement was well captured in a comment about Japan made to me by a former chairman of the Council of Economic Advisers, who told me, "They'll sell us semiconductors and we'll sell them poetry." That production of semiconductors might contribute more than poetry to future productivity gains, overall economic growth, and development of entirely new industries was not a consideration of his. In contrast to this casual unconcern, the Chinese, Singaporese, Japanese, Korean, and many European governments operate on the theory that the structure of a country's economy has a very important impact on its long-term performance.

Adjustment costs are another factor hardly discussed in U.S. economic circles. Most economic models assume away the costs of closed factories, blighted neighborhoods, lost skills, uprooting, moving, and starting up again. Once factories or industries are gone, they almost never come back. The cost of a restart is enormous and the competitive circumstances usually worse. But these costs are rarely considered in analyses of trade agreements and domestic economic policies.

American economists cling to this viewpoint partly becuase they prefer the simpler world of Adam Smith and David Ricardo, with its magic unseen hand and climate-controlled, comparative advantage–based trade. But even more important is American distaste for government, well expressed in the popular line: "We don't want government bureaucrats picking winners and losers." All of the issues I have cited potentially involve possible policy action. If there are important externalities, the government needs to assess and perhaps try to capture them. If there are adjustment costs, maybe there should be policies to abate them. But such steps could be criticized as constituting the hated "industrial policy." So the U.S. government proclaims its devotion to laissez faire and retains no mechanism for considering industry structure issues. The irony is that this in itself is an industry structure decision. Other governments do have industrial policies. The financial incentives offered by China attract investment that might otherwise have been made in the U.S. market. In this case the absence of U.S. policy amounts to a policy to put the plants in China. Because we so hate having U.S. bureaucrats pick winners and losers, we outsource the job to Chinese bureaucrats, all the while reminding ourselves of the glories of the free market and complaining when the Chinese don't comply with our wishes.

CEO Strategies

The U.S. business community simply plays the board as it finds it. American CEOs are potentates in their own right, more powerful than all but a handful of prime ministers and presidents. The American political system, with its susceptibility to lobbying and constant need of political donations, enhances this power. Corporations naturally try to take control of policy decisions that affect them. The U.S. international trade negotiating agenda, for example, is strongly influenced by corporate lobbyists, and complaints are filed before the WTO or other bodies almost entirely at the behest of corporations. Let me emphasize that corporations are U.S. citizens and have every right to lobby the government as they do. But without a microeconomic policy or a trade policy other than to open markets, the questions of what to negotiate for and when and what to complain about are essentially answered by industry.

So U.S. CEOs are accustomed both to telling the U.S. government what they want and to often getting it. Their dealings abroad, however, are quite different. In China there is no rule of law, no democratic congress or parliament, and no such thing as an independent regulatory body. But there are industrial policies and bureaucrats and communist party leaders with enormous discretionary authority. American CEOs need to accommodate the bureaucrats and the party leaders if they want to do business.

A good example is the earlier mentioned IBM sale of its PC division to China's Lenovo. Although the sale was announced in December 2004, it got under way in July 2003, when IBM chairman Sam Palmisano made a special trip to Beijing. Palmisano later told the *New York Times* he was not traveling primarily to initiate talks with Lenovo's chairman. Instead, his first meetings were with top-level Chinese government officials from whom he sought permission to sell to a Chinese company. Palmisano explained that he wanted to help build a modern and truly international Chinese-owned company. The Chinese responded, as he hoped they would, by saying, "That is the future model for where we see China headed."[39] With that green light, he proceeded to negotiate the deal with Lenovo's top executives. Under the agreement, the Chinese government will be a major shareholder along with IBM in China's fifth largest company. According to Palmisano, IBM wants to support China's industrial policies with the expectation that this will pay off big in new business for IBM down the road. The IBM strategy, he says, is "a subtle, sophisticated approach. It is that if you become ingrained in their agenda and become truly local and help them advance, then your opportunities are enlarged. You become part of their strategy."[40]

Not that there is anything wrong with the deal. In a good example of insourcing, Lenovo quickly announced it was moving its headquarters to Armonk, New York, where IBM is based. Furthermore, it will put a group of senior IBM executives in charge of what will become the world's third largest computer company after Dell and Hewlett-Packard, and adopt English as the company language. Here is a case of China outsourcing management to the United States.[41] Said Lenovo chairman Liu Chuanzhi, "The most valuable asset we have acquired through IBM's PC business is its world-class management team and their extensive international experience." This deal could turn out to be a brilliant stroke for IBM, Lenovo, and China.

Perhaps it is also a brilliant stroke for the United States, but no one is analyzing whether it is or not. Of course IBM completed the U.S. formalities required for sales to foreign entities, but Palmisano didn't ask the White House for permission to sell nor did he think about advancing the U.S. strategy or helping U.S. industrial policy succeed. He couldn't, since there is no U.S. strategy or policy. It is assumed that whatever he does will be good for the United States. But the deal itself makes nonsense of that U.S. assumption. First, the U.S. assumption is based on the notion that Palmisano is operating in response to free market forces. But, in this case, he's obviously, to some extent, responding to China's industrial policy. Further, U.S. free trade doctrine is based on the view that the U.S. comparative advantage is precisely what Liu Chuanzhi says it is—the knowledge of modern international management—and that it cannot be easily acquired by developing country companies. Yet Lenovo is doing just that. Again, let me emphasize there is nothing wrong with what either Palmisano or Liu are doing. It's just that it's not at all in keeping with the assumptions that guide U.S. policy.

Tough Times May Come

The interplay of all these factors is pushing toward an unpleasant end. While U.S. consumption and debt continue to mount, productive capacity in both manufacturing and services is moving offshore at a rising rate. Despite a falling dollar, the trade deficit continues to mount. Imports have been rising faster than exports for such a long time that the United States may no longer have the productive capacity to respond quickly to a weaker dollar. As I write in January 2005, we are nearly three years into a dollar correction and the current account deficit just hit a record $60 billion for one month. I can remember when an annual deficit that size was considered unsustainable. Normally a falling dollar should result in more exports, fewer imports, and a move to current account balance along with some increase in inflation. That's what happened in the 1970s and 1980s. But the dollar decline of the early 1990s was accompanied by a shift from current account surplus back to deficit and no inflation. Now the 16 percent dollar decline of the past three years has seen no inflation and a dramatically widening current account deficit. What's going on?

One thing is that the bulk of the U.S. trade deficit is in manufactured goods while the U.S. manufacturing base continues to decline as a percent of GDP. According to Roach, the U.S. manufacturing base may have atrophied to the point that it no longer has the capacity to respond to a weaker dollar by ramping up exports sufficiently to offset the continuing import surges. With imports 52 percent higher than exports, it will be almost impossible to adjust the imbalance with an export surge. The only alternative is a big cut in U.S. consumption.

The falling dollar is likely to be accompanied by rising interest rates. Keep in mind that U.S. consumers have no savings, but the *Wall Street Journal* and other growth mavens have been telling them not to worry because the equity in their homes is really savings. So people have taken out home equity loans to keep the party going. Now a likely rise in interest rates may give consumers a double whammy: reduce the value of their equity while increasing the cost of the loan. To make matters worse, the housing industry could slump, along with capital investment and anything else that is interest sensitive. We're talking recession at the least, maybe worse.

Many economists say the United States can sustain a current account deficit of about 3–4 percent of GDP. I think that's a little high, but let's accept it for the sake of argument. Getting there means cutting the deficit in half, from about $650 billion to $325 billion. Given that many imported products are simply not made in the United States, U.S. incomes might have to fall significantly to reach this number. Of course, it might not be that bad: there will be some increase in exports and foreign countries might stimulate their own domestic consumption. Nevertheless, the future could be difficult for many Americans.

The Old Countries

Japan and Europe face most of the same pressures as the United States, compounded by their own internal difficulties. Outsourcing and offshoring have come to these economies also. According to some reports, Europe is likely to see a million jobs move offshore over the next decade, possibly adding to unemployment rates that already hover around 9 percent.[42] Big companies like Siemens have moved some production to China, and DaimlerChrysler has threatened to move operations offshore to get wage and working hour concessions from workers. Some workers have already opted to go back to working forty hours per week to save their jobs.[43] The German autoworkers union accepted pay cuts from DaimlerChrysler and longer working hours for some workers in exchange for a promise of no layoffs for seven years and a ban on outsourcing the work of security guards and cafeteria workers. Germany is suffering banking and financial woes similar to those that have plagued Japan for over a decade, and European growth over the past ten years has been less than that of the United States.[44] With high unemployment, aging populations, soaring social welfare expenses, little venture capital activity, low rates of adoption of information technology, and rigid labor laws coupled with low labor mobility, Europe will have trouble adjusting to the world of 3 billion new capitalists.

Japan may be in even worse shape. Burdened by a virtually moribund banking and financial sector and mountains of bad debt, its economy over the past decade has also been anemic. Its GDP growth per capita over the past thirteen years has been less than 1 percent annually, the lowest of all the major economies. While its unemployment is lower than Europe's, it is still high for Japan, around 5 percent, a figure that is significantly understated. In the past couple of years, Japan has shown signs of turning around on the basis of an export boom to China, but recently its numbers have looked less robust. Of particular concern is Japan's public debt, currently 163 percent of GDP and rising rapidly. The country could fail to meet its internal pension and social security obligations within the next five years. Here too, work and jobs are moving offshore. Even mighty Toyota is building more cars abroad and importing more parts every year, and Toyota City officials are beginning to think about life with less Toyota.[45] Worker income has been under pressure for over a decade, and lifetime employment is just a memory.

Nevertheless, these two creaky old behemoths may do better than the United States in meeting the challenge of the next ten to fifteen years. Despite Japan's important macroeconomic problems, international companies like Toyota, Sharp, and Sony continue to gobble up market share. In the case of Europe, the numbers can be deceptive. If you adjust the GDP growth rates for population growth to reflect GDP growth per person, the U.S. rate of 2.1 percent over the past ten years is only modestly ahead of the European rate of 1.8 percent. By the same token, if you put the productivity numbers on a per hour basis and adjust for the fact that the EU figures include government workers and the U.S. figures do not, it turns out that Europe's productivity growth has actually been a little higher than America's over the past ten years. Even these figures may overstate the U.S. growth because while spending on software counts as an investment and part of GDP in the U.S. numbers, it is an expense and not included in GDP in the European numbers.

Or take employment. While it grew by 1.3 percent in America over the past decade compared with 1 percent for the Euro area, total European employment has risen since 1977 by 8 percent versus 6 percent in America. In view of American disdain for the welfare state, it is fascinating that in the World Economic Forum's 2004 ranking of the most competitive countries, four were the Nordic countries of Europe, the ones with the biggest welfare states.[46]

So by the time you make all the necessary adjustments, Europe doesn't look so bad.[47] It looks even better when you consider that the gap between rich and poor in Europe and Japan is substantially narrower than in the United States and that the safety net for the poor, the unemployed, and the disadvantaged is infinitely better in Europe and Japan than in America. And neither the Europeans nor the Japanese have 2 percent of their working-age male population in prison.

Moreover, Europe's and Japan's trade with China and the rest of the world, unlike America's, is not all one way. Japan has a surplus with China of $13.5 billion, and while the EU has a deficit of $55 billion, it sells China bullet trains, ships, steel, machine tools, electronic components, silicon, and lots of other capital equipment and high tech components—things Americans either no longer make or no longer make competitively for overseas markets. Manufacturing has declined in Europe but not as much as in America. Although Europe has been buffeted by Japanese, Korean, and now Chinese competition, it has not abandoned the end markets as quickly as the Americans. European companies, for example, stayed in the VCR business and still make a range of consumer electronic products. Unlike U.S. companies, they could quickly increase production if exchange rates and other factors shifted to make that a profitable thing to do. This capability is even greater for the Japanese, who remain dominant in consumer electronics and many other manufacturing industries.

Of the many factors at work here, two stand out: Economists policymakers in Europe and Japan accept the legitimacy of and the need for an economic strategy. They accept the notion that the structure of the economy has a significant influence on its long-term performance and must therefore be studied and attended in policy terms. In both regions there are officials whose job is to worry about economic structure and how various legislative and regulatory proposals might affect it.

The best current example is telecommunications. We saw earlier the rapid advance of Korea, Japan, and Europe in high-speed Internet development and mobile phone technology. In the laggard United States, the regulatory processes in these areas made no allowance for overall economic impact. In Korea, Japan, and Europe, they did. As I write, the *Wall Street Journal* is reporting that the European commissioner for Industry is launching a major effort to make it easier for automakers to produce in Europe. This is pursuant to the resolve of the European Commission to make increasing competitiveness its top goal. As for Japan, it is the inventor of competitiveness policy, and there is no need to comment further.

The second key factor is the European and Japanese concept of the purpose and obligations of the corporation and the responsibility of management. The Daimler Chrysler deal for longer hours and worker pay cuts also included a 9–10 percent pay cut for top management. The *Washington Post* article reporting this deal was caustically disdainful, rhetorically asking how any company could promise not to lay off workers for seven years.[48] For all I know, it may be crazy to promise no layoffs for seven years. But both the promise and the management pay cut imply an intent to stay in the business as a team. When I spoke to Renault chairman Louis Schweizer at his headquarters in Paris, he stressed that the corporation is a part of a community and that it is very difficult for the corporation to succeed if the community is failing. Therefore the long-run interest of the shareholder is also that of the stakeholders. The key term here is "long run." No one can doubt that Saint Gobain, the world's second largest glassmaker, is in it for the long run. Founded in 1665, it is France's oldest industrial company. Under Chairman Jean-Louis Beffa, it has transformed itself from a state-owned business into a publicly held, diversified group with about $40 billion in sales, triple its turnover in 1986 when Beffa took over. Now, early in 2005, he is completing a report to President Chirac on how France, and perhaps Europe, can stimulate growth through technological innovation. I find it fascinating that Chirac, part of Don Rumsfeld's "old Europe," is even interested in the subject. I can think of a number of U.S. CEOs in high-tech companies who wish U.S. presidents would take an interest.

Even more interesting are Beffa's views. He believes that it is important for countries to ensure that inside their borders they have key companies with key technologies. Europe, he says, should follow the lead of Japan more than that of the United States. He also contests the popular U.S. business school notion of "focus" and argues that diversified companies have many benefits.[49] He may be right, he may be wrong. The point is that he has enjoyed great success with an approach very different from that of most U.S. CEOs.

The same is true in spades for Japan. Japanese companies have extensive operations around the world and in China. But you may be sure of two things. They see themselves as long-term entities and as communities within communities. They are in business more for stakeholders than for shareholders, and they definitely believe the government should have competitiveness policies and they should cooperate with them. As I explained earlier, the new countertrend in Japanese business these days is to shift production of high-end products back to Japan from China even as investment in the latter continues. In the Japanese view, the development of products like digital cameras, mobile phones, and flat-display TVs requires continuous collaboration between researchers, engineers, and suppliers. The cost of labor is far less important than getting it right and into the market before anyone else. It is also believed that production in Japan will greatly reduce the risk of loss of intellectual property. This is one reason Japanese companies do far less R&D in China or other overseas locations than U.S. companies.

But let's get to the main game. The major way in which Europe and Japan differ from the United States is that they are not swimming in debt that must be financed by foreigners. Their households are not living on the edge. They don't allow home equity loans. If a crash comes, far fewer of their home owners will lose homes. They have big government budget deficits in many cases, but also the savings to fund them. They are not running big current account deficits, and their currencies are rising and not falling. They are less vulnerable to the vicissitudes of the oil markets. Of course, Japan is somewhat dependent on exports to the U.S. market, but both it and Europe have room to stimulate their economies in case of a big U.S. downturn. This is not to say they will feel no pain in a crisis, but they are in better condition—at least for the short to medium term—to withstand the pain than is the United States. This is not to say they have done a good job running their economies. They have, in fact, done a very poor job. It is only that, contrary to all expectations, Americans are, in some key respects, doing worse.

At What Price Success?

None of this should be taken to mean that China, India, and the other key developing countries will experience an uninterrupted smooth ride to the top. On the contrary, not only will they face many of the same problems as the developed countries, they will also confront enormous challenges resulting uniquely from their own development. Hong Kong, for example, has always been one of my favorite cities. I like to ride the tram to Victoria Peak for the spectacular view across the harbor to Kowloon. At least I used to do this. These days the view is obscured by a cloud of smog that drifts in from factories in China's neighboring Guangdong province. In 2004 Hong Kong had seventy-nine days over 100 (very high) on the air pollution index.[50] Yet Hong Kong is one of the less polluted cities in China.

The new globalization is undoubtedly doing great things for Asia and especially for China and India. But success is coming at the cost of pollution, water shortages, and disease—a cost that could negate the success. To see this you don't even have to go to India or China. Just go to a city on the U.S. West Coast in the summer, and you may see dust blowing in from China's Gobi Desert. Rapid economic growth has cut forest cover in northern and central China by more than half since 1985, and the country's deserts are growing by several hundred thousand square miles annually. Government efforts to replant trees are proving too little too late. The Gobi, which is moving closer to Beijing at a rate of two miles per year, is now less than two hundred miles from the city. Sometimes in the summer the sandstorms in Beijing make you wonder if you mistakenly got off the plane in Saudi Arabia.[51]

But particulate levels in Beijing's air don't come only from the Gobi. China's auto population of 10 million is growing by nearly 2 million a year. It could easily double every three or four years. Given China's huge population, an American rate of vehicle ownership would mean 600 million Chinese cars on the road, or more than the total number of cars in the world today. China is already the world's second largest greenhouse gas emitter and could easily top U.S. emissions if its rate of vehicle ownership gets anywhere near the U.S. level. As some observers have noted, "If China attempts to replicate the U.S. style consumer economy, it will become clear that the U.S. economic model is not environmentally sustainable."[52] The important point is that it would not only be unsustainable for China. It would also be unsustainable for the rest of the world.

Cars and smokestacks are just two of the factors that have made China the home of the world's worst environmental problems. Two-thirds of Chinese cities have air quality below World Health Organization standards, and sixteen of the world's twenty most polluted cities are in China, including Beijing.[53] China's environmental agency calculates that living in Chinese cities does more damage to a person's lungs than smoking two packs of cigarettes a day. The water in five of China's largest rivers is dangerous to touch. But if you live downstream, you don't have to worry about touching it because the rivers dry up before they get there. Beijing, for instance, is in real danger of simply running out of water. Longtime China analyst Jasper Becker says that 600 million people drink water contaminated with human and animal waste.[54]

The country's environmental situation is likely to get worse in the next two decades as 300 million more Chinese are expected to join the 200 million who have already migrated from the countryside to cities. By 2020, the environmental agency estimates that half a million people will die prematurely every year from bronchitis and similar illnesses while many farmers in central China will have to abandon their land to the rapidly advancing deserts. Environmental problems could cut as much as 10 percent from China's GDP.[55]

India's water problems may be even worse than China's. "Pump smashing," where one farmer destroys another's irrigation pump, is becoming a major hazard in the state of Andhra Pradesh. Even worse, angry farmers may destroy the electric company for taking precious water to generate electricity. By 2025 India will have another 400 million people, and three-fourths of the population of about 1.5 billion people will be living in areas with less than the 264,000 gallons per person per year considered essential to sustain economic development.[56] Here, as elsewhere, water is both a cause and an effect of a larger environmental disaster. As in China, the loss of half of India's forest cover has resulted in flooding, loss of water retention, erosion of topsoil, and further pollution of drinking water. Up to 70 percent of people who contract serious illnesses in India do so as the result of contact with polluted water.[57]

India's air pollution is nearly as bad as China's. According to the Center for Science and Environment, deaths due to air pollution in thirty-three Indian cities for which air quality measures are available rose 30 percent in just four years, from 2000 to 2004.[58] As in China, coal is the dominant fuel, and India is the world's third largest producer after China and the United States. The combination of coal and untreated industrial smoke creates hazardous air pollution problems. It also means that Indian greenhouse gas emissions are rising rapidly toward the Chinese and American levels. Because India has one of the highest levels of carbon intensity per dollar of GDP, its emissions could go even higher.[59] Again, the question of whether the world can sustain an Indian modernization along the lines of the American consumer model is one of critical importance for both India and the world.

Of more immediate concern even than the water shortages and air pollution is the AIDS epidemic. The U.S. National Intelligence Council estimates that India has 5–8 million HIV sufferers. Transmission of the disease today is mostly through heterosexual contact with prostitutes, of whom there are some 2–3 million.[60] Given a relatively high rate of female illiteracy, cultural inhibitions about discussing the topic, and an uneven policy response at different levels of government, the outcome of the battle to contain AIDs in India is unclear. Still, the subject is more or less out in the open in Indian public discussion. China is a different story altogether. There the overwhelming majority of cases are undocumented and untreated. The Chinese health ministry estimates a million infected people, but an unnamed UN official told the *New York Times* the number could be as high as 6 million, which would make China perhaps the second largest population of AIDS victims. Nobody knows and therefore not much is being done about it.[61]

Worse, the combination of China's one child policy and technology enabling identification of the sex of the fetus is resulting in abortion of female babies and a growing surplus of men for whom there will be no wives. HIV is primarily transmitted in China by prostitutes. The combination of these two phenomena is not promising.

I could also speak of SARS, the new disease that suddenly appeared in China and spread almost instantly to Hong Kong, Canada, and other parts of the world just a couple of years ago. Others like it will surely follow. But you get the picture. The 3 billion new capitalists are going to do great things for themselves and for the world. But to do so they must successfully overcome immense challenges.

Back to School

Which brings me back to my high school class. My classmates and I were lucky. We chose a good time and place to be born. The new age into which we are rapidly passing will be far more challenging for our children and grandchildren, but also filled with more opportunities.

The recent experience of the Christmas tsunami seems to me a kind of metaphor for the future. On the afternoon of December 28, I was at my house in Maui. Having finished their on line math session with Singapore, my daughter's two kids were hanging out with me and my wife. Suddenly my older son, the skier, who had come in from Tahoe with his family a couple days before, burst through the door, laptop in hand, and said: "Come look at this." "This" was a website with amateur camcorder videos of the waves coming in and obliterating some of the beachside towns. Both the destructive power of the tsunami and the fact that I could see just as those caught up in it had seen it were awesome. Impressive too was the global reach of the disaster. The videos I saw had been taken by an American, but there were also 20,000 Swedes on vacation in the region at the time. Indeed, as a percentage of population, Sweden suffered more victims than some of the countries in the region. Technology held people together as never before. Mobile phones allowed loved ones to reach each other instantly and when the circuits became overloaded, text messages miraculously continued to go through. Most impressive, however, was the effort to help. With our laptops, my son and I quickly found that the Red Cross and the usual charitable organizations were taking donations through their websites. But it was a surprise to find that Amazon.Com was not only taking donations at its website, but that, overnight, it had become one of the major charitable funds. Other companies did the same, and the amounts collected for relief quickly reached record numbers. It was the first catastrophe of the third era of globalization, and it showed a lot about what this new globalization can do.

Yet it also showed some gaping holes. A warning system such as that already in use in the Northern Pacific would have averted most of the death and destruction. Why was there no warning system? Because, with all its potential, globalization has not yet resulted in adequate cooperation among nations and peoples. This is the challenge that will confront our children and grandchildren.

To meet that challenge, they will need far more knowledge of technology and of other people than can be gained from a high school education. To be able to seize the opportunities and meet the challenges, the next generations must truly be able to compete with anyone. Because the playing field is going to be really level.

CHAPTER 11

The Great Shift

The likely emergence of China and India,
as well as others, as new major global players
will transform the geopolitical landscape.
—NATIONAL INTELLIGENCE COUNCIL
2020 PROJECT SUMMARY

For travelers from Europe or the United States, Singapore is the end of the line—it is as far as the plane can go. Because it's the last stop, many of the planes arrive late at night. Or at least you think it's late until you get off the plane to find what looks like half the population of Singapore shopping and playing computer games at the arcades scattered liberally around the giant Changi airport. Not only does the hour seem outlandish, but so does this lively scene in what was once a notorious Japanese World War II prisoner of war camp. It always strikes me as a dramatic example of how good can evolve out of the worst of circumstances.

In a sense, that is what this modern city of Singapore is all about—overcoming adverse circumstances. Founded in 1819 in a marsh at the tip of the Malay Peninsula just north of the equator by the swashbuckling British East India Company man Sir Thomas Stamford Raffles, it was meant to ensure Britain access to the China Sea. It thrived and became the main British base in Southeast Asia. After World War II, it was initially part of Malaysia, but ethnic tension between its largely Chinese population and the Malay majority of the rest of Malaysia resulted in a peaceful separation and the founding of Singapore as an independent city-state in 1965. With a population of 2.3 million, a per capita income of $529, a sweltering climate, and no resources other than a harbor in a strategic location, Singapore was definitely not a candidate for first world membership. But that opinion didn't reckon on either the energy and ingenuity of these overseas Chinese or on their gifted, farsighted leaders headed by senior minister Lee Kuan Yew. Under their guidance, Singapore has become one of the richest cities in the world in the space of forty years with a per capita income of over $21,500 ($37,800 in the United States).[1] The transformation of Singapore's Changi from prison camp to one of the world's great airports is symbolic of what has been achieved. Since Singapore's leaders did not gain this success without a profound grasp of international political and economic trends and a keen sense of which way the wind was blowing, it was to this tiger city-state that I went to gather judgments about the significance of the new forces of globalization for the international balance of power.

If any man now alive deserves to be called the father of his country, it is Minister Lee, who first championed Singapore's separation from Malaysia and its establishment as an independent country. He was the first to understand that English would be the global language of commerce, and made it the fundamental language of the new city-state. He also understood the importance of the American security umbrella and offered the use of harbor facilities when U.S. forces were ejected from the Philippines in 1992. He was among the first to sense the significance of the Japanese development model and to call for "looking east" in search of development guidelines.

When I met with him in the spring of 2004, he noted that the current rise of China is changing the face of Asia. Another top Singapore official said, "China is like a new sun in the solar system," pulling the balance of world power back toward the East for the first time since Portugal's caravels showed up in the Straits of Malacca six hundred years ago. That seemed a more diplomatic way of saying what a Chinese friend in Shanghai had told me the week before: "We've had a couple hundred bad years, but now we're back."

The new importance of China became apparent in August, when the senior minister's son, Lee Hsien Loong, took the reins as prime minister and publically warned Taiwan authorities against support for the increasingly influential pro-independence movement on the island. Just

before taking office, Lee had made a "private and unofficial" visit to Taiwan, as Singaporese officials had been routinely doing for years without comment from mainland Chinese leadership. But this time, Beijing
blasted this unapproved visit by a foreign leader to its "renegade"
province and threatened to delay pending trade talks as punishment.
Lee quickly expressed "regret" that his visit had caused strains with
China, explaining that the trip was necessary to gain firsthand knowledge of Taiwanese thinking. He went on, "I have become more worried
about the cross-strait situation after my visit. There is a real risk of mis-
calculation and mishap." He emphasized that "if Taiwan goes for independence, Singapore will not recognize it. In fact, no Asian country will
recognize it. China will fight. Win or lose, Taiwan will be devastated.
Unfortunately, I only met a few Taiwanese leaders who understood
this. A move by Taiwan towards independence is neither in Singapore's
nor the region's interest." In view of the fact that, because of lack of
space on its own tiny island, Singapore has staged annual military exercises in Taiwan since the 1970s, that was quite a statement.[2]

The BRICs Build a New World

Thus China's economic power is begetting geopolitical power. Just as
Portugal crushed Egypt and Venice by changing the trade routes, so
China is gaining influence by becoming everyone's biggest customer. It
has surpassed the United States as the biggest export market for South
Korea, Taiwan, Japan, Thailand, and Indonesia, and is rapidly increasing trade in Europe and Latin America. Its nominal GDP of $1.4 trillion
dollars now makes it the world's seventh ranked economy, but in terms
of purchasing power, it is already the world's second largest, behind the
United States but well ahead of Japan. (It is also well behind the European Union, the world's largest economic unit—as I explain later in this
chapter.) It is sometimes linked with Brazil, Russia, and India (the so-
called BRIC economies), which are destined to have much greater
weight in the world of the future. In a study done in the fall of 2003, the
investment house Goldman Sachs used demographic projections and a
model of capital accumulation and productivity growth to forecast

GDP growth, per capita income, and currency movements in the BRIC economies until 2050. The study also included comparisons with the current G6 economies: United States, Japan, Germany, United Kingdom, France, and Italy. The results are fascinating and profound. Today the BRIC economies total only 15 percent of the combined GDP of the G6 in current U.S. dollar terms. In less than forty years, however, they will be larger than the G6. By 2025, the BRICs will already be over half the size of the G6; and by 2050, only the United States and Japan will be left among the top six. China overtakes the United States by 2040, India passes Japan in 2030, and Brazil races past Germany by 2035.[3]

But mind you, this is all measured in terms of current or nominal dollars. In terms of purchasing power parity, the BRICs together pass the G6 around 2020. Even more dramatically, by the early 2020s, the annual increase in dollar spending by the BRICs could be twice that of the G6, meaning that they would be far and away the engines of growth of the global economy. Economic power of this magnitude does not exist in a vacuum: it inevitably translates into geopolitical power. In this chapter—a tour through the world's major economies— I'll sketch how the two kinds of power are likely to evolve together.

The Middle Kingdom Comes Back

Unless things go badly off track, the story of the next fifty years will be that of China recovering its historically central position as the Middle Kingdom, with the world's largest population and economy. In terms of purchasing power parity, it could have a larger GDP than the United States as soon as 2020. And in nominal dollar terms, its GDP in 2050 will be $45 trillion versus about $35 trillion for the United States. China will be the world's largest market for virtually everything as well as the biggest recipient of investment from, and the largest investor in, most other countries. It will be a large international creditor, and the yuan could well be the world's money, or at least one of its major reserve currencies.

As well as being big and powerful, the Chinese economy will fund extensive overseas aid projects, becoming perhaps the largest contributor to the United Nations and the largest shareholder in the World Bank and the International Monetary Fund. It will certainly be the single most important country in the World Trade Organization. By 2020, it could be funding a military budget that, in purchasing power parity terms, would be substantially larger than that of the United States and yet still cost less than 3 percent of GDP. Anticipating these developments, nearly all countries are shifting their orbits somewhat toward China.

Australia's adjustment to China is even more interesting than other's. In the summer of 2003 I had a chance to travel around the country and meet with key government, business, academic, and media leaders. What struck me (given that Australia and the United States are formally linked as allies with mutual security obligations in the ANZUS treaty, and that the United States has long been the main guarantor of Australian security) was the comment made not once but many times by various leaders: "Don't ask us to choose between you [America] and China." But that comment was nothing compared with the implications of the starkly different welcomes given soon afterward, first, to President Bush, who visited immediately after the Asia Pacific Economic Conference summit meetings in Bangkok in October 2003, and then, a week later, to China's President Hu Jin Tao. Bush stayed a couple of days, his address to parliament got a chilly reception, and he held no press conferences. Hu toured the country, kissed babies, signed big trade deals to buy Australian commodities, and was welcomed like a conquering hero by parliament. Had you not known otherwise, you would have concluded that Hu's country was the longtime ally and Bush's the threat.

Back in Canberra, Prime Minister John Howard boasted of his "great successes" in building a "very close relationship" with China while strengthening ties with Washington. But doubt was thrown on the strength of those ties when Foreign Minister Alexander Downer said that, if a conflict broke out over Taiwan, Australia would have grave reservations about joining the United States as it had in Iraq. Howard's later attempt to downplay the comment, calling it "completely hypothetical," only enhanced its credibility.[4]

Wherever you go across Asia and the Pacific, the story is pretty much the same. In Thailand, Prime Minister Thaksin Shinawatra, who is of Chinese descent, is talking about building a pipeline across the Kra isthmus to give China quicker access to Middle East oil. Malaysia's exports to China have grown twelvefold in ten years, and it was hardly surprising that the first major overseas visit by the new prime minister, Abdullah Badawi, was to China, with an entourage of eight hundred business executives.[5] While political relations between Beijing and Tokyo remain distant, cultural and economic relations are warming up rapidly. Japanese vacationers take more package tours to China than to the mainland of the United States, and traditional Chinese tea houses are beginning to elbow aside Starbucks for space in Tokyo.[6] In Myanmar, China's influence has direct political consequences. Long at odds with the military government in Yangon (formerly Rangoon), Washington has tried to use trade sanctions to force it to release democracy movement leader Aung Suu Kyi from house arrest. But China torpedoed this effort by signing trade deals with Myanmar worth over $1 billion to replace the $200 million it lost from the U.S. sanctions. Myanmar is too important to China as a source of vital natural resources to be alienated. Beijing has not only kept Myanmar afloat economically but has become the patron of the country's military leaders.[7]

While U.S. military supremacy remains unchallenged, its significance is increasingly eroded by deals like the one signed in the fall of 2004 between China and the Association of Southeast Asian Nations to create the world's largest free trade area by 2010 and to establish an EU-like ASEAN Community by 2020. Not only did the deal help China secure vital sea lanes and access to raw materials, but it also created a major regional entity that excludes the United States and its major allies.

And just as politics follows the money, so does culture. The Bangkok publisher Kitti Jinsiriwanich, whose wildly popular new magazine promotes things Chinese in Thailand, says, "It looks like being Chinese is cool."[8] Vikrom Kromadit, leader of a Thai-Chinese business association, adds, "There are so many cultural and philosophical beliefs the two countries share that I would say no country in the world is as close to China as Thailand." In a recent poll asking Thais whom they considered the country's closest ally, the response was 75 percent for China versus 9 percent for the United States. This sentiment is not limited to Thailand. In Indonesia dragon dancing has suddenly become the rage, while in the Philippines pop stars from Taiwan and mainland China have risen to the top of the ratings. One aspect of China that attracts many Asians is that it is not aggressive. As the Filipino businessman John Gokongwei says, "China isn't interested in military expansion. It will seek tribute through trade, like it did before the Western powers came to Asia."[9]

What is true in Asia is true elsewhere. "The China theme," says Walter Molano of BCP Securities, "has taken on a life of its own. The farther away you go from the United States, the more it has caught on."[10] And you don't even need to go that far from the United States. At the end of 2004, Canadian executives and officials revealed negotiations to strike large deals giving China access to important Canadian oil reserves previously destined exclusively for the U.S. market. "The China outlet would change our dynamic," said Murray Smith, former Alberta Province energy minister.[11] Oil has also been a theme in Iran and the Sudan, two countries on the U.S. blacklist. Although Washington has urged its allies to use economic and diplomatic pressure to stop Iran's nuclear weapons programs, China has concluded understandings with Tehran for tens of billions of dollars of energy deals and announced it would prevent any effort to haul the Iranian nuclear program before the United Nations. Meanwhile, a significant impediment to U.N. action to stop the civil war in the Sudan is Chinese support of the Sudanese government, with which it has concluded energy deals.

Perhaps most significant, however, is what has been happening—or *not* happening—in Washington. The right wing of the Republican Party has long been skeptical of China and strongly favors Taiwanese independence. Conservatives were greatly heartened when the newly elected President George W. Bush, in one of his first official acts, changed the designation of China from "strategic partner" to "strategic competitor." Many of them began to argue that the traditional engagement policy with Beijing had become dangerously out of date. Thus, when Chinese Premier Wen Jia Bao came calling in December 2003, there were high hopes in some Republican circles that Bush would take a hard line in support of Taiwan. No one was more shocked than the China lobby when Bush not only didn't support them but warned Taiwan against any deviation from the long-standing One China formulation.

Of similar significance has been the evolution of U.S. relations with North Korea. Initially the Bush administration refused any but the most minimal contact with Pyongyang. Then it outsourced the handling of the relationship to the Chinese—apparently on the theory that the Chinese had more clout with the North Koreans than Washington did. After decades of trying to freeze China out of the Korean Peninsula, the United States has now put Beijing in the driver's seat on the most sensitive issue in the Pacific. Coupled with the sudden disappearance of the usual expression of U.S. concerns about human rights in China, that step was a measure of Beijing's rapidly growing geopolitical influence.

It was also a measure of of China's financial leverage on the United States. In the 1962 movie *The Manchurian Candidate*, China maneuvers to have a candidate loyal to it win the U.S. presidential election. Today China controls something perhaps more powerful than a president. By buying U.S. Treasury notes, its Central Bank has made itself absolutely essential to prevent a collapse of the U.S. economy. Of course, a collapse would hurt China too, which is why China buys those notes. Still, this situation greatly enhances China's power at the expense of the United States.

Assuming no cataclysmic social or political upheavals, China's power is bound to wax over the next thirty-five years as its economy grows inexorably to become number one. There is, however, a limiting factor. As a result of its one-child policy in metropolitan areas, as well as factors that apparently reduce fertility in all countries as they become rich, China's population will begin to age by 2025 and start contracting by the middle of the century. One worrisome aspect of this trajectory is the fact that a strong cultural preference for sons has led to widespread prenatal sex selection through sonograms and abortion of female fetuses. Thus, in the future, 10–15 percent of the men in China will be unmarriageable because they will find no brides.[12] Since societies full of young men without women are historically aggressive, the combination of rapidly growing power and male majorities is not necessarily desirable—although by 2050 a lot of men will be graybeards.[13]

Slow and Steady Wins the Race

In 1980 India's population of 687 million was about two-thirds that of China, while its per capita income in terms of purchasing power was roughly the same. By 2001 India had 1 billion people compared to China's 1.3 billion, but China's per capita income was now double India's.[14] Because India drove late onto the capitalist road, it will not catch up with China in the next thirty-five years, although all bets are off if China runs into social and political turmoil. The point is that although China is the big winner between now and 2040, India is now driving fast and will pick up all the marbles in the latter half of this century.

The secret to this ultimate success is favorable demographics. India never had a one-child policy, and its fertility rate is far higher than China's. It will pass China in population around 2035 and keep on going, to at least 1.6 billion people, while China contracts. In India, too, sonograms are popular, and there is a growing male-female imbalance. Like China, India has a long list of daunting challenges. But if you're in the race for the long run, it is definitely the country to watch closely.

Even in the short run, however, India is developing great influence and has become a key strategic player. Besides its economic dynamism, its detonation of several nuclear devices in 1998 gave India an instant, if grudging, welcome into the small club of nuclear powers. In the World Trade Organization, it has become a leader of the group of developing countries. Its opposition to what it considered inadequate U.S. proposals to reduce agricultural subsidies played a major role in torpedoing the WTO negotiations in Cancun, Mexico, in 2003 and eventually forcing the United States to improve its offers. India also forced U.S. concessions on drug patents and other intellectual property issues. India, as the world's largest generic drug maker with a large population of poor people who cannot afford expensive proprietary drugs, insisted that in some cases poor countries must be allowed to produce life-saving drugs without paying expensive royalties to patent holders. Initially opposed by the United States, this position eventually won out in the WTO negotiations. On the cultural front, Bollywood (Bombay is India's film center) produces three times as many films per year as Hollywood, and they are increasingly playing to global audiences. Says producer Shekhar Kapur, "America's financial strength helped it export its entertainment and culture. Now an emerging 400 million strong Indian consumer market as well as an economically vibrant Asia, is shifting consumer power to the region. It's now our time to make our culture the prime culture of the world. The time for Bollywood is now."[15] That ambition represents a newly confident India that believes it deserves a seat at the top table.

Despite being the world's largest democracy, India has had distant relations with the United States and the West for most of the past half century. During the Cold War, as a result of its colonial experience and socialist philosophy, it pursued a nonalignment strategy that tied it closer to the Soviets than to the West. India's disdain of free market capitalism and constant conflict over Kashmir with U.S. Cold War ally Pakistan further widened the gap between the two democracies. The nuclear explosions of 1998 turned the gap into a chasm as the U.S. government imposed tough sanctions on trade and finance with India. Despite these governmental differences, however, ties at the individual and institutional level have continued to broaden and deepen. The Indian diaspora found a warm welcome and much success in Silicon Valley and in U.S. universities, where the $13 billion Indians spent in tuition and fees in 2004 was more than the country's total software exports of $12.5 billion.[16] On top of this, the end of the Cold War and and the rise of China have gradually changed all the old calculations. The United States doesn't need Pakistan's support against the Soviets, since there are no Soviets for the Indians to be connected with, and both countries may see the new Chinese power as a potential challenge. For the United States, an alliance with India may be the only way in the long run to preserve its own place at the top table as Asia regains its historically dominant weight in the global economy.

The new importance of India was recognized early. Condoleezza Rice, prior to becoming national security adviser, had written an article in _Foreign Affairs_ noting that India is an element in China's calculations and should be one in America's as well: "India is not a great power yet, but it has the potential to emerge as one."[17] As if to make the wish the father of the fact, in its national security strategy document for 2002, the Bush administration put India in the section of global powers for the very first time. At about the same time, the U.S.-India Defense Policy Group made plans that included joint naval patrols of the Straits of Malacca, workshops on ballistic missile defense, and cooperation in defense technology. Meanwhile, think tanks close to the administration were pointing out that "India is the most overlooked of our potential allies in a strategy to contain China." *Jane's Foreign Report* revealed a classified Defense Department document stating that "India should emerge as a vital component of U.S. strategy."[18] This thinking resulted in a series of joint military exercises and in the Next Step in Strategic Partnership program adopted by the two countries in 2003. Among other things, this program provided for renewed civilian nuclear and space cooperation and liberalization of U.S. high technology transfers.[19] America is taking India very seriously.

So is China. The modern Sino–Indian relationship began in the early 1950s as a kind of love-in between the two one-time victims of colonial oppression. Prime Minister Jawaharlal Nehru preached *hindi-chindi bhai bhai* (Indo-Chinese brotherhood) and tried to preserve it for posterity in a 1954 treaty. The whole thing went bye-bye, however, when India gave safe haven to the Dalai Lama and his followers after China's suppression of Tibet in 1959. In 1962 the last shreds of amity were cut when war broke out after China built—without even mentioning it—a road across what India regarded as its territory. India took a bad licking and immediately launched the nuclear weapons development program that finally bore fruit in 1998. This was an unpleasant surprise for China, as well as Washington, the more so when India's defense minister let it be known that India needed nuclear weapons not so much against Pakistan's nuclear ambitions as the long-term threat from China.

But that was then, and this is now. China has watched with concern the warming of U.S.-Indian relations. Many articles in the Chinese press express a fear that India will do a "China" on China—forge a tacit alliance with the United States, as China did against the Soviets in the 1970s.[20] In China's view, India is a perfect ally for the United States because of its location, British heritage, English-language capability, naval assets, and history of antagonism toward China. Thus the past several years have seen a flurry of diplomatic activity between the two giants, with high-level visits and lots of flowery rhetoric. In the India-Pakistan dispute over Kashmir, China has shifted away from its previous tilt toward Pakistan.

Perhaps more important is the rapidly growing business and technological alliance between the two giants. For example, when India's Infosys Technologies started looking for sites with low-cost, high-quality human resources, there was only one choice—China. Along with Infosys, Tata Consulting Services, Wipro Technologies, and other top Indian companies are now building operations in China as fast as possible. The model currently is to send Indian managers to hire and direct Chinese programmers in low-cost centers far from expensive hubs like Shanghai. But the traffic goes both ways. China's Huawei Technologies, for example, is expanding a research center in Bangalore, where it taps into India's engineering talent pool. As a result of such activity, India–China trade is doubling annually. Says Girija Pande, regional director for Tata Consulting, "These are two countries that are going to be collaborating."[21] In view of India's long geopolitical commitment to a multipolar world, the collaboration may not be strictly commercial.

Finally, two other players are vitally important to India. The European Union—not the United States or China or Japan—is India's largest trading partner and investor, as well as its major source of technology.[22] Consequently an important new interregional framework—the Asia-Europe Meetings (ASEM)—has been established as a vehicle for strengthening the Indo-European connection. At the same time, the Southeast Asian countries of ASEAN have committed to a special annual summit with India. With all competing for its favor, India may find itself the kingmaker or perhaps make itself king.

Asia's Switzerland

In the mid-1980s, when my job involved regular visits with the U.S. ambassador to Japan, Mike Mansfield, he would never fail to remark,

"The U.S.-Japan relationship is the most important bilateral relationship in the world, bar none." At the time, he was correct. Japan seemed to be emerging as the leader of Asia and preparing for a major role on the world stage. It was the world's second largest economy by a wide margin and had become an attractive developmental role model with a lot of "soft power" appeal, partly through its constitutional prohibition on military forces. Japan was the major investor in Southeast Asia and second only to the United States as a market for Asian exports. Despite Tokyo's small military capability, the U.S.-Japan alliance was the foundation of America's Asia strategy. Although it had the means and opportunity to create an Asian community around itself as China is now doing, for a variety of reasons it did not do so.

Today Japan still has the world's second largest economy, but its loss of dynamism and its inward-looking economic policies have greatly diminished its influence. It is not an engine of growth for the rest of Asia, and lingering protectionist policies hinder its ability to respond to or preempt Chinese offers of free trade agreements to Japan's most important Asia-Pacific trading partners. Instead, just as in an earlier era when its growth depended on exports to the U.S. market, Japan has now become heavily dependent on exports to China. Far from being the hub of the Asian economy, Japan is being drawn into China's orbit, despite its own much larger economy. This tendency is likely to increase in the future. Japan has among the worst demographics in the world. Its workforce is already contracting and its population declining. By 2050, there will be only 100 million Japanese, compared to today's 127 million, and within ten years China will pass it in size of GDP.[23]

In the geopolitical arena, Japan remains a highly valued American ally, but the end of the Cold War has decreased its strategic significance. This development has coincided with several shocks for the Japanese. The first was the 1998 launch of North Korea's Nodong ballistic missile over Japan, coupled with that country's continued efforts to develop nuclear weapons. Although Japan has been worried by the U.S. refusal to talk to the North Koreans and by the overall hard-line U.S. approach, even more frustrating has been the fact that U.S. officials have not consulted it on the matter. Nor have they consulted Tokyo about recent U.S. troop reductions in South Korea to fill needs in Iraq. This failure, along with increased U.S. interdependence with China, has raised questions about the true depth of the U.S. commitment to Japan's defense—a concern that has been heightened by continued incidents with China. Prime Minister Koizumi's annual visits to Yasukuni Shrine—which houses the spirits of Japan's war dead, including those convicted of war crimes—provide a continual source of tension. There have also been clashes with Chinese ships around the disputed Senkaku/Diaoyutai islands. Rising energy prices and long-term oil supplies are also increasingly important issues.

In response to all this, Japan has taken some initial steps in the direction of becoming a "normal country." Having long resisted U.S. prodding to enhance its military capabilities, Japan suddenly began to take the idea seriously. It entered into joint development with the Pentagon of a missile defense system, undertook measures to provide for its own spy satellites, beefed up its naval forces with a couple of small aircraft or helicopter carriers, and sent troops to Iraq in support of the U.S.-led occupation. The Diet stunned Japan watchers by adopting a national defense program outline, authorizing the government to dispatch troops anywhere from East Asia to the Middle East for purposes of "national security." In addition to noting the threat from North Korea, the document also directs the government's attention to future military and maritime trends in China. Such direct language is unprecedented for Japan.

Even more unprecedented is open talk of the possibility of Japan's becoming a nuclear power. Although former Prime Minister Yasuhiro Nakasone has long suggested such a course, it got real attention only when chief cabinet secretary Yasuo Fukuda said that "depending on the world situation, circumstances and public opinion could require Japan to possess nuclear weapons."[24]

All this, and especially the dispatch of troops to Iraq, was formally welcomed by Washington. Prime Minister Koizumi became a regular visitor to the Bush ranch, and the president called him the "leader of our strong ally."[25] Many observers saw these actions as efforts by a newly vulnerable Japan to gain favor with its longtime protector. And they were at least marginally helpful to the United States. But they could also be seen in a different light—as steps away from the smothering U.S. embrace. For example, did Koizumi really send troops to Iraq to help America, or was it a good way to break old restraints and set new precedents that would give Tokyo a freer hand? Perhaps a bit of both. But clearly Japan's alignment may increasingly be up for grabs. This likelihood became particularly apparent when, over U.S. objections, Japan entered into extensive negotiations with Iran for exclusive rights to develop its giant Azadegan oil fields. Production is expected to start in 2006, reaching 260,000 barrels a day by 2012.[26] Some Japanese see defiance of U.S. wishes in the Middle East as the key to gaining guaranteed energy supplies.

On the other hand, Japan is financially tied to the United States. To keep its export machine going, it has massively intervened in foreign exchange markets to prop up the dollar and, as we have seen, has become the top accumulator of dollar assets. Of course, this is a double-edged sword: it gives Japan great potential leverage with the United States through any threat to dump dollars, but such dumping would also threaten Japan itself with immense losses.

On its present trajectory, Japan will become the Switzerland of Asia—small, aging, rich, and a bit insular. But it will be more vulnerable than Switzerland because of its enormous dollar holdings, whose value could be inflated away or lost in a collapse of the dollar market. A smart move for Japan would be joining NAFTA and adopting the dollar as its official currency. Such a move could fix the value in yen terms of Japan's dollar assets before either of those eventualities. Since Japan is in effect part of a dollar bloc already, dollarization would bring no real loss of sovereignty. Joining NAFTA would guarantee market access under all circumstances and permanently solve the problem of what to do with excess savings. For the United States, it would solve the problem of no savings while locking Japan into orbit. Since Japan probably won't make this move, however, begin thinking of it as Switzerland.

Acu: Asia's New Money

Before leaving Asia, let us consider one last interesting development— the Asian currency unit, or Acu. The world financial situation is strange in that most of the savings and dollar reserves are in Asia, while the International Monetary Fund, the World Bank, and the major financial markets are in Washington, New York, and London. During the Asian financial crisis of 1997–1998, Japan proposed the creation of an Asian Monetary Fund. Although the idea went nowhere at the time because of U.S. objections, in June 2003, eighteen Asian countries moved to create an Asian Bond Fund as the first step toward a bigger market where Asian countries could issue bonds in their own currencies and Asian institutional funds would buy them.

Meanwhile, although it's not fully convertible, China's yuan is increasingly used as a normal unit of exchange outside China. Indeed, the currency analyst Marc Farber told me, "The yuan is the strongest currency in Asia right now. The problem is there aren't enough in circulation." Clearly Asia could use a common local currency. The Hong Kong Monetary Authority head, Joseph Yam, who believes that the current global financial structure is unstable, has suggested the creation of an Acu to be similar to the European Ecu, which preceded the euro. The Deutsche Bank's chief economist, Norbert Walter, agrees: "Asia is a logical candidate to lead reform of global currency markets by creating a common Asian currency."[27] Such a move would only speed the end of the dollar's hegemony and the shift of wealth and power to Asia.

Latin America: China's New Neighbor

From President James Monroe's enunciation of his eponymous Doctrine in 1823, the United States has looked on Latin and South America as absolutely its sphere of influence. We have invaded, occupied, reoccupied, and otherwise intervened in Latin countries and affairs on countless occasions. More recently, Washington has turned to economic integration. The North American Free Trade Agreement with Canada and Mexico effectively made Mexico an extension of the North American economy, operating increasingly under U.S. influence. A wider Free Trade Area of the Americas (FTAA) has been under negotiation since 1998. The United States initially proposed the idea to extend NAFTA to Central and South America and to cement the American way of economics throughout the hemisphere. Things are not, however, going exactly as planned. To begin with, NAFTA has only partially fulfilled its promise. While most analysts agree that Mexico is better off than it would have been with no deal, few see great progress. Real wages in Mexico are no higher now than when the agreement was adopted. The good news for Americans was that there was no "sucking sound" of escaping jobs—but that was the bad news for Mexico, which saw no net increase in jobs.[28] Today the sucking sound in Mexico is jobs leaving for China. In the past five years China has surpassed Mexico as an exporter to the U.S. market, and factories that initially came to Mexico because of NAFTA are closing and moving to China. Mexico is caught in the middle. Its wages are too high to compete with China, but it is not integrated enough or high-tech enough to be fully a part of the U.S. industries that are better able to fend off the Chinese.

As a result, the rest of Latin and South America are not wildly enthusiastic about the FTAA discussions. Adding to their lack of enthusiasm, Japan and the EU have also been negotiating free trade deals with Mexico and the Mercosur free trade agreement countries of Brazil, Argentina, Paraguay, and Uruguay. These deals are less intrusive than the proposed FTAA and permit these countries to become less dependent on the U.S. market.

The really big developments are the rise of Brazil and the arrival of China in South America. Long known as the "eternal country of the future," Brazil at long last seems to be fulfilling its destiny. In the past seven years, exports have nearly tripled as a percentage of GDP, partly as a result of massive investment in everything from soybean cultivation to steel and aircraft. While coffee accounted for over half of exports thirty years ago, today manufactured goods make up the majority of exports, with coffee at less than 2 percent. Stable, honest government, deregulation, privatization, better corporate governance, currency devaluation, and better international debt arrangements have put the Brazilian economy on track to overtake Germany by 2035. Brazil is projected to continue growing rapidly in the second half of the century and eventually become one of the Big Five, along with India, China, the United States, and the European Union. Perhaps more importantly, Brazil is expected to continue to produce world champion soccer teams.

China has significantly powered this growth. For example, during the peak of the soybean harvest, 2,600 trucks and 400 railcars line up every day to deliver their loads at Brazil's southern port of Paraguana, which are then shipped to China. Between 2000 and 2003, Brazil's exports to China jumped from about $2.5 billion to over $10 billion. And it's not only soybeans. Iron ore production is exploding while alumina output will soon double.[29] Cotton, sugar, uranium, timber, manganese, zinc, and airplanes are also on the list of soaring exports to China. At the same time, China is investing in railways, ports, highways, gas pipelines, and other energy-related projects.

Nor is it only Brazil's story. All of South America is increasingly dancing to a Chinese beat. Chile, Peru, Bolivia, and Venezuela are doing big deals with China in copper, oil, and other commodities. In March 2004 Dominica cut ties with Taiwan in return for a $112 million aid package from Beijing. Later that year, China signed long term oil supply deals with Venezuela, undermining Washington's efforts to pressure the Venezuelan government for more democracy. In November 2004 the peripatetic President Hu received another hero's welcome while touring Brazil, Argentina, Chile, and Cuba. In Argentina, which is barely on speaking terms with Washington and Wall Street, he announced a $20 billion investment in oil and gas exploration, communications satellite construction, and railway improvement—a huge boost for a country battered by financial collapse since 2001. While many in Latin America are disappointed with the United States and have even begun to lose faith in democracy, China is giving new hope for Latin America to become a viable part of the world. Moreover, it is doing so without moralizing or attaching geopolitical conditions.

Nowhere is this difference so much appreciated as in Brazil. Always resentful of U.S. preaching and resistant to U.S. trade deals, it has begun to flex its muscles. It has leaked the notion of a strategic alliance with Beijing and made clear that it is cultivating closer China relations as a way of offsetting U.S. dominance.[30] The European Union is Brazil's largest economic partner, and here, too, Brazil cultivates close relations. It led the way in concluding a free trade deal between the

European Union and Mercosur in filing and winning two key legal actions against U.S. agricultural subsidies, and in creating the G20 alliance of developing countries in the WTO. As the National Security Council's former Latin America adviser Richard Feinberg says, "South America is obviously drifting."[31]

Europe: Mr. Welch Meets Mr. Monti

Looking for Europe on a globe, you see a lot of lines and different colored areas bearing the names France, Netherlands, Germany, Britain, Italy, Poland, and Spain. You will find no "Europe" as such—which has been the perspective of much of the world for a long time. Even the Goldman Sachs projections for GDP mentioned at the start of this chapter were for BRICs overtaking Italy, France, Gemany, and the G6, but there was no mention of Europe. Major multinational companies almost invariably speak of the German market or the Italian market and compare them with the U.S., the Chinese, or another national market. No one seems to have discovered Europe.

But Jack Welch has. According to the author T. R. Reid, in late 2000 Welch was preparing to retire from General Electric after a storied career that made him the iconic symbol of the hard-driving, no-nonsense, value-driven American business leader.[32] Suddenly, at the last minute in his career, word leaked that avionics maker Honeywell was about to be taken over by United Technologies. Learning of this late on a Thursday afternoon, Welch called Honeywell's chairman first thing Friday morning to discuss a counteroffer. Too late, said the executive assistant who took the call: the board was already meeting in executive session to accept the United Technologies offer. The deal was done.

Welch wasn't an icon for nothing. Storming the hallways, he found a GE secretary who knew a Honeywell secretary, and eventually a handwritten note from Welch offering to top the United Technologies offer by $5 billion was faxed to Honeywell headquarters and passed into the board meeting. That afternoon, the deal was really done, but not the one everybody expected. GE—not United Technologies—was taking over Honeywell. So put another one on the board for Jack. Right?

Not so fast. This was a really big deal, $42 billion.[33] Many of the industries covered by the two companies have few competitors. Since their merger might create an illegal monopoly, the deal had to be cleared by the Antitrust Division of the U.S. Department of Justice. But Welch had the smartest lawyers and economists around, and they told him "no sweat" with Justice. They were right. The biggest industrial merger in history sailed through the approval process with hardly a dent.

But wait. There's another approval process. Brussels. That's where the Directorate General for Competition of the European Union has its offices. Though GE and Honeywell are American companies, they have operations in most of the European countries, and this deal couldn't go forward in any of them without the approval of the Directorate General for Competition of the European Union. This could be a little more sweat. The Europeans have a theory about antitrust that is like the old American theory before the Americans discovered the miraculous efficiency of big companies. The Europeans think monopolies are bad news. Still, Jack, who hadn't gotten where he was without being persuasive and charming, flew to Brussels to have lunch with the director-general, Mario Monti.

"Mario, call me Jack," said Jack when they met.

"Mr. Welch," responded Mario, "we have a regulatory proceeding under way. I feel the proper approach would be to keep things on a more formal basis. You can call me Signor Monti."

It went downhill from there. Mr. Welch kept making concessions, offering to sell off this division or that subsidiary, and Sgr. Monti kept asking for more. Finally, when Mr. Welch had given all he could without destroying the rationale for the deal, it still wasn't enough. Sgr. Monti called later to tell Mr. Welch that he would recommend against to his bosses on the European Commission.

"The deal is over," he said. "Now I can say to you, 'Good-bye, Jack.'"

If there was no deal in Europe, the whole thing made no business sense. But Welch was not the kind of guy to give up just because some bureaucrat told him it was over. He called President Bush, who was then flying on Air Force One to a summit meeting with European leaders in Sweden. Since the president would be meeting with all the top leaders who were Monti's bosses, Welch asked him to pressure them to overrule Monti. The president did, and that really was the end of the deal—in both Europe and the United States.[34]

The European Union is a single, increasingly powerful entity. It comprises twenty-five countries with a combined population of 456 million and a GDP of $12.6 trillion—compared with the U.S. population of 293 million and GDP of $11.5 trillion. In addition to being the world's largest economy, the EU is also the largest trader of goods and services. It has a president, a parliament, a draft constitution, a cabinet, a central bank, a currency, a bill of rights, a unified patent office, a court system with power to overrule any national court, embassies and ambassadors around the globe, a 60,000 member army independent of NATO or any outside authority, a space agency with 200 satellites in orbit including its own spy satellites, a flag, an anthem, and a national day. Citizens of Europe use a standard license plate and carry standard birth certificates and passports. Although the EU as such does not have a seat on the U.N. Security Council or in the IMF, its twenty-five members (Austria, Belgium, Cyprus, the Czech Republic, Denmark, Estonia, Finland, France, Germany, Greece, Hungary, Ireland, Italy, Latvia, Lithuania, Luxembourg, Malta, the Netherlands, Poland, Portugal, Slovakia, Slovenia, Spain, Sweden, and the United Kingdom) have many seats in these and other international institutions.

There is a tendency to see Europe as economically and geopolitically sclerotic. Both assessments are dangerously wrong. Let's start with economics. Since the mid-1990s, U.S. GDP growth has been faster than Europe's. In 2004, for example, the U.S. growth was 4.5 percent versus about 2 percent for Europe. But during the first five years of this period, the United States was experiencing the financial bubble mentioned earlier; and, as we saw, all U.S. growth has been fueled by enormous growth in debt at all levels. Since the mid-1980s, Europe's growth is higher on average than that of the United States. Much has been made of recent U.S. gains in productivity growth. In the 2000–2003 period, U.S. labor productivity growth was 2.6 percent annually, compared with about 1 percent for Europe.[35] But from 1989 to 2000, U.S. annual productivity growth was only 1.7 percent compared with Europe's 1.9 percent. Moreover, these comparisons ignore the fact that, in terms of GDP produced per hour worked, the EU has long been ahead of the United States. Of the largest 140 global companies, 61 are European, while only 50 are American and 29 are Japanese.[36] Three of the top six chemical manufacturers are European, as are fourteen of the top twenty banks, eight of the ten top insurance companies, the two top food and consumer goods companies, and three of the five top engineering companies. So, though not without problems, Europe should not be underrated.

In global trade, the European Trade commissioner is perhaps the world's most powerful figure, speaking for the world's largest trading bloc. If Jack Welch learned about Europe from Mario Monti, the U.S. Congress learned about it from then EU trade commissioner Pascal Lamy. For years, the U.S. tax system has provided for a tax rebate on export earnings. Claiming this rebate constituted an illegal subsidy, Lamy asked the U.S. government authorities to change it. When Washington stonewalled—Who is this Lamy guy to tell the U.S. Congress what's a subsidy?—Lamy filed a case at the WTO and, after winning, threatened to impose sanctions on $4 billion of U.S. exports to Europe unless Congress changed the tax law. With gritted teeth, the U.S. Congress changed the law.

New Year's Day 2002 was one of the most significant days in world financial history as EU countries threw away their marks, francs, lira, and guilders, and adopted the euro as their currency. In doing so, they set the stage for a tectonic financial shift. Before the establishment of the euro, there had been no real alternative to the dollar. Now there was—and is, with the result we saw earlier of the Russians, OPEC, and other countries having either moved or thinking about moving a large portion of their reserves out of dollars and into euros. Since Europe is the biggest customer for OPEC oil, it would make a lot of sense for OPEC to price oil in euros. Most analysts believe that if the UK and Sweden eventually adopt the euro along with the rest of Europe, OPEC will move to euro pricing—and thus end the dollar's days as the main international money.

Europe is economically very powerful and is gaining geopolitical power for the simple reason that everybody wants to join. Waiting in the wings to join the present twenty-five members are Romania, Turkey, Bulgaria, Ukraine, Croatia, and the former Yugoslav Republic of Macedonia. At some point even Russia may want to join. To become a member of the EU, a country has to become a democracy, enforce a rule of law, adopt market economics, adopt the euro as its currency, and implement the body of EU law that has been established over the past forty years. By joining, a country becomes part of the world's second largest democratic entity (after India) as well as its largest market. By spreading throughout Europe to the borders of the Middle East and Russia, the EU has established a zone of democracy, peace, and stability in a region that has been the source of history's worst wars. Maybe Europe doesn't have a lot of army divisions because it doesn't need them. Or to look at it differently, how big would the U.S. army have to be if Europe were its old self? This new EU is by far the biggest foreign aid donor and has more troops engaged in peacekeeping in places like Afghanistan than any other nation, including the United States.

Europe's appeal lies not only in the prospect it offers of economic development but also in the cultural attractions of the European model.[37] This new Europe is diverse, tolerant, inclusive, as concerned with quality of life as with rate of growth. It emphasizes community relationships and obligations, sustainable development, and global cooperation through dialogue and negotiation. It's about interdependence rather than autonomy, about peace rather than war, about cooperation rather than conflict. Its form of governance is peculiarly modern. In an increasingly networked world, it operates more by convening and arranging conversations than by issuing orders. It is a process for solving "problems without frontiers," in which the concept of nationality and flag-waving patriotism are subordinated to the exigencies of a wider community. This is arguably a more appealing dream than the American one. It can be universal, while the American dream is tied tightly to America and its peculiar conditions. Combined with its economic and financial might, this approach to governance gives Europe great power beyond its material means.

When tensions arose in 2002 between the United States and Europe over the invasion of Iraq, defense secretary Donald Rumsfeld spoke of an "old Europe" that opposed U.S. policies and of a "new Europe" that backed them. A year and a half later, however, the countries of "new Europe" had all eagerly signed up to join the EU, while pulling their troops out of Iraq as soon as their initial commitments were completed.

A deep division has arisen in the old Western alliance. Pew Research Center polls show dramatically declining opinions of the United States all across Europe. Germany went from 78 percent favorable in 1998 to 38 percent in 2004. In France the numbers were similar; and even in Great Britain, 55 percent said they see America as a threat to global peace. In Greece, Spain, Finland, and Sweden, the United States was seen as more menacing than Iran or North Korea. In Poland, perhaps the European country closest to the United States, the first postcommunist president, Lech Walesa, said, "America failed its exam as a superpower. They are a military and economic superpower but not morally or politically anymore. This is a tragedy for us."[38] It could also be a tragedy for America.

The EU will not become a superpower like the United States, with carrier battle groups deployed around the world. But over the next ten to fifteen years, as it consolidates and adds new members, it will have a significant impact on the balance of power. After that, however, disastrous demographics will begin to sap Europe's vitality. At the moment, the elderly make up 16 percent of the EU population; within five years, they will make up 27 percent.[39] The total population will peak around 2022, and by 2050 will have contracted by 13 percent from its 2000 total.[40] Italy will lose a fifth of its population; Spain, more than a fifth. Germany will also shrink dramatically. The current median age of 37.7 years will rise to 52.3 by 2050,[41] and the working-age population will fall to 50 percent of the total.[42] Like Japan, this is going to be a really old and tired society unless it gets massive immigration.

Europe is already receiving large inflows of legal and illegal immigrants, mostly from North Africa and the Middle East. Nonnationals now compose about 7 percent of the population of Germany and France and 5 percent of the EU as a whole.[43] But assimilation is proving difficult. In France the question whether Muslim girls may wear headscarves in schools has been the subject of a national commission and presidential decision; some countries are voting to restrict further immigration. The German press is full of discussion about the *leitkultur* (main culture) and the need to adhere to it. In the Netherlands a popular film producer and author was murdered by an Islamic extremist for making a film critical of Islamic attitudes toward women. It is not clear when—or even whether—Europe will learn the knack of peacefully assimilating large numbers of outsiders. If it does, it will be the most powerful entity in the world. If it does not, it will gradually decline and die.

The United States: Vulnerable at the Bridge Table

Think of the major countries and the EU as players in a game of bridge. Of course, bridge is a game for only four players, but we'll stretch the rules a little. If you had your choice of whose hand you'd like to play, you'd almost surely pick the American. It has all the aces. The U.S. GDP may be a bit behind that of the EU, but it's more than twice as large as Japan's, the next largest single-country economy. And U.S. overall productivity is the highest. The United States is still the overall leader in technology. It has the best universities and spends by far the most money on R&D. It is the financial capital of the world, and the global economy runs on its money. It spends more than the rest of the world combined on defense and, not surprisingly, has overwhelming military superiority. It has twelve aircraft carrier battle groups patrolling the oceans of the world; no other country even has one. It can fly its army anywhere in the world in twenty-four hours, as no other country could dream of doing. It has the highest per capita income of the major nations. It is blessed with a large, beautiful territory full of important minerals and fertile farmland. At nearly 300 million, its population is the third largest—or fourth, if you count the EU as one.

Significantly, its demographics are pretty good. It will age a bit, but nothing like Japan and Europe or even China, and its population keeps on growing. By 2050 today's 293 million Americans will have increased to 400 million; and, in the second half of the century, America will rapidly pass the EU in population. By 2050 the age of the median American will creep up to 40, compared with 43 for China, 48 for Europe, and 53 for Japan (India will be 38). Finally, until very recently, the United States enjoyed enormous reservoirs of goodwill throughout the world. What more could you want? Go for a slam. These cards should be pretty easy to play.

But the United States is playing them as badly as possible—as though it was the only player that mattered: saving is down drastically, the U.S. net saving that was 11 percent of GDP in the 1960s having declined to near zero today, and households being in debt up to their eyeballs, after borrowing against inflated home equity values to maintain themselves in a style many can't really afford. The government has also gone into record debt, with budget deficits over 4 percent of GDP, rising—according to General Accounting Office projections—to 8 percent over the next ten to fifteen years. This debt is not being used to invest in new infrastructure, plant, or equipment to generate future wealth. Federal spending on physical capital, R&D, and education and training, which averaged over 6 percent of GDP in the 1960s and 1970s, is now well under 3 percent of GDP. To look at it another way, future-oriented outlays that accounted for 32 percent of total federal spending in 1965 have fallen to 14 percent today.[44] Instead, the spending is going into benefits for individuals, which are going to rise dramatically as baby boomers retire and need more medical attention. Nor has private infrastructure been maintained. The labs and facilities of our world-class universities are beginning to look antiquated compared with those being installed in Asia and Europe.

As for education, it is even worse than the poor performance of U.S. students on international tests of math and science knowledge imply. American students actually do progressively less well the longer they stay in school. Few study a foreign language or can find Greenland on a map. Teachers are paid poorly and accorded less honor and respect relative to other professionals in the United States than in most other countries. Not surprisingly, they increasingly come from the lower half of their university class and frequently—particularly in science and math—are not certified in the subjects they are assigned to teach. The United States has a crazy-quilt school district system funded mostly by local property taxes: if you live in a rich area, the schools are likely to be reasonably good; but God help you if you live in the central city or in a really poor area. There is no standardization of curricula or of expected results or any way of ensuring that students in Los Angeles are at roughly the same level as those in Palo Alto. In short, this rich, powerful country is educating its children less well than many other countries and less well than it did in the past.

In the international arena, the United States has insisted on owning the game but has not been overly concerned that everyone play by the rules. The fact that the dollar is still the world's money means that, however the cards are dealt, America always holds trumps: it removes all restraint on how much America buys abroad and how much debt it accumulates both at home and abroad. For this reason, the U.S. government generally likes a strong dollar because that means Americans can buy and borrow more. A strong dollar also favors Wall Street and the whole financial industry, which is very powerful in Washington. While both Wall Street and Washington say they are strongly opposed to industrial policies in which the government picks winners and losers, the strong dollar is a general government policy with a clear winner. But there are also losers. Since any U.S. firm providing goods or services in a competitive international market will be disadvantaged by an overly strong dollar, it is not surprising that U.S. companies have increasingly moved their operations offshore and that the U.S. trade deficit is rising inexorably. The long-held assumption that U.S. exports of robust services and high-tech products would so dominate world markets as to balance trade has been seriously undermined by the third wave of globalization. Instead, much of the technology developed in U.S. universities and funded by taxpayer money is likely to be commercialized abroad.

Further exacerbating the situation is the fact that, despite its embrace of free trade, America is relatively unconcerned about creating the conditions necessary for realizing that doctrine. As owner of the playing field, whose tilt it thinks it can pretty much shift at will, America doesn't necessarily pay much attention to that tilt. Wedded as it is to the Ricardian view that one-way free trade is fine, it feels that we shouldn't get too upset if other countries want to sell and not buy. If they want to manage currency values to keep their exports cheap or subsidize their exports and dump in our market, it's a kind of a gift to our consumers. Take it and be happy. If plants close and move abroad or software services are offshored, don't worry. Just move up the ladder to something more sophisticated, high-tech, and entrepreneurial. Although this philosophy has the pluses and minuses we have considered, it surely accelerates the offshore movement of U.S. productive capacity.

Further accelerating that movement is what happens when U.S. businesses interact with governments whose industrial policies focus on financial investment incentives. Businessmen who are sovereigns of their own domains in America and disdain U.S. officials will be very sensitive to the wishes of China's leaders; they show respect even in tiny Singapore. Investments that in the United States would be made in a truly free market get made elsewhere through large financial inducements and subtle but powerful political pressures. Yet the U.S. government accepts this practice as the optimal working of the market.

One reason the U.S. government is complacent about this situation is that it is being lobbied by the very business leaders who are the recipients of the approvals in Beijing and elsewhere. Another is that it has no understanding of the linkages between industries and technologies. The scenario that losing the ability to make a VCR means losing out on the development of charge-coupled devices, which in turn means losing out on development of digital cameras and so forth, is not a matter of discussion in many U.S. circles. Thus there is little understanding of the impact of economies of scale, intellectual property, and the barriers to subsequent entry that arise simply from the existence of a prior entrant. As a result, the United States accepts asymmetric investment and trade conditions that further exacerbate U.S. deficits, which in turn result in enormous piles of U.S. Treasury bonds sitting in the coffers of foreign central banks, where they give foreign leaders—particularly those in Japan, China, Korea, Singapore, and the EU—enormous influence over U.S. decisions of all kinds.

A card that the United States has played particularly poorly is the respect and liking in which we were held by the world for decades. This favorable opinion has declined dramatically in recent years. In the age of the third wave of globalization, when the world is ever more interdependent and everyone is effectively in everyone else's living room, the U.S. insistence on acting like the Lone Ranger and asserting absolute autonomy of decision and action is simply disliked—as the public opinion polls reflect.

When you add to the trade deficits the rising American dependence on foreign oil and the recent decline in respect and liking for the United States, the result is that the President of the United States, the head of the most powerful country the world has ever seen, is in a very tight box. In every part of the world and in every arena—strategic, political, economic—the United States will find its capacity for action increasingly restricted and its range of options reduced. We still possess a strong, though not overwhelming, hand, but we will have to start to play our cards a good deal better.

Consider, for example, that you have just been elected president and are now receiving your first intelligence briefing.

Briefer: Mr. President, the first situation to be aware of is what's developing in Taiwan. The Taiwanese have voted for formal independence from mainland China and are requesting that we send the Seventh Fleet to visit Taiwanese waters to warn China against any precipitate action. However, the State Department has just been informed by the Chinese ambassador here in Washington that any move of the fleet toward Taiwan will be regarded as hostile by Beijing, which will immediately begin dumping its reserves of Treasuries on the open market.

The Japanese are apparently aware of the Chinese threat, because there is already evidence of Japanese selling off some of their Treasuries, and the dollar is falling rapidly in Europe, where the markets have been open now for several hours.

Iran has announced plans to test a nuclear device. Japan, China, and the EU, all of which are heavily dependent on Iranian oil, have urged us privately not to make a big deal out of it.

In Moscow President Putin is mad about NATO's invitation to Ukraine to join and has sent a personal note to you demanding that you rescind the invitation. If not, he says he'll start dumping dollars. Russia doesn't buy much from the U.S. and doesn't really need the dollars. So this is a credible threat.

The Saudis are really unhappy about our pressure on the royal family to open up and democratize. They have initiated discussion at OPEC headquarters in Vienna on pricing oil in euros or a basket of currencies rather than dollars.

Finally, the drought in the Midwest has been so devastating that it looks like we're going to have to import soybeans from Brazil. The price is already in the stratosphere.

Otherwise, things are pretty quiet. Congratulations on your inauguration, Mr. President.

Who would want to be president with such perilous issues facing him or her at the start of the term? More to the point, do we Americans want to allow things to get so bad? We need to wake up to these issues so that America learns to play the game with due respect for its own people as well as the other players at the table.

CHAPTER 12

To Ride the Third Wave

> The dominant leadership mood of the day
> is to whistle past the graveyard.
> —JIM HOAGLAND
> *WASHINGTON POST*

As they rang in the new year in January 1914, European celebrants were on top of the world. It was the best of times. The globalization they had launched five hundred years before had brought them worldwide empires and wealth far beyond anything Prince Henry could have imagined when he sent his captains from Sagres searching for the riches of the Indies. The economy was truly global, and new technology—in the form of the airplane, radio, and automobile—was dramatically shrinking time and distance. Technology was also raising productivity at a spectacular rate, and new forms of business corporations were beginning to exploit the technology on a global scale. French was the international language, the royal families were intermarried; the elites gathered annually at the posh watering places of the day, and there was no end in sight to the good times. But the global system had serious flaws that few recognized. The technology and industrial development that created such wealth also set powerful new forces in motion that would severely test the system. Historians have long sought the cause of World War I and tried to allocate blame. But the truth is that none and all were to blame. The countries were programmed to act in certain ways: each had its own logic. But their logic combined made no sense, although none could or would see that. As spring and then summer came, Europe of 1914 was an accident waiting to happen.

We may be in a similar situation today. I am not predicting a disaster along the lines of the Great War. I don't anticipate war or chaos, although they are possible. What I see is an apparently successful global system with serious flaws. The hegemony of the floating dollar allows many of the major players to be irresponsible. Americans consume too much and save too little while Asians save too much and consume too little. Some are playing a mercantilist or quasi-mercantilist game while others are playing more or less free trade and open markets. Yet all are pretending that all are playing the free trade game. The potential for misunderstanding and conflict is enormous. New technology in the form of the Internet and other developments examined in this volume are shrinking the globe into a single community by negating time and distance. It is also unleashing new forces that are powering a new kind of globalization. As in 1914, these new forces have the potential for great creativity and progress. But in further stressing the flaws in the current global system, they could precipitate a serious crisis that would then feed on itself.

Each of today's players, including the great business and nongovernmental organizations, has its own logic. It is understandable that Americans consume so much and that Asians save so much and that everyone likes the dollar's hegemony and that business responds to the powers that be. But when these factors combine, the logic is illogical and ultimately unsustainable. It is an accident waiting to happen. To prevent it from happening, I offer the following suggestions at a time when the president's National Intelligence Council notes, "At no time since the formation of the Western alliance system in 1949 have the shape and nature of international alignments been in such a state of flux."[1]

The United States

Although America has not yet caught on, its relative economic superiority and power are rapidly slipping away. Far from leading the world on a global march to freedom, the United States could find itself hard-pressed to maintain a reasonable standard of living and defend its vital interests. While America still has the best cards, it will have to hold on to them—and learn to play them a lot better. Unfortunately, the hand and the position of play have deteriorated since I first wrote about these issues nearly twenty years ago in *Trading Places: How We Allowed Japan to Take the Lead*. Maintaining a unipolar, hegemonic leadership is out of the question. It is no longer possible nor desirable for the long-term welfare of Americans. But there is much America can and should do to mitigate the impact of wage competition, maintain the promise of opportunity at the heart of the American Dream, provide for a continually rising standard of living more equally distributed, and continue to influence the course of global affairs.

The first step is to realize that there is a problem. America needs to recognize that many of the assumptions guiding its economic policy are at odds with the realities of today's global economy. Its performance in a broad range of areas—including saving, education, energy and water conservation, critical infrastructure, R&D investment, and workforce upskilling—is far below the standard of many other nations. America needs to understand that its refusal to have a broad competitiveness policy is, in fact, a policy. And it gives leading U.S. CEOs no choice but to play into the strategies of other countries. This policy, according to its proponents, leaves decisions to the unseen hand of the market. Actually, however, it leaves them to the highly visible hands of lobbyists and foreign policymakers. It is a policy that ultimately leads to impoverishment.

I have been involved in several efforts to identify principles of national competitiveness. The first one is always that a nation's industries cannot remain competitive internationally if the nation's overall economic environment is not competitive. It is impossible, for example, to have successful world-class competitors based in economies characterized by hyperinflation or lack of crucial infrastructure or low educational achievement. The first priority of American leaders—even more important than fighting terror or spreading liberty—should be to ensure long-term U.S. competitiveness. Without it, nothing else will make any difference. The president should establish an independent blue ribbon commission—headed by the chairman of the Federal Reserve or another major figure and including leaders from government, private industry, academia, and the media—to assess and make recommendations for shoring up America's long-term competitive potential. Once the problem is squarely faced, a number of crucial measures must be considered in respect to the ongoing issues of the dollar; savings, taxes, and spending; pensions, health care, and wage insurance; education; structural competitiveness; energy; and bilateral international initiatives.

Role of the Dollar

To preempt the gathering financial crisis and ensure a sounder basis for the third wave of globalization, the United States should take the lead in a global effort to reduce the role of the dollar. It must do so gradually and cautiously. Because the whole system now depends on U.S. consumption and the dirty floating of the dollar, any sudden or unilateral change could precipitate disaster. As a first step, the United States might convene a new Bretton Woods Conference of key global leaders to devise a plan. The U.S. government might announce beforehand the measures it would take to begin balancing the federal budget and creating more savings in the U.S. economy. It could then ask other major countries to come to the meeting with plans for raising consumption and stimulating their own economies. The initial objective of the conference would be to agree on joint implementation of these plans. It must be joint, since action by only one side would be worse than no action at all.

To Create New Money

The second step could be to create an international planning commission, perhaps in the IMF, to develop a scheme for eventual adoption of a new international currency. This might involve interim steps like pricing oil and other key commodities in a basket of currencies including the yen, dollar, euro, and renminbi. Mechanisms for continued coordination of fiscal and monetary policy would also have to be developed.

An alternative reserve currency unit already exists in the form of IMF special drawing rights, or SDRs. These were originally created in 1969 to support the Bretton Woods fixed exchange rate system. Although the collapse of the Bretton Woods system in 1973 and the advent of the current floating exchange rate system obviated the original purpose of the SDRs, they are still used today as the IMF's unit of account, and some countries hold in their reserves SDRs that can be exchanged for IMF member country currencies, just like dollars or gold. The value of the SDR is presently based on a basket of currencies that includes the euro, the yen, the pound sterling, and the dollar, which provides a tie to present market values. Consequently it might provide a vehicle for moving away from today's largely dollar-based system. Or perhaps some other vehicle would be preferable. The point is ultimately to get away from dollar hegemony.

Such a step away from the dollar as the world's money would be a big one for Americans, given our pride in our country and, by extension, the dollar. But in the long run, discretion is the better part of valor. The dollar's present role makes Americans feel good in the short term, but ultimately it will kill us. The way to maximize long-term welfare and power is to reduce the role of the dollar as fast as possible. I don't mean that the dollar should cease being prominent; only that it should not be the only player.

Energy

After changing the dollar's role, the single most important step the United States could take to preserve its long-term welfare and power would be to declare energy independence—and mean it. Reducing both energy intensity (energy per dollar of GDP) and dependence on foreign energy supplies must be given the highest priority. We have seen the likely cost (in terms of the trade deficit and reduced growth, as well as in vulnerability to global political developments) of not doing so. The good news is that reductions would be easy to make. For example, the miles per gallon of the U.S. light vehicle fleet doubled between 1978 and 1987 in response to new laws requiring better gas efficiency. Since 1987, while other countries have continued to improve the efficiency of their fleets, the United States has gone backward. Why? Because SUVs, being technically classified as trucks, are exempt from the gas mileage requirements. As Americans have shifted en masse to driving SUVs, the fleet mileage has declined from 26.5 miles per gallon to about 19 miles per gallon. Just applying the mileage regulations to SUVs would significantly reduce U.S. oil dependence. Some of America's best energy analysts at the Rocky Mountain Institute have estimated the country could be completely off oil by 2025.[2] Even if they are only half right, the result would be truly revolutionary. Here are some key elements of the strategy—none of which involve gasoline taxes or even new fuel efficiency regulations.

Lighter, Stronger Vehicles

The United States today gets twice as much output from a barrel of oil as it did in 1975. Using the latest technologies, we could double oil efficiency again with an investment of only $12 per barrel of oil that now costs $35 per barrel and may well cost $80 or more by 2025. The key is to use advanced composite materials and lightweight steel that can double present hybrid car and light truck efficiency while also improving safety and performance. Not only would the vehicle's total extra cost be repaid from fuel savings in about three years, but the factories to produce them would be smaller and cheaper as well.

Revenue and size-neutral "feebates" could induce customers to shift quickly to these vehicles by combining fees on inefficient vehicles with rebates on efficient ones.

A scrap-and-replace program could lease superefficient cars to low-income Americans, who tend to own most of the gas guzzlers, which could then be scrapped.

Pentagon Energy Leadership

The Pentagon uses huge amounts of oil and drives new technologies. The need for agility, rapid deployment, and better logistics make it logical for the U.S. military to take the lead in developing these new technologies and techniques. In the service of energy efficiency, we should use smart procurement and targeted technology acquisition, two old techniques for driving development that have proven their success.

Federal Financing

By the same token, federal loan guarantees could help speed up the $70 billion retooling investment necessary for the auto industry and its suppliers to make ultralight vehicles. At the same time, there should be loan guarantees for airlines to buy more efficient new airplanes and for truckers to get gas-sipping heavy trucks.

Biomass

Much of the money for such measures could be obtained from saving on farm subsidies by promoting development of a major biofuels industry. New cellulose-to-ethanol conversion technology can double previous yields at less cost in capital and energy. Replacing hydrocarbons with plant-derived carbohydrates could displace about one-fourth of U.S. oil consumption and strengthen rural America by boosting farm income by tens of billions of dollars annually.

Get Smart

Finally, better use of off-peak consumption incentives for electric usage, fully synchronized traffic lights, on-ramp metering, wider usage of new highway paving materials, electronic tolls, and other already known techniques could complete America's declaration of energy independence.

Savings, Taxes, and Spending

Savings Our Way to Health

To ensure long-term economic health, the United States needs to pay attention to saving and paying as it goes. The federal budget deficit must be brought under control, and the public needs to get back to the

8–10 percent personal savings rates that prevailed between 1960 and 1990. In other words, something must be done about savings incentives, taxes, and spending. Right now the U.S. tax code looks like a "picking winners and losers," policy written by the housing industry and foreign exporters to the U.S. market. The mortgage interest deduction, by favoring housing over all other investments, distorts allocation of U.S. capital. It might be an acceptable price to pay if it were just to help people own a home. But it isn't. The deduction is also available for your vacation mansion at the beach or in Aspen. It also allows you to take a tax deductible home equity loan to pay for your new suit or a vacation in Aruba. This system fosters greater debt and contributes to the trade deficit and the volatility of the dollar. A modest step would be to halt home equity loans and disallow the mortgage interest deduction on second homes. We can continue to help young people get a foothold in the American Dream, but we must stop making it easier for millionaires to build luxury mansions.

Tax the Spender

The current U.S. tax system is a monstrosity of deductions, exclusions, and special allowances that few can understand and that fails in just about all its objectives. For example, GE recently announced an 18 percent increase in 2004 earnings, due to a surprisingly low tax rate. The corporate tax rate is 35 percent, but GE actually paid only 11.2 percent as a result of all the special provisions.[3] This is not a criticism of GE. Few corporations actually pay the full tax rate—not because they cheat but because they, just like individuals, work hard to find deductions. The problem is not the corporations. It's the tax code. So let's change it.

Instead of taxing income, America should be taxing consumption. That's right. We should junk the corporate income tax and abolish the personal income tax for most people. In its place, we should introduce one of three possible consumption taxes. We could simply add a national sales tax to the final price of most goods and services we buy at the retail level, just as most states do today. An alternative would be the so-called valued-added tax (VAT), under which businesses pay the tax at each stage of production and pass the cost on to consumers in the form of higher prices. The VAT is used throughout Europe. A secondary aspect of the VAT is that it is rebated on exports. Finally, the Feds could collect the money through a system of withholding and annual returns, as they do now. Under this "consumed income tax," you the taxpayer add up all your income, subtract all that you have saved and invested, and pay tax on what is left.

All of these measures have pros and cons that would have to be carefully weighed in designing an actual new system. Doing it right means eliminating interest deductions and other tax breaks along with introducing the new system. If done right, the tax code would be much simpler: it would eliminate double taxation of capital income and sharply reduce the use of tax shelters. Most economists also think it would add a few tenths of a percent to growth each year. Beyond that, it's fair. If you work and save, and I work and don't, why should you pay more tax than I do over your lifetime? The fact that such a tax would tend to have the poor paying more of their income in taxes than the rich could be addressed in two ways: one would be an income tax that would kick in at $100,000 of income or more, combined with a higher estate tax.

Control the Drivers

The big drivers of federal spending are going to be health care, social security, interest on the federal debt, and defense. We can and must address the interest issue by taking measures to reduce the debt. In the end, health care will almost certainly require a national health insurance system of some kind. The sooner we move in that direction, the less the eventual cost will probably be. Social security can be handled relatively easily by extending the retirement age and raising the base on which social security tax is paid. Or we could introduce private social security accounts, but only if the transition to these accounts is fully funded by taxes without recourse to more borrowing. Finally, the United States should not try to maintain a hegemonic military position from a relatively declining position of economic power. It will be in our interest to strengthen alliances and multilateral organizations like the United Nations so that others may bear a burden commensurate with their rising power. The United States should plan on cutting defense spending and reducing commitments over the long term.

Safe Safety Nets

American employees of all types are going to be living in an uncertain, rapidly changing, unforgiving environment. The old model of a career with one company and a defined benefit pension and indexed health care in retirement belongs in a museum. Today you're likely to outlive your company. It's also likely that you won't want to or won't be able to stay with your company for a long time even if it survives. It's becoming a jungle out there in the workplace. For the employee, this puts a premium on flexibility, on being able to roll with the punches and move quickly and easily from one position and one company to another. Society also has a stake in this kind of flexibility. It minimizes unemployment and social welfare payments and maximizes overall production and government tax receipts.

Portable Health Care and Pensions

But there's a problem. Key parts of most workers' personal safety nets, such as pensions and health care plans, are tightly organized around the company currently employing them. These plans are not flexible, having been in part designed to keep workers where they are. Both government and corporations need to give serious thought to creating portable systems. A universal pension plan based on deductions from workers' paychecks and voluntary matching payments by employers would create flexibility and might, at the same time, raise savings by bringing all workers into the system. Also crucial is a scheme for portable health care plans. The single consideration that ties people most tightly to their job and their company is the health care plan. Losing the plan is frequently the most devastating part of losing a job. Cobra provisions that allow a person who has been laid off to pay out of his or her own pockets to maintain an existing health care plan are inadequate because the cost is often prohibitive, especially for someone who has no income. If America wishes to minimize the downside of globalization's third wave, it will have to find a way of creating a portable health care program, no matter how complex the task.

Wage Insurance

One problem in losing a job is how to find a new one—something as good as or better than the one you lost. But sometimes the choice is between taking a job that pays less or staying out of work in the hope that something better will turn up. A new experiment called wage insurance is now being tried as part of the U.S. government's long-standing Trade Adjustment Assistance program. This program for people who have lost their jobs due to imports has long paid them to get retraining and assistance in finding new work. Now there is a new twist. If a new job pays less than the old job, the program will make up half the differential for a period of time. This kind of wage insurance can speed movement to new employment by cushioning the shock of less pay and giving a worker a chance to move up in the new job before the program assistance is withdrawn. One important question is why it should be available only to those laid off as a result of foreign trade. This program should be available to all laid-off workers, as it would greatly improve the flexibility of the U.S. workforce.

Education

The problems of the U.S. education system have been under discussion for some time but without—to judge by students' international test scores—much evident progress toward their solution. Reform of the whole system might well be the focus of another presidential blue ribbon commission. Here are a few observations and simple recommendations.

Discipline

I have learned three important lessons from observing my daughter's experience with home-schooling her two children. First, home-schooling is the new growth industry in America. There are now about 1.2 million home-schooled students, and the number is growing by nearly 100,000 annually. Second, a lot of good, inexpensive material is available for these programs, and the kids can and do learn much more than those in conventional classrooms. Test scores consistently show home-schooled kids significantly outperforming their peers in public school. Third, according to surveys by the Department of Education, the chief motivating factor for home-schooling is "concern about the environment of other schools."[4] When I asked my daughter what that meant, Anne explained that the middle school to which her kids would be assigned has two police on duty at all times. Said she, "I really don't want my kids in a place where they have to be guarded by cops all the time. How can kids learn in a place like that?" Good question. Apparently a lot of other parents are asking it too.

Discipline would seem to be the minimum requirement for a place of learning. Why can't we have it in our schools? For starters, we need to think seriously about empowering teachers and administrators to establish discipline and respect in the classrooms without fear of lawsuits. Without both, nothing else is possible.

Higher Pay, Greater Flexibility

Another key issue is the quality of people we attract into teaching. Sometimes I wonder why we have hundreds of thousands of good, dedicated teachers in this country when we pay them so poorly, allow students to disrespect them, and give them little status in the community. As a result, all too frequently our schools lack the teachers they need—particularly for math and science teaching, where too many people are teaching subjects for which they were never prepared. In this regard, two solutions come to mind. First, we should pay teachers as if we really believed that our children are our most precious possessions and need to be educated and cared for accordingly. If a newly minted MBA can make well over $100,000, why can't a newly minted teacher with a master's degree make at least $75,000? Why can't a master teacher with long seniority make $250,000? If we pay that much to the people who design our cars and computers, why can't we pay that much to the people who design our kids?

Certification is the second issue. There are legitimate reasons for requiring certification, but some flexibility is needed. Too much talent goes to waste in our communities. Let's figure out how to tap it so that people in the neighborhood who are expert teachers in key subjects can have a supplemental role in our schools.

In the 1960s, I studied Japanese in graduate school on a grant fully funded by the National Defense Education Act. The act was aimed at increasing the number of students studying exotic foreign languages, of which there was then a serious dearth. Today, with the declining enrollment in science and engineering courses that are the building blocks for a high-tech economy and society, we should consider something, like a National Antiterrorist Education Act, to fully fund anyone studying for a science or engineering degree. To further add to our pool of future technologists, we might also consider automatically extending permanent residence status to foreign students who come here for advanced study to make it easier for them to stay once they have graduated.

Lifetime Education

Permanent education is going to be the name of the game in the world of 3 billion new capitalists. Since employees at all levels and at all stages of their careers will find it increasingly necessary to upgrade and augment their knowledge and skills, they should be helped through training credits, other financial incentives, and the necessary infrastructure. For example, our community colleges should be wired to all the great centers of learning as well as extensively throughout our communities.

Subsidize Education, Not Cotton

This all takes money, but it shouldn't be too difficult to find some. In 2004 we spent about $3 billion on subsidies to 25,000 U.S. cotton farmers whose average net worth is about $1 million. That's just one crop. Some states spend more money on helping young people go into farming than they do on helping fund new high-tech ventures. Let's take some of the farm subsidy money and put it into education for a real win-win solution.

Build Strong Foundations

All microeconomic and international trade issues can be covered by the broad term "structural competitiveness," the area no one has charge of in the United States. We need to have someone constantly studying the building blocks of our economy, looking at how they fit together, and how they might be affected by all the regulatory, legislative, and trade and other factors at work. South Korea is far ahead of the United States in the application of Internet and broadband technology because that country's leaders approached regulatory issues from the perspective of how this technology could enhance economic growth and competitiveness. The United States dealt with the regulatory issues primarily as matters of fairness and competition. No one in the United States was charged with getting the most out of this new technology in terms of growth, productivity, and competitiveness. By the same token, no U.S. official is looking at the financial investment incentives being offered by foreign governments to entice U.S. firms or considering counteroffers to keep technology and those jobs in the United States. Nor is any U.S. official calculating the long-term damage to the U.S. economy of manipulated exchange rates or considering how to respond.

Put Someone in Charge

In seeking someone with real power to be in charge of this stuff, the office of the vice president might be a good place to lodge the overall responsibility. Below that, how about combining the departments of Commerce, Energy, and Transportation, along with NASA, into one Department of International Industry and Commerce. The vice president would chair a president's council on competitiveness that would include the secretary of this new department, along with the secretaries of Treasury, Defense, Justice, and State and the U.S. Trade Representative. Whatever we do, however we organize it, the main thing is to take the economic nuts and bolts.

Feed the Ecosystem of Competitiveness

In the rules for national competitiveness noted earlier, the key point was infrastructure or, as the PCAST report calls it, an ecosystem of competitiveness. Far from being a few venture capital companies or semiconductor producers, Silicon Valley is a densely interwoven network of universities, law firms, venture capitalists, R&D centers, local government officials, major companies, and small start-ups. In some measure, all depend on each other. Being competitive, therefore, requires just as much attention to the key interrelationships as to the single elements themselves. From this perspective, what happens to important end-use markets or to key intellectual property rights or to university research can be critical to the viability of the whole ecosystem and, ultimately, to the nation's ability to remain competitive. The operation of the system is not necessarily linear. In other words, the disappearance of important companies might have as much impact on the number of students enrolled in the university engineering courses as the decline in that number might have on the ability of the companies to remain competitive.

Moreover, the development of these ecosystems is evolutionary, not revolutionary. The full impact of today's developments might not be felt for a decade or more. The fact that this view (initially an intuitive one that sprang from our experience in high-tech industries and international trade) has since been confirmed mathematically by the work of Gomory and Baumol should demonstrate both the legitimacy and the absolute necessity of the government's concerning itself with these developments. Rather than being protectionist or even tending toward picking winners and losers, such concern is their antithesis and would aim to prevent the protectionism and mercantilism that so frequently distort these competitive ecosystems.

Stop Mercantilism

In this context, the United States must respond to interventions in foreign currency markets that distort trade and investment decisions by acting as indirect subsidies. Because such currency policies can nullify and impair the concessions made in WTO agreements and may therefore be in violation of those agreements, the U.S. government must challenge possible violations. The WTO must be persuaded to deal with currency policies that undermine that organization's entire basis.

In the same way, the U.S. government should actively review the investment incentives other governments are offering to attract major installations from U.S. companies. It is one thing for a factory or an R&D center to be located in a particular place owing to market considerations, but entirely another if the place has been chosen mainly because of tax holidays and other subsidies. The United States should not sit benignly by as perfectly competitive operations are moved overseas in response to such subsidies. We should counter with our own incentives. Some state governments try to do this, but their resources are obviously more limited than those of the federal government. The U.S. government ought to know at least as much about the investment thinking of its companies as the Chinese, Singaporese, and other governments routinely do. Just as foreign economic development boards actively work to promote investment in their jurisdictions, so the U.S. government ought to be working to promote investment in the United States.

Upgrade Infrastructure

A final issue that is of huge importance but little discussed is infrastructure, both physical and institutional. Why are many foreign companies doing their initial public offerings in the United States? Because the U.S. financial markets and corporate governance rules are the most transparent and the best. Still, there is room for improvement, as Enron and other scandals clearly demonstrated. But they are an essential part of what makes New York the financial capital of the world. To be competitive, America needs to keep improving its financial infrastructure while upgrading institutions like the Centers for Disease Control, the National Institutes of Health, and research universities around the country.

The U.S. government also needs to take a hard look at the country's physical infrastructure. People who travel abroad often have a slight feeling of returning to a developing country. While most foreign cities have a fast rail connection from the airport to downtown, most U.S. cities do not. The whole U.S. air traffic system, from the airlines to air traffic control technology, is obviously under stress. In Europe and Japan, rail is fast, comfortable, convenient, and efficient. U.S. rail travel is torture. Among international travelers, the U.S. telephone system has become a bit of a joke. My mobile phone works better in Bombay than in Washington, D.C. Many of our municipal water systems are getting close to one hundred years old, and the blackout of 2003 showed the weaknesses in our electric grid. We cannot be competitive with a second-rate infrastructure. The U.S. government needs to make improvement a top priority.

Bilateral International Initiatives

Although its relative power and influence is in decline, the United States at this moment remains overwhelmingly the most important country on the globe. The unusually fluid international alignments present a once-in-a-lifetime opportunity for the United States to use its still vast power to reset the global table in ways that will favor its interests for a long time to come. Five specific initiatives should be pursued in respect to NAFTA, Japan, the European Union, India, and China.

NAFTA

This trade agreement should be turned into an economic and, eventually, a political union along the lines of the EU. It is critically important to all of North America that Mexico succeed. This will require greater integration with Canada and the United States than is possible or likely under NAFTA. Steps should be taken toward the full integration of the three economies and the adoption of the dollar as the official currency in both Mexico and Canada—in order to relieve both of the costs of dollar fluctuations while also creating a more efficient market for all.

Japan

The NAFTA countries should invite Japan to join, and Japan should also be invited to adopt the dollar as its currency. Here what may seem like madness has a method. Japan, as we know, holds a lot of dollar assets and worries about their long-term value. Its economy is already highly integrated with the U.S. economy, and it has strong links to Canada and Mexico, with which it recently concluded a free trade agreement. It suffers a heavy cost burden as the result of dollar/yen fluctuations and is under constant uncertainty about the possibility of a protectionist backlash in the U.S. Congress. All these uncertainties and costs could be eliminated if it joined NAFTA and dollarized. In addition, dollarization would enable Japan to negotiate a conversion value for its dollar assets that would guarantee their long-term worth. For the United States, this deal would marry Japan's surpluses with U.S. deficits and create a dollar zone in trade balance with the rest of the world. It would also serve to keep Japan in the U.S. orbit and prevent it from slipping into China's.

European Union

Far from trying to divide the EU, the United States should do its best to unite it and encourage its expansion, along with the broad adoption of the euro as an international currency. For example, the United

States might encourage the EU to incorporate not only Turkey but Russia as well. A bigger, stronger EU means a partner with somewhat similar values to share global burdens. A widely used euro means a necessary discipline on U.S. finances but also a more widely engaged EU likely to want to cooperate with Washington on global problems. Every effort should be made to develop NATO into a truly bilateral military force that can enable joint power projection on a global basis. Russia in the EU would guarantee Moscow's future democratic development and eliminate it as a potential threat while also relieving EU dependence on Middle Eastern oil. The EU is a natural partner for the United States: we need to promote that partnership and thereby enhance our influence.

India

India is special to the United States for several reasons. It is the largest democratic country, and the success of its democracy is important to democracy globally. Its business leaders are already well acclimated to U.S. values and practices. Both economies are based on English common law and can integrate quite easily. Done properly, economic integration can help both countries solve enormous problems. For America, the rising costs of health care and aging might be ameliorated. For India, access to critical technology and know-how could be enhanced. In view of India's positive demographics and likely eventual emergence as the world's biggest economy, development of a close relationship with India could extend and enhance American influence and welfare. The United States should foster a special relationship with India by negotiating a free trade agreement and perhaps eventually inviting India into NAFTA as well.

China

Right now, however, the most important bilateral relationship in the world is that between the United States and China. It will be a difficult

and complex relationship for a long time. It is in America's interest for
China to succeed. The most dangerous thing for the world of the future
would be a failing China. Imagine a China with hundreds of millions of
people desperate to escape upheaval and catastrophe, or a rogue China
resembling North Korea. To avoid such scenarios, we must work for
China's success. But we must do so with our eyes wide open, recognizing the element of competition between the two countries and keeping
U.S. interests clearly in mind. It is of particular importance that China
cope successfully with its pollution, energy, and water scarcity problems. Here there is great potential for joint R&D and the application of
U.S. technologies and techniques. The U.S. government should propose
a couple of major joint projects along these lines.

If I Were Riding Some Other Country's Surfboard

However rash it may be to put myself in the shoes of some of the key
players in globalization today, I am nonetheless going to do so and offer a few suggestions:

OPEC.   Give serious thought to the idea of pricing oil in a basket of
currencies that would include yens, dollars, euros, and renminbis.

EU.   Keep pressing ahead. Your new constitution is far from ideal,
but it is as good as it is likely to get, and should be adopted as fast as
possible.

In view of growing EU dependence on Russian gas and oil as well as
Russia's shaky commitment to democracy, develop a close relationship with Russia, including its eventual membership in the EU. Though
geographically a big country, Russia's economy is about the size of
Holland's, which should make digesting it easier.

Despite the difficulties of accepting Turkey into the EU, in the end
doing so seems to me the wise thing. Excluding Turkey is not going to
solve the continuing Islamization of Europe, while including it might
actually help with that issue. In any case, it certainly helps assuage Europe's disastrous population decline.

In regard to demographics, Europe needs to encourage population growth. How about substantial government grants of money to people who have babies, or making it profitable for people who have children and costly for those who don't; taxing childless couples (married or unmarried) and giving those who have children tax holidays. Europe might also encourage immigration from the Americas, including both Latin America and the United States, which still have growing populations. Indeed, many Americans might like the prospect of living in and becoming citizens of Europe. So have your recruiters at work in the Americas, India, and other similarly growing countries.

Europe, especially the United Kingdom, has a long, extensive involvement with India, and the EU is still India's largest trading partner. Make every effort to continue this. The UK in particular should be doing all in its power to attract Indian students to UK universities and take advantage of U.S. visa restrictions on foreign students.

Using the euro more as an international reserve currency would have certain advantages. For starters, it would reduce both the need to earn dollars and much of the uncertainty and volatility in financial markets. At the same time, insist that other major economies like Japan and China refrain from currency management and play more of an international currency role.

Europe needs to have the same concern as the United States about the outward movement of important industries and the broad array of financial incentives being used to entice that movement. Counter vigorously such incentives while joining with the United States to bring some WTO discipline to bear on them.

Many EU economies need more demand and less saving—a situation that might be helped by a cut in the VAT, along with extensive deregulation.

The welfare states don't have to be abolished, but they do need adjustment. Sweden and Finland have shown the way by becoming very competitive while maintaining the key elements of their welfare states. Since people are living longer, they may well retire later. The option to work more than the minimum number of hours should also be available to those who are bored with too much time off the job.

Japan.   Seriously consider joining NAFTA and eventual dollarization of the economy—especially to avoid the alternative of greater integration into the Chinese market and eventual renminbiazation. As a second option, consider using your presently great but gradually diminishing power to establish an Acu anchored by the yen. This course would create great potential leverage in the inevitable future bargaining with China.

Since Japan shares Europe's demographic problem without the potential sources of immigration available to the EU, it is even more imperative that Japan make it profitable to have babies. Seriously consider taxes on singles and childless couples and tax breaks for those who have children. In addition, how about imitating Singapore by promoting immigration from China and other growing countries like the Philippines? The Americas are also a possible recruiting ground, as they are for Europe.

Japanese private consumption has needed a boost for a long time. Since most of the incentives in Japan are aligned against private consumption, try to realign them. Start with land use and taxation and housing. Change the land use and tax laws to encourage the sale of undeveloped land for housing purposes. Also, make public the selling price of properties and create a national multiple listing service that would make public the asking price for properties on sale. Cut agriculture subsidies way back, and change the zoning of agricultural land to accommodate more and better housing. Since new and bigger houses need a lot of things like telephones, furniture, TVs, and appliances, the new demand for them would greatly stimulate the economy.

Also consider reversing the standard assumptions of the Japanese bureaucracy, in which everything is forbidden unless explicitly allowed. Try allowing everything in terms of licenses, certifications, and so forth that is not explicitly prohibited. Consider introducing the right of privately initiated legal proceedings against cartels and price fixing arrangements, with tough penalties for proven violations of the law.

To reform corporate governance, consider measures to give shareholders more power in corporate governance and also require that a majority of board members of a corporation come from outside its management ranks and closely allied corporations. Also, try to continue unwinding cross-shareholding arrangements between allied corporations.

China.   Definitely continue the charm offensive in Asia, Latin America, Africa, and elsewhere. Despite its high savings rate, China has a gross misallocation of capital. India is getting about the same growth rate by investing half the capital of China. For the long term China risks looking like Japan, with a savings and investment rate that is too high and consumption that is too low. You should be thinking about how to adjust this problem; you can't depend on export-led growth forever, as Japan has.

China, even more than the United States, needs to reduce energy intensity and dependence on overseas supplies. It also desperately needs to cut emissions and reduce dirty coal usage. Make every effort to avoid development along the lines of U.S. consumer society. Have people take public transport as much as possible and make it costly to use private autos. Highly desirable would be development of a network of intercity high-speed rail lines and extensive subway and tram lines in the municipalities. The same technologies and techniques that would make the U.S. oil independent would also do wonders for China's future. Press the United States and other advanced countries to do joint development of these technologies—especially because production of ultralightweight vehicles and related products is likely to become a major growth industry.

Heroic measures are already being taken to deal with growing water problems. Here again there is opportunity for joint development based on application of water conservation techniques and technologies already extant in several developed countries.

It might be wise for China to offer to negotiate a free trade agreement with Japan and to work with Japan to develop an Acu. This course would tend to ensure access to the Japanese market, ease the way for the renminbi eventually to become an international reserve currency, and also tend to lock Japan into a Chinese, rather than an American, orbit.

India.   The growth of the service and software industries has been and will continue to be extraordinary, but it is not sufficient to carry India where it needs to go. India might be wise to study China carefully and imitate China's emphasis on building infrastructure by allowing private companies to build and collect tolls on roads and bridges. It could also offer the kinds of financial incentives China offers to attract important manufacturing and high-tech installations from U.S., European, and Japanese companies.

India will likely have to decide eventually for either the euro, the dollar, or an Acu zone. Which will be best is unclear, but chances are it will probably be the Acu. Like China, however, India should make every effort to adopt a non-U.S. development model. Also engage in joint development projects with the United States, Europe, and Japan on reducing energy intensity and dependence and on water conservation and pollution abatement.

Brazil.   Brazil is on a roll and should keep doing what it is doing. A free trade agreement with China and also Japan might be a good idea. On the energy side, Brazil has a lot of interesting ethanol and alternative energy technology that could be valuable to China, India, and even the United States. Joint development projects might be rewarding.

Pollution and devastation of the rain forest are serious problems. Because their effects extend beyond Brazil, there is potential help available for solving them. Make every effort to get this help from the multinational institutions as well as from the United States, the EU, and Japan individually.

Conclusion: To Catch the Tide

Long ago as a Swarthmore College student, I listened to Scott Paper Company chairman and Swarthmore benefactor Thomas B. McCabe tell the winners of his scholarship that the purpose of elite institutions of higher learning is to train leaders. Leadership, he emphasized, is what it's all about. I have pondered that statement many times in the intervening forty-five years as I have met a number of world leaders and have asked myself what exactly is leadership. It is good to have intelligent leaders, but intelligence is not leadership. Leaders may be in a position of high office, but all those who obtain these positions are not leaders. Just think of the high officials of 1914, blindly plunging the young men of Europe into the blood bath of World War I. Eloquence is a wonderful gift for a leader, but those who eloquently mouth the conventional wisdom are not leaders.

Essentially, a true leader strives to discover the facts, connect the dots, follow where they lead, and determine how best to face the problem they present, and then shape events and persuade people to embrace the results.

Six centuries ago, Portugal's Prince Henry (the Navigator) was bold enough to connect certain dots, to think outside the box and so lead our forebears to the Far East and the New World. We too must think outside the box. The fact that we are now riding a new wave of globalization with 3 billion new surfers presents a unique opportunity for a still powerful America to turn from illusions of empire and exercise the ingenious entrepreneurial leadership that has long characterized it. To do so, we must be mindful of Shakespeare's lines in *Julius Caesar*:

There is a tide in the affairs of men, which taken at the flood leads on to fortune; omitted, all the voyage of their life is bound in shallows and miseries. On such a full sea are we now afloat, and we must take the current when it serves, or lose our ventures.

CHAPTER 1

1. "The Business Week Global 1000," *BusinessWeek*, July 26, 2004, pp. 87–93; Merrill Lynch, "International Stock Investing," *Merrill Lynch Investment Managers L.P.*, 2004, http://www.mlim.ml.com/content/Private/pdfs/pi_intl_stock_inv.pdf.

2. "Strengthening Our Alliance with the United States," *Consolidating and Expanding Our Bilateral and Regional Relationships*, Australian Government Department of Foreign Affairs and Trade, http://www.dfat.gov.au/ani/chapter_6.html.

3. Daniel J. Boorstin, *The Discoverers: A History of Man's Search to Know His World and Himself* (New York: Random House, 1985), p. 163.

4. Boorstin, *Discoverers*, p. 178.

5. Martin Wolf, *Why Globalization Works* (New Haven: Yale University Press, 2004), p. 113.

6. Social Security Online; National Average Wage Index, http://www.ssa.gov/OACT/COLA/AWI.html.

7. Mark Landler, "Sidelined by U.S. and Asia, Singing the Euro Blues," *New York Times*, December 12, 2004, sec. 4, p. 6.

8. Bureau of Economic Analysis, http://www.bea.doc.gov.

9. Congressional Budget Office, "The Budget and Economic Outlook: Fiscal Years 2006 to 2015," *Historical Budget Data*, January 2005.

10. National Intelligence Council, *Mapping the Global Future: Report of the National Intelligence Council's 2020 Project*, December 2004.

CHAPTER 2

1. William R. Doener, "The Comeback Comrade," *Time*, January 6, 1986, p. 42.

2. Jos Gamble, "Shanghainese Consumerism," *Asia Pacific Business Review*, Spring 2001, p. 91.

3. Todd Crowell and Thomas Hon Wing Polin, "Asian of the Century: Politics and Government: Deng Xiaoping," Asiaweek.com, December 10, 1999, http://www.asiaweek.com/asiaweek/features/aoc/aoc.deng.html.

4. Nicholas Lardy, "Do China's Abusive Labor Practices Encourage Outsourcing and Drive Down American Wages?" Senate Democratic Policy Committee Hearing, March 29, 2004.

5. Bureau of East Asian and Pacific Affairs, U.S. Department of State, Background Notes: China, October 1997, http://www.umsl.edu/services/govdocs/backgroundnotes/34.htm.

6. "China's College Graduates to Exceed Two Million in 2003," *People's Daily Online*, updated March 28, 2002, http://www.english.people.com.cn/200203/26/eng20020326_92866.shtml.

7. Andrew Targowski and Christopher Korth, "China or NAFTA: The World's Largest Market in the Twenty-First Century?" *Advances in Competitiveness Research*, November 1, 2003, p. 92.

8. Allen Zhang, "Hidden Dragon: Unleashing China's Private Sector," PricewaterhouseCoopers, 2003, http://www.pwcglobal.com/extweb/newcolth.nsf/docid/3D15C57A6D220BB985256CF6007B9607.

9. "WTO Successfully Concludes Negotiations on China's Entry," WTO News: 2001 Press Releases, Press/243, World Trade Organization, http://www.wto.org/english/news_e/prs01_e/pr243_e.htm.

10. Trade and Development Center, http://www.topics.developmentgateway.org.

11. Trade and Development Center.

12. Trade and Development Center.

13. H. K. Pradhan, "Country Experiences of India on External Debt Management," Regional Workshop on Capacity Building for External Debt Management in the Era of Rapid Globalization, Bangkok, Thailand, July 7, 2004.

14. Soutik Biswas, "India's Architect of Reforms," BBC News, May 22, 2004, http://www.news.bbc.co.uk/1/hi/world/south_asia/3725357.stm.

15. Richard T. Griffiths, "From Arpanet to World Wide Web," History of the Internet, http://www.let.leidenuniv.nl/history/ivh/chap2.htm.

16. Griffiths, "Arpanet."

CHAPTER 3

1. Alexandra Harney and Dan Roberts, "Midnight in Memphis, New Dawn in China," *Financial Times*, August 9, 2004, p. 15.

2. Douglas Kiker, "Bush Econ Adviser: Outsourcing OK," CBS News.com,

February 13, 2004, http://www.cbsnews.com/stories/2004/02/13/opinion/main 600351.shtml.

3. The Call Center School, interview by author, February 14, 2005.

4. Christine Taylor, "Two-Time Baldrige Winner Shares Secrets of Success: Employees, Customer, and Values Are Key," *Quality in Manufacturing*, January–February 1999.

5. Rob Koepp, *Clusters of Creativity: Enduring Lessons on Innovation and Entrepreneurship from Silicon Valley and Europe's Silicon Fen* (Hoboken, N.J.: Wiley, 2003).

6. Austin Weber, "Contract Manufacturing on the Rise: Outsourcing Assembly Is No Longer Just a Short-Term Fad," *Assembly*, September 1, 2002.

7. Harvard Business School, *Zenith Radio Corp. v. The United States: 1977* (Boston: HBS Case Services, Harvard Business School, 1978), p. 27.

8. Harvard Business School, *Zenith*, pp. 9–10.

CHAPTER 4

1. "The Dragon and the Eagle," *Economist*, September 30, 2004, p. 6.

2. Clay Chandler, "Inside the New China: Part Communist, Part Capitalist—and Full Speed Ahead," *Fortune*, April 4, 2004.

3. Andrew Targowski and Christopher Korth, "China or NAFTA: The World's Largest Market in the Twenty-first Century?" *Advances in Competitiveness Research*, November 1, 2003.

4. David Hale and Lyric Hughes Hale, "China Takes Off," *Foreign Affairs*, November–December 2003, p. 38.

5. World Bank, *World Development Indicators 2004*, http://www.world bank.org/data/onlinedatabases/onlinedatabases.html.

6. Peter S. Goodman, "China's Silk Noose Tightens: Italy's Textile Industry Feels Squeeze from Low-Cost Competitor," *Washington Post*, December 18, 2003, p. E6.

7. Christopher Rhoads, "Into the Fray: Threat from China Unravels Italy's Cloth Trade," *Wall Street Journal*, December 17, 2003, p. A1.

8. Goodman, "China's Silk Noose."

9. Abigail Goldman and Nancy Cleeland, "The Wal-Mart Effect: An Empire Built on Bargains Remakes the Working World," *Los Angeles Times*, November 23, 2003, p. A1.

10. Nancy Cleeland, Evelyn Iritani, and Tyler Marshal, "The Wal-Mart Effect: Scouring the Globe to Give Shoppers an $8.63 Polo Shirt," *Los Angeles Times*, November 24, 2003, p. A1.

11. Peter S. Goodman and Philip P. Pan, "Chinese Workers Pay for Wal-Mart's Low Prices: Retailer Squeezes Its Asian Suppliers to Cut Costs," *Washington Post*, February 8, 2004, p. A1.

12. Goodman and Pan, "Chinese Workers," p. A1.

13. Goldman and Cleeland, "Wal-Mart Effect."

14. Ito-Yokado, *Corporate Social Responsibility Report* 2003, p. 19, http://www.itoyokado.iyg.co.jp/company/eco/pdfs/ItoYokadoCSR2003_p18_19.pdf.

15. Goodman and Pan,"Chinese Workers."

16. Evelyn Iritani, "China's Next Challenge: Mastering the Microchip," *Los Angeles Times*, October 22, 2002, p. A1.

17. Iritani, "China's Next Challenge."

18. Jason Dean, "Upgrade Plan: Long a Low-Tech Power, China Sets Its Sights on Chip Making," *Wall Street Journal*, February 17, 2004, p. A1.

19. Iritani, "China's Next Challenge."

20. Iritani, "China's Next Challenge."

21. International Monetary Fund, *IMF World Economic Outlook 2004*, http://www.imf.org/external/pubs/ft/weo/2004/01.

22. "The Dragon and the Eagle," *Economist*, September 30, 2004, p. 4.

23. "The Dragon and the Eagle," p. 8; Economic Strategy Institute estimates.

24. Hale, "China Takes Off," p. 38.

25. Hale, "China Takes Off," p. 36.

26. Hale, "China Takes Off," p. 36.

27. Jim Hemmerling, Boston Consulting Group, interview by author, Shanghai, June 5, 2004.

28. Jim Jarrett, Intel, interview by author, Santa Clara, September 16, 2004.

29. "Haier's Purpose: China's Global Brand?" *Economist*, May 18, 2004.

30. Clay Chandler, "Inside the New China," *Fortune*, October 4, 2004.

31. George Stalk and Dave Young, "Globalization Cost Advantage," *Washington Times*, August 24, 2004, p. A15.

32. Stalk and Young, "Globalization Cost Advantage."

33. Ted C. Fishman, "The Chinese Century," *New York Times Magazine*, April 4, 2004, p. 30.

34. Fishman, "Chinese Century."

35. Jim Gradoville, American Chamber of Commerce in Beijing, interview by author, Beijing, June 2004.

36. Fishman, "Chinese Century," p. 31.

37. David Pilling and Richard McGregor,"Crossing the Divide," *Financial Times*, March 30, 2004.

38. Ken Belson, "Japanese Capital and Jobs Flowing to China," *New York Times*, February 17, 2004, p. C1.

39. Daniel Altman, "China: Partner, Rival or Both," *New York Times*, March 2, 2003, p. 30.

CHAPTER 5

1. C. R. Subramanian, *India and the Computer: A Study of Planned Development* (New Delhi: Oxford University Press, 1992), p. 133.

2. Daniel Yergin, PBS documentary, *The Commanding Heights*.

3. Srinivas Konakanchi, "Infosys Takes the Leap," *Silicon India*, May 1991.

4. Yergin, *Commanding Heights*.

5. Balaji Parthasarathy, "Globalizing Information Technology: The Domestic Policy Context for India's Software Production and Exports," *Iterations*, May 3, 2004.

6. Parthsarathy, "Globalizing," p. 2.

7. International Labor Organization (ILO), *World Employment Report 2001: Life at Work in the Information Economy*, http://www.ilo.org/public/english/support/publ/wer/index2.htm.

8. Jay Solomon, "India's New Coup in Outsourcing: Inpatient Care," *Wall Street Journal*, April 26, 2004, p. A1.

9. Solomon, "India's New Coup," p. A1.

10. Solomon, "India's New Coup," p. A1.

11. Solomon, "India's New Coup," p. A1.

12. Richard Rappaport, "Bangalore," *Wired*, April 2002.

13. Heather Timmons, "Reuters Plans to Triple Jobs in India," *New York Times*, October 8, 2004, p. W1.

14. Heather Tomlinson, "Scheme to Process NHS Clinical Tests in India," *Guardian*, July 9, 2004, p. 1.

15. Carol Matlack and Manjeet Kripalani, "Job Exports: Europe's Turn," *Business Week Europe Edition*, April 19, 2004.

16. Matlack and Kripalani, "Job Exports."

17. Rob Atkinson, *Understanding the Offshore Challenge*, Progressive Policy Institute, May 28, 2004, p. 7.

18. Kripalani and Engardio, "Rise of India."

19. Kripalani and Engardio, "Rise of India."

20. National Association of Software and Service Companies, "Indian Software and Services Industry: NASSCOM Analysis," NASSCOM, http://www.nasscom.org/download/IndianITIndustryFactsheet.pdf.

21. "Out of India," *60 Minutes*, August 1, 2004.

22. Pete Engardio and Manjeet Kripalani, "The New Global Job Shift," *BusinessWeek*, February 3, 2003.

23. Celia W. Dugger, "India's Unwired Villages Mired in the Distant Past," *New York Times*, March 19, 2000.

24. Eric Bellman, "Indians Answer Cell Phones," *Wall Street Journal*, September 23, 2004.

25. Amy Waldman, "Indian Soybean Farmers Join Global Village," *New York Times*, January 1, 2004.

26. Manjeet Kripalani and Stephen Baker, "Will Outsourcing Hurt America's Supremacy?" *BusinessWeek*, January 1, 2004.

CHAPTER 6

1. Stephen Baker and Manjeet Kripalani, "Will Outsourcing Hurt America's Supremacy?" *BusinessWeek*, March 1, 2004, p. 84.

2. Kenneth Flamm, *Mismanaged Trade: Strategic Policy and the Semiconductor Industry* (Brooking Institution Press, 1996), p. 47.

3. Kenneth Flamm, *Creating the Computer: Government, Industry, and High Technology* (Brookings Institution Press, 1988), p. 94.

4. Paul Carroll, *Big Blues: The Unmaking of IBM* (New York: Crown, 1993), p. 20.

5. Carroll, *Big Blues*, pp. 22–23.

6. Carroll, *Big Blues*, p. 21.

7. Richard S. Rosenbloom and Karen J. Freeze, "Ampex Corporation and Video Innovation," *Research on Technological Innovation, Management, and Policy* (Harvard Business School, 1985), 2:116.

8. Rosenbloom and Freeze, "Ampex Corporation," 2:166.

9. Rosenbloom and Freeze, "Ampex Corporation," 2:166.

10. Richard Elkus Jr., interview by author, September 11, 2004.

11. Clyde Prestowitz Jr., *Trading Places* (New York: Basic, 1988).

12. National Automobile Dealers Association, *Newsroom: AutoExec Magazine: 2004 NADA Data Report*, p. 51, http://www.nada.org/Content/Navigation Menu/Newsroom/NADAData/20043/NADA_Data_2004.pdf.

13. President's Council of Advisors on Science and Technology, *Sustaining the Nation's Innovation Ecosystems, Information Technology, Manufacturing, and Competitiveness*, January 30, 2004, p. 7.

14. Semiconductor Industry Association, *Industry Facts and Figures*, http://www.sia_online.org/pre_facts.cfm.

15. Charles W. Wessner, Ph.D., The National Academies, statement before

the Armed Services Committee, U.S. House of Representatives, July 8, 2004, http://www.7.nationalacademies.org/ocga/testimony/TopOfPage.

16. *Sustaining the Nation's Innovation Ecosystems*, p. 2.

17. "$600 Million over 10 Years for IBM's 'Trusted Foundry'; Chip Industry's Shift Overseas Elicits National Security Agency, Defense Department Response," *Manufacturing and Technology News*, February 3, 2004, p. 1.

18. Alex Salkever, "Innovation Is a Symbiotic Cycle," *BusinessWeek Online*, March 16, 2004, http://www.businessweek.com/technology/content/mar2004/tc20040316_9616_tc166.htm.

19. "The U.S. Military 'Owns the Night' on the Battlefield, But Not for Long, Says Industry Pioneer," *Manufacturing and Technology News*, October 3, 2003, p. 2.

20. *Sustaining the Nation's Innovation Ecosystems*, p. 10.

21. *Sustaining the Nation's Innovation Ecosystems*, p. 14.

22. *Sustaining the Nation's Innovation Ecosystems*, p. 14.

23. Alex Salkever, "Gunning for the U.S. in Technology" *BusinessWeek Online*, March 16, 2004, http://www.businessweekeurope.com/technology/content/mar2004/tc20040316_6114_tc166.htm; *Third European Report on S&T Indicators, 2003: Toward a Knowledge-based Economy*, March 2003. European Commission, http://www.cordis.lu/indicators/third_report.htm; National Science Foundation, Office of Legislative and Public Affairs, *News for the News Media*, NSF PR 00-24 (NSB00-128) CD Rom 2000.

24. Council on Competitiveness, *U.S. Competitiveness 2001: Strengths, Vulnerabilities, and Long-Term Priorities*, http://www.compete.org/pdf/Highlights.pdf.

25. National Center for Education Statistics, *Pursuing Excellence: Comparisons of International Eighth Grade Mathematics and Science Achievement from a U.S. Perspective, 1995 and 1999*, December 2003.

26. *Third European Report on S&T Indicators, 2003*.

27. Salkever, "Gunning for the U.S. in Technology."

28. William J. Broad, "U.S. Is Losing Its Dominance in the Sciences," *New York Times*, May 3, 2004, p. A1.

29. Lou Uchitelle, "Basic Research Is Losing Out as Companies Stress Results," *New York Times*, October 8, 1996, p. A1.

CHAPTER 7

1. Arik Hesseldahl, "Get Ready to Call iTunes," Forbes.com, December 16, 2004, http://www.forbes.com/personaltech/2004/12/16/cx_ah_1216aapl.html.

2. "Worldwide Semiconductor Revenue Growth Slows in Second Half of

Year," *Gartner, Inc.*, December 21, 2004, http://www3.gartner.com/press_releases/asset_116344_11.html.

3. World Trade Organization, *International Trade Statistics 2004*, http://www.wto.org/english/res_e/statis_e.htm.

4. "Korea Increases Investment in Manufacturing R&D to Combat China's Growth," *Manufacturing and Technology News*, July 7, 2004, p. 1.

5. Olga Kharif, "Challengers to America's Science Crown," *BusinessWeek Online*, March 16, 2004.

6. Michael Dobbs, "In a Global Test of Math Skills, U.S. Students Behind the Curve," *Washington Post*, December 7, 2004, p. Al.

7. Seah Park, "South Korea Wants Tech Kept at Home," *Wall Street Journal*, November 23, 2004, p. A17.

8. Park, "South Korea," p. A17.

9. Ian Rowley with Hiroko Tashiro, "So Much for Hollowing Out," *BusinessWeek*, October 11, 2001, p. 64.

10. World Trade Organization, *International Trade Statistics 2004*.

11. Michiyo Nakamoto, "Consumer Demand for DVDs, Mobile Phones, and Cameras . . . ," *Financial Times*, August 6, 2004, p. 11.

12. Dobbs, "Global Test," p. A1.

13. Pete Engardio et al., "Scouring the Planet for Brainiacs," *BusinessWeek*, October 11, 2004.

14. Saritha Rai, "In India, a Hi-Tech Outpost for U.S. Patents," *New York Times*, December 15, 2003, p. C4.

15. Jeff Chu, "How to Plug Europe's Brain Drain," *Time* Europe, April 20, 2004.

16. Chu, "How to Plug Europe's Brain Drain."

17. *Third European Report on S&T Indicators*.

18. "Aufstieg zum Weltmacht," *Der Spiegel*, special issue, May 2004, p 53.

19. Dobbs, "Global Test."

20. Engardio et al., "Scouring the Planet."

21. John Carey, "Flying High?" *BusinessWeek*, October 11, 2004, p. 116.

22. Carey, "Flying High?"

23. Carey, "Flying High?"

24. Carey, "Flying High?"

25. "MIT's Chief on America's Slide and How to Fix It," *BusinessWeek*, October 4, 2004.

26. Andy Grove, keynote address to Business Software Alliance, Washington, D.C., October 9, 2003.

CHAPTER 8

1. Amory Lovins et al., *Winning the Oil Endgame* (Snowmass, CO: Rocky Mountain Institute, 2004), p. 7.

2. Lovins et al., *Winning*, p. xiii.

3. Lovins et al., *Winning*, p. 8.

4. Tim Appenzeller, "The End of Cheap Oil," *National Geographic Magazine*, June 2004, p. 87.

5. Appenzeller, "The End of Cheap Oil," p. 87.

6. Energy Information Administration, *Annual Energy Outlook 2005: Forecast Tables*, Table 20, http://www.eia.doe.gov/oiaf/aeo/excel/aeotab–20.xls.

7. *Annual Energy Outlook 2005: Forecast Tables*, Table 20.

8. *Annual Energy Outlook 2005: Forecast Tables*, Table 20.

9. Charles T. Maxwell, "The Gathering Storm," *Barron's*, November 15, 2004, p. 20.

10. Appenzeller, "The End of Cheap Oil," p. 88.

11. Appenzeller, "The End of Cheap Oil," p. 90.

12. Maxwell, "Gathering Storm," p. 47.

13. Lovins et al., *Winning*, p. 10.

14. Lovins et al., *Winning*, p. 10.

15. Doug Tsuruoka, "China's Ever-Growing Needs May Result in a Global Shortage," *Investor's Business Daily*, January 26, 2005, p. A1.

16. Tsuruoka, "China's Ever-Growing Needs."

17. Alberto Jerardo, "The U.S. Ag Trade Balance: More Than Just a Number," *Amber Waves of Grain*, February 2004.

18. Jason Stein, "Some State Farmers Respond Creatively to Threat from Brazil," *Wisconsin State Journal*, July 6, 2004, p. A1.

19. Griff Witte and Nell Henderson, "U.S. Food Imports Increase, May Match Exports This Year," *Washington Post*, November 25, 2004, p. E1.

20. Witte and Henderson, "U.S. Food Imports Increase," p. E1.

21. Jerardo, "U.S. Ag Trade Balance."

22. Juliet Eilperin, "Arid Arizona Points to Global Warming as Culprit," *Washington Post*, February 6, 2005, p. A3.

23. Eilperin, "Arid Arizona," p. A3.

24. Eilperin, "Arid Arizona," p. A3.

25. Eilperin, "Arid Arizona," p. A3.

26. David Pimental et al., "Water Resources: Agriculture and Environmental Issues," *BioScience*, October 2004, pp. 909–918.

27. "Water Shortages," *Kiplinger Agriculture Letter*, October 15, 2004.

28. "More Water Woes," *Omaha World Herald*, September 20, 2004, p. B6.

CHAPTER 9

1. Carol Loomis, "America's Growing Trade Deficit," *Fortune*, November 10, 2003, p. 106.

2. Alan Greenspan, "The Mortgage Market and Consumer Debt," remarks before the annual convention of America's Community Bankers, Washington, D.C., October 19, 2004, http://www.federalreserve.gov/boarddocs/speeches/2004/20041019/default.htm.

3. Teruhiko Mano, "Decline in Savings Rate a Warning to Reform-Resistant Politicians," *Japan Times Online*, June 28, 2004, http://www.202.221.217.59/print/business/nb06_2004/nb20040628a1.htm.

4. "Credit Cards: Use and Consumer Attitudes, 1970–2000," *Federal Reserve Bulletin*, September 2000, pp. 623–634.

5. Median family income includes all wages, salaries, and tips, income from self-employment, interest, rent, government cash assistance, dividends, and all other income.

6. Lawrence Mishel, Jared Bernstein, and Sylvia Allegretto, *State of Working America, 2004/2005* (Washington, D.C.: Economic Policy Institute, 2005), Table 1.6, p. 48.

7. Mishel, Bernstein, and Allegretto, *State of Working America*, Table 1.9, p. 56.

8. W. Michael Cox and Richard Alms, "Defining Poverty Up," *Wall Street Journal*, November 2, 1999, A26.

9. Office of Management and Budget, *Budget of the United States Government*, Fiscal Year 2005, Historical Tables, Table 1.3, http://www.whitehouse.gov/omb/budget/fy2005/sheets/hist01z3.xls.

10. Congressional Budget Office, *The Budget and Economic Outlook: An Update*, September 2004.

11. Paul Krugman, ed., *Strategic Trade Policy and the New International Economics* (Cambridge: MIT Press, 1986), pp. 12–13.

12. Ralph E. Gomory and William Baumol, *Global Trade and Conflicting National Interests* (Cambridge: MIT Press, 2000), p. 5.

13. Gomory and Baumol, *Strategic Trade Policy*, p. 4.

14. Paul Craig Roberts, "The Harsh Truth About Outsourcing," *Business-Week*, March 22, 2004, p. 48.

15. Lester C. Thurow, "Do Only Economic Illiterates Argue That Trade Can

Destroy Jobs and Lower America's National Income?" *Social Research: The Worldly Philosophers at Fifty*, March 2004.

16. Paul A. Samuelson, "Where Ricardo and Mill Rebut and Confirm Arguments of Mainstream Economists Supporting Globalization," *Journal of Economic Perspectives*, Summer 2004, 135–146.

17. David W. Gumpert, "U.S. Programmers at Overseas Salaries," *BusinessWeek Online*, December 2, 2003.

18. Roberts, "Harsh Truth," p. 48.

19. Brian Bremner and Pete Engardio, "The Makings of a Meltdown; Why the Danger of a Stampede Away from the Dollar Remains," *BusinessWeek*, December 13, 2004.

20. Andrew Balls, "Strong U.S. Growth for Ten More Years," *Financial Times*, December 14, 2004.

21. Henry Kaufman, "Why There Can Be No Alternative to the Dollar," *Financial Times*, December 9, 2004, p. 19.

22. Catherine Mann, "Perspectives on U.S. Current Account Sustainability," *Journal of Economic Perspectives*, Summer 2002, pp. 131–152.

23. Martin Wolf, "The Eurozone May One Day Outperform the Dollarzone," *Financial Times*, June 25, 2003, p. 19.

24. Lee Scheier, "Call It a Day, America; Some Think It's Time We Quit Working So Hard and Start Playing a Little More," *Chicago Tribune*, May 5, 2002.

25. Sam F. Ghattas, "IMF Forecasts Pick Up in U.S. Economic Growth, but Budget Deficit a Concern," Associated Press, September 18, 2003.

26. Craig Karmin, "Stock Investors Ignore the Positive; Dow Falls Nearly 70," *Wall Street Journal*, May 7, 2004, C1.

27. Stephen Roach, "Coping with the Global Labor Arbitrage," Morgan Stanley Global Economic Forum, February 9, 2004, http://www.morgan stanley.com/GEFdata/digests/20040209_mon.html.

28. Adam Bell, "Cabarrus County, N.C., Jobless News Only Good at First Glance," *Charlotte Observer*, December 6, 2004.

29. Japan, Ministry of Finance, *International Reserves/Foreign Currency Liquidity*, January 2005, http://www.mof.go.jp/1c006.htm.

30. "Soros Warns of Dollar Plunge," BBC News, June 28, 2002, http://www.news.bbc.co.uk/1/hi/business/2072100.stm.

31. Chris Giles and Steve Johnson, "Dollar Down as Moscow Trails Case for Euros," *Financial Times*, November 24, 2004, p. 17.

32. Rebecca Buckman and Jason Singer, "Euro for Asia Gains in Allure: Re-

gional or 'Trading' Currency Might Be Steadying Factor," *Wall Street Journal*, October 3, 2003, p. C16.

CHAPTER 10

1. United Nations Conference on Trade and Development (UNCTAD) *World Investment Report 2004*, annex tables B1, B2.

2. Progressive Policy Institute, Trade Fact of the Week, "Foreign Direct Investment in the United States fell to $30 Billion Last Year," September 29, 2004.

3. Dennis Redmond, "Novartis Abandons Europe for New England," *Financial Times*, May 8, 2002.

4. Tom Murphy, "The American Autobahn," *Ward's Auto World*, June 1, 1998.

5. "Former President Bush to Join Samsung to Launch Chip Plant Upgrade," *TateAustin News*, May 2, 2003.

6. Hamish McRae, "Prague Is the New Bangalore," *Independent on Sunday*, October 17, 2004.

7. McRae, "Prague," p. 15.

8. UNCTAD, *Word Investment Report*, 2004.

9. Rich Miller and Pete Engardio, "Is It China's Fault?" *BusinessWeek*, October 13, 2003.

10. Chris Condon and Rick Butler, "A Chill East Wind," *BusinessWeek*, September 1, 2003.

11. Ted Fishman, "The Chinese Century," *New York Times* Magazine, July 4, 2004.

12. David Pilling, "Crossing the Divide," *Financial Times*, March 30, 2004.

13. Ken Belson, "Japanese Capital and Jobs Flowing to China, *New York Times*, February 17, 2004.

14. Jim Hemmerling, interview by author, Shanghai, June 29, 2004.

15. Dan Altman, "China: Partner, Rival, or Both," *New York Times*, March 2, 2003.

16. Altman, "China."

17. Greg Schneider, "Info Tech Employment," *Washington Post*, November 9, 2004, p. A1.

18. Schneider, "Info Tech Employment."

19. Rob Atkinson, *Understanding the Outsourcing Challenge*, Progressive Policy Institute, May 2004.

20. Manjeet Kripalani and Pete Engardio, "Rise of India," *BusinessWeek*, December 8, 2003, p. 66.

21. Pete Engardio, Aaron Bernstein, and Manjeet Kripalani, "New Global Job Shift," *BusinessWeek*, February 3, 2003.

22. Engardio, Bernstein, and Kripalani, "New Global Job Shift."

23. Chris Gentle, *The Cusp of a Revolution: How Offshoring Will Transform the Financial Services Industry*, Deloitte Research, April 2003.

24. Global Insight, *Offshore IT Outsourcing and the U.S. Economy*, March 2004, http://www.globalinsight.com/MultiClientStudy/MultiClientStudyDetail 846.htm.

25. John C. McCarthy, Christine Ferrusi Ross, William Martorelli, Christopher Mines, Adam Brown, "Near-Term Growth of Offshoring Accelerating: Resizing US Services Jobs Going Offshore," *Forrester*, May 14, 2004, http://www.forrester.com/Research/Document/Excerpt/0,7211,34426,00.html; Ashok Deo Bardhan and Cynthia Kroll, "The New Wave of Outsourcing," Fisher Center for Real Estate and Urban Economics–UC Berkeley, Fall 2003, http://www.haas.berkeley.edu/news/Research_Report_Fall_2003.pdf .

26. Jyoti Thottam et al., "Is Your Job Going Abroad?" *Time*, March 1, 2004, p. 26.

27. Census Bureau, cited in Lou Uchitelle, "It's Not New Jobs, It's All Jobs," *New York Times*, August 29, 2004.

28. Kripalani and Engardio, "Rise of India."

29. Roach, interview by author, November 10, 2004.

30. "Job Forebodings," *Washington Times*, April 19, 2004.

31. Stephen Roach, "More Jobs, Worse Work," *New York Times*, July 22, 2004.

32. Stephen Roach, "Coping with the Global Labor Arbitrage," Morgan Stanley, Global Economic Forum, February 9, 2004, http://www.morgan stanley.com/GEFdata/digests/20040209_mon.html.

33. Atkinson, *Understanding the Outsourcing Challenge*.

34. Lawrence Mishel, Jared Bernstein, and Sylvia Allegretto, *State of Working America*, 2004/2005 (Washington, D.C.: Economic Policy Institute, 2005), p. 67

35. *State of Working America*, p. 214.

36. Jon Hilsenrath and Sholnn Freeman, "Affluent Advantage," *Wall Street Journal*, July 20, 2007, p. A1.

37. Jonathan Krim and Griff Witte, "Average Wage Earners Fall Behind: New Job Market Makes More Demands but Fewer Promises," *Washington Post*, December 31, 2004.

38. Martin Wolf, "America on the Comfortable Path to Ruin," *Financial Times*, August 18, 2004.

39. Steve Lohr, "IBM Sought China Partnership, Not Just a Sale," *New York Times*, December 13, 2004, p. C1.

40. Lohr, "IBM Sought China Partnership."

41. David Barboza, "Outsourcing to the U.S.," *New York Times*, December 25, 2004, p. 1.

42. Chris Nuttall, "Europe Set to Move 1 M Jobs Abroad," *Financial Times*, August 16, 2004, p. 6.

43. "Showdown in the Ruhr Valley," *Business Week*, December 1, 2004, p. 54.

44. "Mirror Mirror on the Wall," *Economist*, June 19, 2004.

45. Ken Belson, "Rethinking the Town Toyota Built," *New York Times*, October 21, 2003, p. C1.

46. Andrew Balls, "Nordic Nations Top," *Financial Times*, October 14, 2004, p. 5.

47. "Mirror Mirror on the Wall."

48. Steve Pearlstein, "Can Old Europe Preserve Its Prosperity?" *Washington Post*, August 6, 2004, p. E1.

49. Peter Marsh, "France's Successful Throwback," *Financial Times*, January 4, 2005, p. 6.

50. Stan Sesser, "Air Pollution Is Big Concern in Asia," *Wall Street Journal*, November 24, 2004, p. B2A.

51. Joshua Kurlantzick, "China's Blurred Horizon," *Washington Post*, September 19, 2004.

52. Lester Brown and Chris Flavin, "China's Challenge to the United States and to the Earth," *World Watch*, September–October 1996.

53. Elizabeth Economy, *Living on Earth*, NPR (Somerville, Mass.: Stanley Studios).

54. Kurlantzick, "China's Blurred Horizon."

55. Kurlantzick, "China's Blurred Horizon."

56. "Nor Any Drop to Drink," *Economist*, August 24, 2002, p. 31.

57. Ashish Khotari, et al., "Impact of Environmental Degradation," February 24, 2005, http://www.infochangeindia.org/environmentlbp.jsp.

58. Khotari, et al., "Impact of Environmental Degradation."

59. EIA Country Analysis Brief, February 2004, http://www.eia.doe.gov/emeu/cabs/indiaenv.html.

60. Nicholas Eberstadt, "The Future of AIDs," *Foreign Affairs*, November/December 2002.

61. Eberstadt, "The Future of AIDs."

CHAPTER 11

1. *International Financial Statistics Yearbook 2004* (Washington, D.C.: International Monetary Fund, 2004).

2. John Burton, "Singapore Warns Taiwan on Independence," *Financial Times*, August 23, 2004.

3. Dominic Wilson and Roopa Purushothaman, *Dreaming with BRICs: The Path to 2050*, Goldman Sachs Global Economic Paper no. 99, October 1, 2003.

4. Jane Perlez, "Across Asia, Beijing's Star Is in Ascendance," *New York Times*, August 28, 2004.

5. Perlez, "Across Asia."

6. David Pilling and Richard McGregor, "Crossing the Divide," *Financial Times*, March 30, 2004.

7. Perlez, "Across Asia."

8. James Hookway, "Now It's Hip to Be Chinese," *Wall Street Journal*, March 16, 2004, p. A18.

9. Hookway, "Hip to Be Chinese."

10. Richard Lapper, "Latin America Dances to China Beat," *Financial Times*, November 11, 2004.

11. Simon Romero, "Canada's Oil: China in Line as U.S. Rival," *New York Times*, December 23, 2004, p. A1.

12. Ben Wattenberg, *Fewer: How the New Demography of Depopulation Will Shape Our Future* (Chicago: Ivan R. Dee, 2004), p. 44.

13. Andrew Ward, "South Korea Feels the Chill in China's Growing Shadow," *Financial Times*, September 25, 2003, p. 24.

14. "Two Systems, One Grand Rivalry," *Economist*, June 19, 2003.

15. Sumathi Bala, "Bollywood Dreams Going Global," *Financial Times*, August 28, 2004, p. W6.

16. Chidanand Rajghatta, "Sommelier, Soprano, Tailor," *Times of India*, November 20, 2004.

17. C. Raja Moshan, "For New Delhi, It's as Good as It Gets," *India Express*, November 16, 2004, p. 1.

18. Conn Hallinan, "U.S. and India: A Dangerous Alliance," *Foreign Policy in Focus*, May 6, 2003.

19. Moshan, "For New Delhi."

20. Venu Rajamony, "India-China-U.S. Triangle," *CSIS*, March 15, 2002.

21. Rebecca Buckman, "India Finds Able Ally," *Wall Street Journal*, p. A8.

22. Gurmeet Kanwal, "Power Politics: India's Quest for Great Power Status," *The Statesman, India*, February 4, 2003.

23. National Institute of Population and Social Security Research, *Population Projections for Japan, 2001–2050*, http://www.ipss.go.jp/pp_newest/e/ppfj02/ppfj02.pdf.

24. Irene Kunii, "Why Japan Just Might Build Nukes," *Business Week*, January 20, 2003.

25. Department of State, Washington File, "Bush, Koizumi Discuss Strong Dollar," transcript, http://www.usembassy_china.org.cn/shanghai/pas/hyper/2004/nov/22/epf112.htm.

26. Richard Hanson, "Japan, Iran Sign Major Oil Deal, U.S. Dismayed," *Asia Times Online*, February 20, 2004.

27. Walter Norbert, "Create a Common Asian Currency by 2025," *Asahi Shimbun*, May 12, 2003.

28. Celia Dugger, "Report Finds Few Benefits for Mexico in NAFTA," *New York Times*, November 19, 2003, p. A9.

29. Larry Rohter, "China Widens Economic Role in Latin America," *New York Times*, November 20, 2004, p. A6.

30. Rohter, "China Widens Economic Role."

31. Rohter, "China Widens Economic Role."

32. T. R. Reid, *The United States of Europe* (New York: Penguin, 2004) pp. 95–109. I am indebted to Reid for this insightful account of Welch meeting Europe.

33. "GE-Honeywell Deal Nears Collapse," BBC News, June 14, 2001, http://news.bbc.co.uk/1/hi/business/1386896.stm.

34. Reid, *The United States of Europe*, pp. 95–109.

35. Lawrence Mishel, Jared Bernstein, and Sylvia Allegretto, *State of Working America, 2004/2005* (Washington, D.C.: Economic Policy Institute, 2005), p. 387.

36. Jeremy Rifkin, *The European Dream* (New York: Tarcher/Penguin, 2004), p. 66.

37. Rifkin, *European Dream*, p. 66.

38. Andrew Higgins, "At Expense of U.S. Nations of Europe Are Drawing Closer Together," *Wall Street Journal*, December 23, 2004, p. A1.

39. European Commission, *The Social Situation in the EU, 2002*, May 22, 2002, pp. 11 cl, 61 cl, 63 cl, c2, http://www.europa.eu.int/comm/employment-social/news/2002/jun/inbrief_en.pdf.

40. Martin Wolf, "The Challenge Facing Old Europe," *Financial Times*, March 4, 2003.

41. Richard Bernstein, "An Aging Europe May Find Itself on the Sidelines," *New York Times*, June 29, 2003.

42. Dominic Wilson and Roopa Purushothaman, *Dreaming with the BRICs: The Path to 2050*, Global Economics Paper no. 99, Goldman Sachs, October 1, 2003.

43. Rifkin, *European Dream*, p. 251.

44. Peter Peterson, *Running on Empty* (New York: Farrar, Straus & Giroux, 2004), pp. 45–47.

CHAPTER 12

1. National Intelligence Council, *Mapping the Global Future: National Intelligence Council 2020 Project*, December 2004, executive summary.

2. Amory B. Lovins and Kyle Datta, *Winning the Oil Endgame* (Snowmass, CO: Rocky Mountain Institute, 2004).

3. Stephen Taub, "Why GE Pays Little in Taxes," CFO.com, January 26, 2005.

4. U.S. Department of Education, National Center for Education Statistics, *1.1 Million Home-Schooled Students*, July 2004.

Bhagwati, Jagdish. *In Defense of Globalization*. New York: Oxford Univ. Press, 2004.

Boorstin, Daniel J. *The Discoverers: A History of Man's Search to Know His World and Himself*. New York: Random House, 1985.

Carroll, Paul. *Big Blue: The Unmaking of IBM*. New York: Crown Publishers, 1993.

Cox, W. Michael and Richard Alms. *Myths of Rich and Poor: Why We're Better Off Than We Think*. New York: Basic Books, 2000.

Duncan, Richard. *The Dollar Crisis*. Singapore: Wiley, 2003.

Fingleton, Eamonn. *Unsustainable*. New York: Nation Books, 1993.

Fingleton, Eamonn. *In Praise of Hard Industries*. New York: Houghton Mifflin, 1999.

Fishman, Katharine Davis. *The Computer Establishment*. New York: Harper and Row, 1981.

Flamm, Kenneth. *Creating the Computer: Government, Industry and High Technology*. Washington, D.C.: Brookings Institution Press, 1988.

Flamm, Kenneth. *Mismanaged Trade? Strategic Policy and the Semiconductor Industry*. Washington, D.C.: Brookings Institution Press, 1996.

Garton Ash, Timothy. *Free World*. New York: Random House, 2004.

Gomory, Ralph E. and William Baumol. *Global Trade and Conflicting National Interests*. Cambridge, Mass.: MIT Press, 2000.

Greider, William. *One World Ready or Not*. New York: Simon & Schuster, 1997.

Jackson, Tim. *Inside Intel*. New York: Dutton, 1997.

Jacobs, Michael T. *Short Term America*. Cambridge, Mass.: Harvard Business School Press, 1991.

Koepp, Rob. *Clusters of Creativity: Enduring Lessons on Innovation and Entrepreneurship from Silicon Valley and Europe's Silicon Fen*. Hoboken, NJ: John Wiley & Sons, January 2003.

Koo, Richard C. *Balance Sheet Recession*. Singapore: Wiley, 2003.

Kotlikoff, Laurence J. and Burns, Scott. *The Coming Generational Storm*. Cambridge, Mass.: MIT Press, 2004.

Krugman, Paul (ed). *Strategic Trade Policy and the New International Economics.* Cambridge, Mass.: MIT Press, 1986.

Longworth, Richard C. *Global Squeeze.* Chicago: Contemporary Books, 1998.

Lovins, Amory B., E. Kyle Datta, Odd-Even Bustnes, Jonathan G. Koomey, and Nathan J. Glasgow. *Winning the Oil Endgame.* Snowmass, Colo.: Rocky Mountain Institute, 2004.

Malabre, Alfred L. Jr. *Beyond Our Means.* New York: Random House, 1987.

Mandel, Michael J. *Rational Exuberance.* New York: Harper Business, 2004.

Mishel, Lawrence, Jared Bernstein, and Sylvia Allegretto. *The State of Working America 2004/05.* Ithaca, NY: Cornell University Press, 2005.

Peterson, Peter. *Running on Empty.* New York: Farrar, Strauss and Giroux, 2004.

Prestowitz, Clyde, Jr. *Trading Places.* New York: Basic Books, 1988.

Prestowitz, Clyde. *Powernomics: Economics and Strategy After the Cold War.* Lanham, Md.: Madison Books, 1991.

Pugh, Emerson W. *Building IBM.* Cambridge, Mass.: MIT Press, 1995.

Reid, T. R. *The United States of Europe.* New York: Penguin Press, 2004.

Rifkin, Jeremy. *The European Dream.* New York: Penguin Group USA, 2004.

Serling, Robert J. *Legend and Legacy.* St. Martin's Press, New York, 1992.

Smith, Hedrick. *Rethinking America.* New York: Random House, 1995.

Talbott, Strobe. *Engaging India.* Washington D.C.: Brookings, 2004.

Ward, Diane Raines. *Water Wars.* New York: Riverhead Books, 2002.

Warren, Elizabeth and Amelia Warren Tyagi. *The Two Income Trap.* New York: Basic Books, 2003.

Wattenberg, Ben. *Fewer: How the New Demography of Depopulation Will Shape Our Future.* Chicago: Ivan R. Dee, 2004.

Wolf, Martin. *Why Globalization Works.* New Haven, CT: Yale University Press, 2004.

Yergin, Daniel and Joseph Stanislaw. *The Commanding Heights.* New York: Touchstone, 1998.

ACKNOWLEDGMENTS

I could not have written this book without the help of hundreds of people who kindly met with me and shared their insights and opinions. The list is too long to mention each person here, but I wish to thank all who shared their time and thoughts in interviews, e-mails, and phone calls.

For persuading me do the project in the first place, I owe a lot to two special people. One is my elder son, Chummy, whose interest in snow removal and comment about the difficulty of moving snow to India, provided an initial insight. The other is my long-time friend Richard Elkus, Jr., the developer of the original VCR, who for more than thirty years has thought deeply about what it takes to be competitive.

I am also deeply indebted to former Intel Chairman Andy Grove and present Intel Chairman Craig Barrett. For more than twenty years, we have been having a discussion about competitiveness, technological leadership, and globalization, and I have learned a great deal from them and their colleagues at Intel. I also deeply appreciate their encouragement and support over the years. I should also mention Intel Vice President Jim Jarrett whose interest and willingness to help have been indispensable. I must also express my deep gratitude to former Motorola Chairman Robert Galvin who has been a long time source of advice, encouragement, and wisdom.

A number of people worked long and tirelessly in researching and helping to organize the manuscript. In particular, I am deeply indebted to Ulrika, "Riki," Swanson, who oversaw and coordinated the full research effort and the intern army. She is without a doubt the best researcher in Washington. I must also express my deep appreciation to economist Robert Cohen, who has been generous with his time, support, and guidance. I also want to thank Hiromi Murakami who contributed much help on research in Asia and served as my note taker on several Asian trips. Franck Journoud contributed to the research on Europe and was the note taker on my European trips. Gladys Scott provided essential administrative support, and special thanks are due to Monica "Queen" Bridgewater who kept the office under control in the face of extraordinary demands. Nathan Brownback proved adept at finding the right statistics at the right moment. To my indefatigable interns: Alexandra Clegg, Charlie Gourlis, Anshuman Kar, David Jinjolia, Frank Qi, Jennifer Agopsowicz, Rebecca Kleinman, Michael Wahl, Britt Cecconi, Michael Fioretto, Jennifer Lee, Jessica Matsko, Jennifer Li, Christopher Kan, Brian Regan, Daniya Tamendarova, Thibaut Muzart, Maurice Wong, Jennifer Buntman, Jeff Kozlowicki, Adrienne Hadley, and Laura Jones, I also express my gratitude.

As always, Ambassador Chas Freeman of Projects International served as a great guide to China. My old college friend and President of the U.S.-China Business Council Bob Kapp was immensely helpful in arranging contacts in China and putting his staff at my disposal. Joseph Ha, Vice President of Nike, went way beyond the call of duty in arranging plant tours and meetings in Shanghai and in following up on my many questions. In Beijing, Craig Allen of the U.S. Embassy was generous with his time and support. Patrick Powers of the U.S.-China Business Council was very helpful, as were Tan Wee Theng of Intel, Yue Xiaoyong of the Ministry of Foreign Affairs, Robert Wang of the U.S. Embassy, Wang Jisi of the Institute of American Studies, and Anthony Kuhn of the *Far Eastern Economic Review*. In Shanghai, John Chang Chien was very generous with his time at Nike's Harry Johnson shoe factory as was Richard Chang at SMIC. I am very grateful to Vivian Fang of the U.S.-China Business Council who provided wonderful support for meetings and gathering information. Special thanks are due to Jonathan Heimer, a truly outstanding Foreign Service Officer at the U.S. Consulate in Shanghai who organized a number of key visits for me at the very last moment and on a weekend. In Hangzhou, I am most grateful for the help of Fu Du'er, the Deputy Director General of the Zhejiang Province Foreign Trade and Economic Cooperation Bureau. I also wish to thank Beijing University Professor Fan Shiming for his advice and assistance. Izabella Zhu was extremely helpful and gave generously of her time as an interpreter and guide, and Yuan Jian, Vice

President of the China Institute of International Studies was very kind and helpful. My old friend and mentor Peter Bottelier also gave excellent advice and guidance. I am indebted to Thomas Shoesmith for his hospitality in Shanghai and also to Stephen Casale. I am also grateful to my long time friend Jim Gradoville for his advice and assistance, and I would like to thank Mr. and Mrs. Dean Ho for their kind assistance. Yang Jiemian of the Shanghai Institute for International Relations was also generous with both time and support.

Mike Clark, former of the U.S.-India Business Council and now CEO of GTL Limited, has been a great teacher and guide to India. I must also thank Tarun Das, Kiran Pasricha, and Basu Dev of the Confederation of Indian Industries for their assistance in arranging key meetings. John Peters, Minister Counselor for Commercial Affairs of the U.S. Embassy in New Delhi was of immense assistance as was Richard Rothman, the Commercial Attache at the U.S. Consulate in Mumbai. Raman Roy, Chairman of Wipro Spectramind, was most helpful, and I am grateful to Mike Gadbaw for his assistance in organizing key visits to GE in India. GE India CEO Scott Bayman was also most helpful. At Texas Instruments, I wish to thank John Boidoc, Bobby Mitra, and Harish M for their kind help. Steve Roach at Morgan Stanley kindly arranged for me to meet with his people in Mumbai, and I need to thank Intel India CEO Ketan Sampat for organizing meetings with his key executives. Charles Morrison, President of the East West Center in Honolulu, was most helpful. I am also indebted to Konrad Seitz, former German Ambassador to India and to Joerg Wolf, head of the Konrad Adenauer Stiftung offices in New Delhi. Pete Engardio and Manjeet Kripilani of BusinessWeek were also extremely helpful.

I am grateful to Ambassador Heng Chee Chan of Singapore for her assistance and support and also to long-time friend Ira Wolf who arranged key meetings in Singapore and Hong Kong. As always Pat Mulloy was very helpful in reading the entire manuscript and making important factual corrections. Paul O'Day was also generous with his advice as were Robert Cohen and Rob Westcott. I must thank my old colleague and friend Scott Hallford for his insights and advice on China and also for keeping me company during a long night at the FedEx tower in Memphis. As always I benefited greatly from the insights of

New York Times columnist Tom Friedman and also from the guidance of Arnie Nachmanoff.

I was blessed again by having Bill Frucht as my editor. He is knowledgeable, creative, sympathetic, persistent, insightful, and a good friend as well as a great editor. I must also think my old friend and writing instructor Phoebe Hoss from whom I have learned so much and with whom I have had such good fun.

While all these people gave generously of their time, views, and information, I am responsible for what has been written. I hope it will provide some useful insights, and I take complete responsibility for any errors or omissions.

Last, but very far from least, I must thank my muse, advisor, critic, editor, researcher, tea brewer, constant companion, and best friend—my wife, Carol Ann Prestowitz.